God's Message...

REPENT!!

Karen L. Howard

Table of Contents

"And it shall come to pass, that in all the land, saith the LORD, two parts therein shall be cut off and die; but the third shall be left therein. And I will bring the third part through the fire, and will refine them as silver is refined, and will try them as gold is tried: they shall call on my name, and I will hear them: I will say, It is my people: and they shall say, The LORD is my God." Zechariah 13:8-9

"... there is no God else besides me; a just God and a saviour, there is none besides me. Look unto me, and be ye saved, all the ends of the earth: for I am God, and there is none else." Isaiah 45:21-22

"Therefore I will judge you... every one according to his ways, saith the Lord GOD. Repent, and turn yourselves from all your transgressions; so iniquity shall not be your ruin." Ezekiel 18:30

"... Thus saith the Lord GOD; Repent, and turn yourselves from your idols; and turn away your faces from all your abominations." Ezekiel 14:6

Ten Commandments: Words to Live By

I have touched on this subject in both **Books 1** and **2**, but have yet to really dig in and explore the true meanings of each one of God's Commandments thus far.

In **Book 2,** after quoting the **Ten Commandments** I stated, **"These are not just words... they are words to live by that have consequences if they are not followed."**

What people fail to realize though, is that they have deeper meanings than what we all take at face value.

Let's start with the first one, which is the most important of all... Exodus 20, beginning with verse 2 states;

#1 *"I am the LORD thy God, which have brought thee out of the land of Egypt, out of the house of bondage. 3)* **Thou shalt have no other gods before me."**

Given the fact that this is #1 on His list leads me to believe that it is, by far, the most important of all to God. The Old Testament is full of verses in which God states repeatedly that we are not to worship other gods. The following are just a few examples of this very thing.

"Ye shall not go after other gods, of the gods of the people which are round about you;" Deuteronomy 6:14

"Thou shalt have none other gods before me." Deuteronomy 5:7

"Ye shall not go after other gods, of the gods of the people which are round about you;" Deuteronomy 6:14

"For they will turn away thy son from following me, that they may serve other gods: so will the anger of the LORD be kindled against you, and destroy thee suddenly." Deuteronomy 7:4

"And it shall be, if thou do at all forget the LORD thy God, and walk after other gods, and serve them, and worship them, I testify

against you this day that ye shall surely perish." Deuteronomy 8:19

"And a curse, if ye will not obey the commandments of the LORD your God, but turn aside out of the way which I command you this day, to go after other gods, which ye have not known." Deuteronomy 11:28

"And thou shalt not go aside from any of the words which I command thee this day, to the right hand, or to the left, to go after other gods to serve them." Deuteronomy 28:14

"For they went and served other gods, and worshipped them, gods whom they knew not, and whom he had not given unto them: And the anger of the LORD was kindled against this land, to bring upon it all the curses that are written in this book:" Deuteronomy 29:26-27

"But if thine heart turn away, so that thou wilt not hear, but shalt be drawn away, and worship other gods, and serve them;" Deuteronomy 30:17

"And I will surely hide my face in that day for all the evils which they shall have wrought, in that they are turned unto other gods." Deuteronomy 31:18

"But if ye turn away, and forsake my statutes and my commandments, which I have set before you, and shall go and serve other gods, and worship them;" 2 Chronicles 7:19

"But if ye shall at all turn from following me, ye or your children, and will not keep my commandments and my statutes which I have set before you, but go and serve other gods, and worship them:" 1 Kings 9:6

"And had commanded him concerning this thing, that he should not go after other gods: but he kept not that which the LORD commanded." 1 Kings 11:10

"Then they shall answer, Because they have forsaken the covenant of the LORD their God, and worshipped other gods, and served them." Jeremiah 22:9

"And go not after other gods to serve them, and to worship them, and provoke me not to anger with the works of your hands; and I will do you no hurt." Jeremiah 25:6

"Because of their wickedness which they have committed to provoke me to anger, in that they went to burn incense, and to serve other gods, whom they knew not, neither they, ye, nor your fathers." Jeremiah 44:3

I can keep going, but I think I've made my point. However, for those that have access to a computer, I encourage you to pull up the **King James Bible Online** and type **worshipping other gods** in the **Search the Bible** field. In doing so you will see that there is at least 20 (plus) pages of verses listed that pertains to this topic. It's incredible the number of times that the Bible speaks of how we are not to worship other gods, and yet it continues.

In fact, lets add one more...

"And the children of Israel did evil again in the sight of the LORD, and served Baalim, and Ashtaroth, and the gods of Syria, and the gods of Zidon, and the gods of Moab, and the gods of the children of Ammon, and the gods of the Philistines, and forsook the LORD, and served not him." Judges 10:6

Of these listed, there is still one missing. Look at Judges 16:23, *"Then the lords of the Philistines gathered them together for to offer a great sacrifice unto Dagon their god, and to rejoice: for they said, Our god hath delivered Samson our enemy into our hand."*

The significance of **Dagon** is found in the back of my 1945 King James Bible in the **New and Practical Plan of Self-Pronunciation** section. Under the word **Dagon** it states "**fish**"!! Hmmm! Who do we know that the **fish** symbol is associated with? Jesus!

I had always wondered why the Christian population was displaying that symbol on their cars, jewelry and other apparel. Am I saying that Jesus is Dagon? I'll let you answer that for yourself.

One scripture that I will include can be found in Deuteronomy. Look at chapter 18, beginning with verse 18, it states; *"I will raise* *them up a Prophet from among their brethren, like unto thee, and will put my words in his mouth; and he shall speak unto them all that I shall command him.* 19) And it shall come to pass, that whosoever will not hearken unto my words which he shall speak in my name, I will require it of him.* 20)* **But the prophet, which shall presume to speak a word in my name, which I have not commanded him to speak, or that shall speak in the name of other gods, even that prophet shall die."**

This is a very significant scripture! And clearly it is speaking of Jesus based on the black stars (*) placed at the end of verses 18 & 19. But they failed to place one at the end of verse 20, the most important one of all!

God has made it abundantly clear that **He is the One and Only**, and **He needs No Help!**

I realize that this is the third time now that I've shared these verses, but I never get tired of reading them over and over. And, anyone that truly loves the LORD God, should love rereading them as well. So, here we go...

Isaiah 42:8, ***"I am the LORD; that is my name: and <u>my glory will I not give to another, neither my praise to graven images</u>."***

Deuteronomy 4:35, *"Unto thee it was shewed, that thou mightest know that* **the LORD he is God; there is none else beside him."**

Deuteronomy 4:39, *"Know therefore this day, and consider it in thine heart,* **that the LORD he is God in heaven above and upon the earth beneath: there is none else."**

Deuteronomy 32:39, *"See now that* ***I, even I, am he, and there is no god with me****: I kill, and I make alive; I wound, and I heal:* ***neither is there any that can deliver out of my hand."***

II Samuel 7:22, ***"Wherefore thou art great, O LORD God: for there is none like thee, neither is there any God beside thee"***.

I Kings 8:60, *"That all the people of the earth may know that **the LORD is God, and that there is none else.**"*

I Chronicles 17:20, ***"O LORD, there is none like thee, neither is there any God beside thee."***

Isaiah 41:13, ***"For I the LORD thy God will hold thy right hand,*** *saying unto thee, **Fear not; I will help thee.** 14) **Fear not... I will help thee,** saith the LORD, and **thy redeemer...**".*

Isaiah 43:10, *"Ye are my witnesses, saith the LORD, and my servant whom I have chosen: that ye may know and believe me, and understand that I am he: **before me there was no God formed, neither shall there be after me.**"*

Isaiah 44:6, *"Thus saith the LORD ... **I am the first, and I am the last; and besides me there is no God.**"*

Isaiah 44:8, ***"Is there a God besides me? Yea, there is no God, I know not any."***

Isaiah 45:5, ***"I am the LORD, and there is none else, there is no God besides me".***

Isaiah 45:6, *" ... **that there is none besides me. I am the LORD, and there is none else.**"*

Isaiah 45:18, *"thus saith the LORD that created the heavens; God himself that formed the earth and made it... **I am the LORD; and there is none else.**"*

Isaiah 46:9, *"Remember the former things of old: **For I am God, and there is none else; I am God, and there is none like me.**"*

Isaiah 48:11, ***"... I will not give my glory unto another."***

Hosea 13:4, *"Yet I am the LORD thy God from the land of Egypt, and **thou shalt know no god but me: for there is no saviour beside me.**"*

Clearly these verses can't be repeated enough, because if they were, people would stop worshipping Jesus! Or whomever else they worship.

In fact, let's add on more. Exodus 23:13, *"... **and make no mention of the name of other gods, neither let it be heard out of thy mouth.**"*

He doesn't even want us to speak their names! And even though I have to use their names in my books, I try never to speak them aloud.

Furthermore, God tells us numerous times that He is a **jealous God.** Which, evidently people don't take too seriously.

Look at Exodus 20:5. He states; *"Thou shalt not bow down thyself to them, nor serve them: **for I the LORD thy God am a jealous God**, visiting the iniquity of the fathers upon the children unto the third and fourth generation of them that hate me;"*

Now, Exodus 34:14, ***"For thou shalt worship no other god: for the LORD, whose name is Jealous, is a jealous God:"***

Deuteronomy 4:24, *"For the LORD thy God is a consuming fire, **even a jealous God.**"*

Deuteronomy 5:9, *"Thou shalt not bow down thyself unto them, nor serve them: **for I the LORD thy God am a jealous God...**".*

Deuteronomy 29:20, *"The LORD will not spare him, but then **the anger of the LORD and his jealousy shall smoke against that man,** and all the curses that are written in this book shall lie upon him, and the LORD shall blot out his name from under heaven."*

Deuteronomy 32:16, ***"They provoked him to jealousy with strange gods,** with abominations provoked they him to anger."*

Joshua 24:19, *"And Joshua said unto the people, Ye cannot serve the LORD: for he is a holy God; **he is a jealous God**; he will not forgive your transgressions nor your sins. 20) **If ye forsake the LORD, and serve strange gods, then he will turn and do you hurt, and consume you,** after that he hath done you good."*

1st Kings 14:22, *"And Judah did evil in the sight of the LORD, **and they provoked him to jealousy with their sins which they had committed**, above all that their fathers had done."*

Psalm 78:58, *"For they provoked him to anger with their high places, **and moved him to jealousy with their graven images.**"*

Psalm 79:5, *"**How long, LORD? wilt thou be angry for ever? shall thy jealousy burn like fire?**"*

Once again, I can keep going. And, can you even imagine the extent of his jealousy and anger at this day and time? Talk about the **Wrath of God!!**

I have provided several Biblical examples of God's punishment of His people for breaking, not just His Laws, Statutes and Testimonies, but His Covenant as well. And it has been weighing on my heart, here lately, of another example. One that's hard to talk about, but I'm reminded of daily. The **Holocaust**.

Was the **Holocaust** yet another punishment by God, inflicted upon His people for their disobedience? Was Hitler the **servant** that God used to implement His wrath?

A quote from Jewfaq.org regarding the **Holocaust** states; "It is believed that **six million Jews, one third of all Jews in the world, were killed** during this time **and millions more suffered**."

It was a horrible atrocity! But, so was the siege by Sennacherib of Assyria, and Nebuchadnezzar of Babylon, and Titus of Rome. Numerous Biblical accounts! And, aside from that, I feel certain that there are numerous other sieges and plagues that have befallen Israel throughout the centuries.

Look at Lamentations 4, written by Jeremiah after Babylon decimated Jerusalem. Verse 6 states; *"**For the punishment of the iniquity of the daughter of my people is greater than the punishment of the sin of Sodom, that was overthrown as in a moment, and no hands stayed on her. 7) Her Nazarites were purer than snow, they were whiter than milk,** they were more ruddy in body than rubies, their polishing was of sapphire: 8) **Their visage is blacker than a coal; they are not known in the streets: their skin**

cleaveth to their bones; it is withered, it is become like a stick. 9)
They that be slain with the sword are better than they that be
slain with hunger: for these pine away, stricken through for want
of the fruits of the field... 11) The LORD hath accomplished his
fury; he hath poured out his fierce anger, and hath kindled a fire
in Zion, and it hath devoured the foundations thereof."

This sounds like it was every bit as horrific as that of the Holocaust. One more scripture, verse 14; *"They have wandered as blind men in the streets, **they have polluted themselves with blood, so that men could not touch their garments. 15) They cried unto them, Depart ye; it is unclean; depart, depart, touch not:"**.*

Knowing how blood made them unclean, they deliberately **polluted themselves with blood**, just to keep from being robbed or assaulted by others. Moses even prophesied and warned them that these things would happen.

Deuteronomy 4, beginning with verse 25 states; *"**When thou shalt beget children, and children's children, and ye shall have remained long in the land, and shall corrupt yourselves**, and make a graven image, or the likeness of any thing, and shall do evil in the sight of the LORD thy God, to provoke him to anger: 26) I call heaven and earth to witness against you this day, **that ye shall soon utterly perish from off the land** whereunto ye go over Jordan to possess it; **ye shall not prolong your days upon it, but shall utterly be destroyed. 27) And the LORD shall scatter you among the nations, and ye shall be left few in number among the heathen**, whither the LORD shall lead you."*

This has, and still is happening. And why does God single out the Jewish people more so than the rest?

Moses tells us in Deuteronomy 4, beginning with verse 5; *"Behold, I have taught you statutes and judgments, even as the LORD my God commanded me, that ye should do so in the land whither ye go to possess it. 6) **Keep therefore and do them; for this is your wisdom and your understanding in the sight of the nations, which shall hear all these statutes, and say, Surely this great nation is a wise and understanding people. 7) For what nation is there so great, who hath God so nigh unto them,** as the LORD our God is in all*

*things that we call upon him for? 8) **And what nation is there so
great, that hath statutes and judgments so righteous as all this
law, which I set before you this day? 9) Only take heed to thyself,
and keep thy soul diligently,** lest thou forget the things which thine
eyes have seen, and lest they depart from thy heart all the days of
thy life: **but teach them thy sons, and thy sons' sons;"***

Look also at Deuteronomy 7:6, *"**For thou art a holy people unto
the LORD thy God: the LORD thy God hath chosen thee to be a
special people unto himself, above all people that are upon the
face of the earth.**"*

They are His chosen people! And the majority of His people have
still not learned their lessons. If they had, there would be no
worship of Jesus within their religion... **No Judeo-Christianity**!

According to the Wikipedia, "The term **Judeo-Christian** is used to
group Christianity and Judaism together... or due to the
commonalities in Judeo-Christian ethics shared by the two
religions. The term 'Judaeo Christian' first appeared in the 19th
century as **a word for Jewish converts to Christianity**."

As I stated in **Book 2**, I remember years ago, the Jewish people
used to be much more staunch in their beliefs. But, as time has
passed, they have slowly succumbed to the Christian Saviour.
Why?

Also, what's up with the Jewish calendar? The following is an
excerpt from **Book 2**, where I addressed this problem then. I
stated;

"A quick side note, the question was posted on Quora.com
regarding what the month of **Abib** is called today? Mark B.
Fischer responded, 'Abib (Aviv), which means spring... is the first
month of the Jewish. **When the Jews were exiled to Babylonia,
they adopted the Babylonian names of the months, and Abib
became Nisan.**'

This is evident with the Jewish calendar. #1, the first month of
the year, as we were just told in Exodus 12:2, should be Abib

(Nisan). However, when researching online, numerous sites state that Tishrei is the first month.

I find this contradiction to be in violation of God's explicit instructions given in Exodus 12:2, stating; *'This month shall be unto you the beginning of months: it shall be the first month of the year to you.'* Why is this not in compliance?

And #2, if **Abib** (Nisan) is the first month (according to scripture), why is the 4th month named **Tammuz** (also Tamuz), which is the name of the reincarnated Nimrod that we previously discussed in chapter 2? Why?

I can understand that 70 years of captivity would cause people to adopt some of the customs of their captors, but knowing the truth about the real identity of **Tammuz** should have triggered a desire to correct the name at some point there after! Not only correct the name but correct the layout of the entire calendar!"

In short, **Tammuz** was the original "christ child", per'se. Wikipedia states; "Hislop asserted that Semiramis was a queen consort and the mother of Nimrod, builder of the Bible's Tower of Babel. He said that Semiramis and Nimrod's incestuous male offspring was the Akkadian deity **Tammuz**, and that **all divine pairings in religions were retellings of this story**." (Wikipedia)

The highlights and details of both these stories are provided in **Book 2**, for those that may be interested to know more.

And, why do they have the 6 pointed star as they're symbol? Look at Amos 5:26, *"But ye have borne the tabernacle of your Moloch and Chiun your images, the star of your god, which ye made to yourselves."*

An article found at **m.facebook.com>media>set** states; "A bull's head is enclosed in a six-pointed star, and surrounded by letters composing the name **Rempha**, the planetary genius of Saturn, according to the alphabet of the Magi. The bull represents **Moloch** worship and ultimately, **Satan** worship. **The six-pointed star represents Satan, not the Star of David**."

The Wikipedia states; "The **Star of David** (Hebrew: מָגֵן דָּוִד,

romanized: *Magen David*, lit. 'Shield of David') is a generally recognized symbol of both Jewish identity and Judaism. Its shape is that of a hexagram: the compound of two equilateral triangles. A derivation of the **seal of Solomon**, which was used for decorative purposes by **Muslims** and **Kabbalistic Jews**, its adoption as a distinctive symbol for the **Jewish people** and their religion dates back to 17th century **Prague**."

Checking now, **Kabbalistic Jews**, an article titled, **The power of language in Jewish Kabbalah and magic**, found at British Library, bl.uk. It states; "Jewish mysticism is an umbrella term which covers a range of theories regarding the Godhead, as well as practices and beliefs extending beyond the requirements of standard Judaism. The term **Kabbalah** refers to a particular variety of Jewish mysticism, which first emerged in the 12th-century CE in Provence and Catalonia. It was concerned with the inner structure and processes taking place within the divine realms, on whose metaphysical dynamics the Kabbalists tried to exert influence."

As far as it being the **seal of Solomon**, if you've read the Bible, you know what happened to Solomon. In **Books 1 & 2**, I elaborate further about his fall from grace, and his ties to Freemasonry.

1st Kings 11:6 states, *"And **Solomon did evil in the sight of the LORD**, and went not fully after the LORD, as did David his father. 7) **Then did Solomon build a high place for Chemosh**, the abomination of **Moab**, in the hill that is before Jerusalem, **and for Molech**, the abomination of the children of **Ammon**. 8) **And likewise did he for all his strange wives, which burnt incense and sacrificed unto their gods."*

For those that are not aware, **Moab** and **Ammon** are Lot's sons by his two daughters. Beginning with verse 32 of Genesis, chapter 19, Lot's daughters hatch a plan to get their father drunk on wine and lay with him, so they can **preserve the seed of their father.**

Then, verse 36 states, *"**Thus were both the daughters of Lot with child by their father**. 37) And **the firstborn bare a son, and called his name Moab**: the same is the father of the Moabites unto this*

14

day. 38) And *the younger, she also bare a son, and called his name Benammi: the same is the father of the children of* <u>*Ammon*</u> *unto this day."*

Sin is a vicious cycle, leading to more and more sin!

We left off with the Kabbalists, but prior to that, the six pointed star, or the **hexagon,** i.e., the **Star of David**. Which it's not! How many times must His people be punished for their failure to obey? I am not trying to point a finger, I am merely trying to understand.

But one thing that I do understand is that all of the inhabitants of the world will pay. Not just His chosen people, but everyone! No one will escape His wrath that worship other gods... **And that includes Jesus**!

Look at Deuteronomy 31:17, *"Then my anger shall be kindled against them in that day, and I will forsake them, and I will hide my face from them, and they shall be devoured, and many evils and troubles shall befall them; so that they will say in that day, Are not these evils come upon us, because our God is not among us?"*

I believe this statement to be so true!

His second Commandment, found in Exodus 20, verse 4, states;

#2 *"Thou shalt not make unto thee any graven image, or <u>any likeness of any thing that is in heaven above, or that is in the earth beneath, or that is in the water under the earth</u>: 5) Thou shalt not bow down thyself to them, nor serve them: for I the LORD thy God am a jealous God, visiting the iniquity of the fathers upon the children unto the third and fourth generation of them that hate me; 6) And shewing mercy unto thousands of them that love me, and keep my commandments."*

The following is a quote from **Book 1**, which my thoughts on the matter have not changed, so let's go with it!

"Now look again at the second commandment and think about all of the various pictures and figurines, nicknacks, whatnots, and yard decorations, the list is endless involving the sun, the moon, astrological signs, Buddha, you name it – we've got it! Monuments and statues, angels and demons, mythical gods and superheroes – there's just no end to it! We worship our 'movie stars', our 'music idols', and most of all, Jesus!! Think about it. And please don't try to justify it – just own it! I was the same way, and I'm still trying to purge my home of all the seemingly innocent décor I have, until God makes me look again. And let's not forget about our jewelry that we wear, and clothing that is full of imagery that we worship, and tattoos on our bodies... and stars!!

Stars are everywhere!! Revelation, chapter 1, verse 20; *'The mystery of the seven stars which thou sawest in my right hand, and the seven golden candlesticks. **The seven <u>stars are the angels</u>** of the seven churches...'.* **'Stars' are angels!**"

Have you ever paid attention to the **Paramount** logo... the motion picture studio? It's a mountain peak with 22 stars that circle over the top of it, from one side of the peak to the other. But, if you visualize the stars that would be necessary to finish off the complete circle, the ones that are touching the ground, it would be 11 more. Those 11 upon the ground represents the 1/3 that fell from heaven. Again, stars are angels. 33 stars total, 22 in the sky, 11 on the ground! Everything means something. Google **picture of Paramount logo**. Check it out! That's their way of honouring the 1/3. Which explains how they've been so successful!

And let's not forget the **crosses!** Statues of crosses, huge crosses on church properties! They're everywhere! Necklaces, bracelets, earrings, rings, tatoos, all sorts of decorations and adornments that bear crosses.

The main problem that I see, is that most people overlook the actual **literal interpretation** of most scripture in the Bible. Look at that portion of verse 4 which I have underlined.

<u>*"any likeness of any thing that is in heaven above, or that is in the earth beneath, or that is in the water under the earth".*</u>

Now, think about pictures and paintings of landscapes, clouds, seascapes, flowers, fruit, animals, marine life, sunsets, lightning bolts, winter scenes, snow capped mountains, volcanic eruptions... the list is extensive!

Another example that comes to mind, is all of the souvenirs that I've brought home from my vacations to beaches, Gatlinburg, Theme Parks, the Caribbean Islands, and other tourist attractions throughout the states. Postcards, stuffed animals, figurines, Tee shirts and refrigerator magnets of sharks, crabs, bears, and numerous other **likenesses.** The snares are everywhere, we just don't recognize them for what they are.

The definition of the word **likeness**, once again means, #2 "the semblance, guise, or outward appearance of." #3 "a portrait or representation."

With that said, think about all of the photographs that we take of our children, families, and loved ones. I don't know about you, but I have albums full of them! I have wondered on many occasions if our photographs were considered **likenesses**, or **images**?? But looking at the literal interpretation, as I sit here writing, I now know that it does.

Think about how we just love to look at family pictures... We put them in frames and hang them on walls and display them on tops of furniture. We post them all over Social Media. We have albums and scrapbooks, collages and life size posters.

Think about all of the smartphones with cameras, and everybody taking **selfies**! Talk about **Vanity**!

People can say, **that's not what it means**, all they want. But, **it is!** Then some will say, **But... that's not what it means to me!** It is what it is, regardless of what it is to you! We've all been lied to so we would be more accepting, and truly we have taken the bait!

Look at Deuteronomy 4, beginning with verse 16, it states; *"Lest ye corrupt yourselves, and make you a **graven image**, <u>the similitude of any figure, the likeness of</u> male or female, 17) The likeness of any beast that is on the earth, the likeness of any winged fowl that flieth in the air, 18) The likeness of any thing that creepeth on the ground, the likeness of any fish that is in the waters* *beneath the earth: 19) And lest thou lift up thine eyes unto heaven, and when thou seest the sun, and the moon, and the stars, even all the host of heaven, shouldest be driven to worship them, and serve them, which the LORD thy God hath divided unto all nations under the whole heaven."*

The Wikipedia defines **worship** as; "showing regard with great respect, honor or devotion... Worship may involve one or more of activities such as **veneration**, **adoration**, **praise**, **supplication**, **devotion**, **prostration**, or **submission**."

The definition of **adoration** means; 1. "**the act of admiring strongly**". Synonyms: **idolisation, idolization**

2: "a feeling of **profound love** and **admiration**". Synonyms: **worship**. (Vocabulary.com)

When God tells us that we are not to **prostrate** ourselves before other gods or idols, it means bow down. **Prostration** is defined as "the state of lying stretched out on the ground with one's face downward." (Oxford Languages)

Given these definitions, it's easy to see how we all have crossed that line on many occasions, as far as adoring, or idolizing goes. I know that I have in the past. I can't tell you how many times I have said... **I just love it!!** And, many times, those things that I have loved too much, always seemed to get ruined! And now I know why!

One last thought on the matter... Think about the **Statue of Liberty**. That's a colossal **graven image**!

According to **Dictionary.com**, "The name Lucifer, which means **'bearer of light'** or **'morning star'**, refers to his former splendor as the greatest of the angels."

Now, what is Lady Liberty holding in her hand? A **torch**. And what do you see atop her head? A **seven pointed (horned) crown**.

Bear in mind that angels are said to be **androgynous** creatures, **partly male and partly female in appearance**. (Oxford Languages). That explains the **androgynous** appearance of the **Baphomet** deity worshipped by various cults and Satanists, dating back to, and including the **Knights Templar**.

The "Sabbatic Goat" image, drawn by Eliphas Levi, is a human torso with female breasts, and both male and female genitalia. It has the head of a goat, with two long horns protruding. A pentagram on its forehead. And, has the lower body and legs of a goat.

As I have stated, and elaborated about, in **Book 1**, America's first president, George Washington, was a **Freemason**. Not just him, but since the office was established in 1789, 14 men out of 44 (45, including Donald Trump) have been members of the same Secret Society, or their affiliates. This doesn't even include George H.W. Bush and George W. Bush being members of the **Skull and Bones**.

I have yet to find any credible sources regarding Joe Biden. But I did discover that many have the same suspicions as I.

I have even included a quote, in both books, taken from the Freemason databank, made by General Albert Pike. Pike was the Grand Commander, and sovereign pontiff of Universal Freemasonry, and during his address to the 23 Supreme Councils of the world he states; **"the Masonic religion should be by all of us initiates of the high degrees, maintained in the purity of the luciferian doctrine."**

I have provided much history in **Book 1**, not only about Secret Societies and how they are all connected to one another. But their ulterior motives, and their preparation for their **Supreme Being's** arrival, as well. I encourage anyone that has not read it, to check it out, or educate yourself further about these cults.

Regardless, the Statue of Liberty was a gift from France, and presented to the U.S. on July 4, 1881. It was designed by Frederic Auguste Bartholdi. (Wikipedia)

An article from **harvardpress.typepad.com**, dated Oct 28, 2018, states; "Frederic Auguste Bartholdi, the State's Alsatian architect, and his collaborators are sometimes said to be members of a secret society, the **Illuminati, clandestinely working to undermine the pillars of order (property, national states, religion)."**

It is said that Lady Liberty represents **freedom from God**! Which, as we've been taught, our forefathers first came to this country seeking "**political liberty**. They wanted **religious freedom** and economic opportunity." (americanhistory.si.edu)

I believe that they were looking for a fresh start somewhere. In a place that they would be able to, not only worship the god of their choosing, but be free to make their own laws according to their hearts desire.

God has said numerous times...

Exodus 23:24, *"**Thou shalt not bow down to their gods, nor serve them, nor do after their works: but thou shalt utterly overthrow them, and quite break down their images.**"*

Leviticus 19:4, *"**Turn ye not unto idols, nor make to yourselves molten gods: I am the LORD your God.**"*

Leviticus 26:1, *"**Ye shall make you no idols nor graven image, neither rear you up a standing image, neither shall ye set up any image of stone in your land, to bow down unto it**: for I am the LORD your God."*

Deuteronomy 7:25-26, *"**The graven images of their gods shall ye burn with fire: thou shalt not desire the silver or gold that is on them, nor take it unto thee, lest thou be snared therein**: for it is an abomination to the LORD thy God. 26) **Neither shalt thou bring an abomination into thine house, lest thou be a cursed thing like it**: but thou shalt utterly detest it, and thou shalt utterly abhor it; for it is a cursed thing."*

Deuteronomy 27:15, *"**Cursed be the man that maketh any graven or molten image, an abomination unto the LORD,** the work of the hands of the craftsman, **and putteth it in a secret place.**"*

They may have started out hiding the god that they worshipped, but then they finally figured out how to cleverly disguise him. Aside from the statues of Jesus and Mary that are everywhere, not excluding Buddha, Krishna and all of the other gods and deities, but now they've turned them into Super Heroes!

Movies about Thor, Ragnarok, and Loki, which are pagan gods from Norse mythology. And we have Superman, Iron Man, Batman, Dr. Strange, Silver Surfer, and many more, who's characters are all based on the fallen Angel's supernatural powers or abilities.

And the same is true of books, comic books, video games, clothing, shoes, toys and dolls in their likenesses. As well as vampires, werewolves, ghosts, and demons like Freddy Kruger, Michael Meyers, Jason Voorhees... the list is extensive!

And we love it!! I used to thoroughly enjoy all of the Marvel movies, and Vampire Diaries, and Twilight!! I grew up watching Batman back when he was played by Adam West, in the 60's. So, I speak from experience, being guilty myself.

But there's the snare! They have made it enjoyable for us to become attached to our favourite super heroes, and fall in love with our handsome vampires. They may have made evil look cute for our children... but for us, desirable!

We must open our eyes and realize what we are really seeing. I heard something several years ago, another one of those things that I wrote down and hung on to. It said...

Real eyes, realize, real lies. Hmmm!

Moving on...

God's third Commandment, found in Exodus 20, verse 7, states;

#3 *"Thou shalt not take the name of the LORD thy God in vain; for the LORD will not hold him guiltless that taketh his name in vain."*

Also, Leviticus 19:12, *"And **ye shall not swear by my name falsely, neither shalt thou profane the name of thy God**: I am the LORD."*

I've always thought that **taking the LORD's name in vain**, meant using it in a profane way... Like saying it along with **damn it**! Or swearing by His name. But that's not all there is to it.

I stumbled upon an article in **The Gadsden Times**, titled, **What does it mean to take the Lord's name in vain?** It was published on June 11, 2004, and proved to be most enlightening.

It states, "Many believe that it simply means not to curse using God's name. Though that is certainly inappropriate and showing the utmost disrespect for Him, that is not all that is meant by this command."

I'm glad to see that I'm not the only one that had that same interpretation.

It continues, "Another way we can take His name in vain is to use it casually in phrases such as 'Oh, my God!'... Even phrases like 'Thank God' or 'Praise the Lord' are often used in a less than sincere and reverent manner. These type phrases are commonly used in daily speech without really giving any thought to God. For the most part, they have become simply figures of speech."

I, too, have always refrained from saying "Oh, my God!" And taught my children, and grandchildren, not to, as well. I have, on many occasions, said "Thank God", but meant it! However, I do see the writer's point.

"We can also take God's name in vain when we use it to swear an oath such as 'I swear to God'. If we lie or do not follow through on the oath, we have taken His name in vain."

The article then provides the meaning of the word "**vain**". "Webster's defines vain as 1) **having no real value or significance; worthless, empty, idle, hollow**, etc.; 2) **without force or effect; futile, fruitless, unprofitable, unavailing**, etc.".

One last quote states, "... **Many bear His name without it having any real effect on their life. What God is saying is that we should not claim His name without living under His lordship. Taking the Lord's name in vain is another way of saying 'false believer' or 'hypocrite'."**

That last quote was my reason for including this article. I would never have considered that otherwise. That is so true!

The Wikipedia tells us that "It is common Jewish practice to restrict the use of the names of God to a liturgical context. In casual conversation some Jews, even when not speaking Hebrew, will call

God **HaShem** (Hebrew: הַ שֵׁ ם *haššēm*), literally 'the name'; often abbreviated to 'ה [*h'*]) is a title used in Judaism to refer to God."

"Judaism considers some names of God so holy that, once written, they should not be erased."

So, now we see that the Jews have an even more advanced understanding than everything stated thus far. Truly, there are layers of interpretation!

I have a couple scriptures to share in which God addresses **swearing**, which I feel strongly is referring to profanity. The first is found in Leviticus chapter 5. Verse 1 states; ***"And if a soul sin, and hear the voice of swearing, and is a witness, whether he hath seen or known of it; if he do not utter it, then he shall bear his iniquity."***

I understand this to mean, if someone uses profanity in your presence, you should call it out. Let that person know that you don't appreciate it, that it's offensive, and to please not speak those words in your presence. If we say nothing about it, the sin is on us.

I know that confrontation can be difficult, and I have kept quiet many times because of it. But after reading this scripture, I now know that I would rather God's wrath be on that person for speaking it, as opposed to it being on me for allowing it.

Look now at Leviticus 24, beginning with verse 10 states; *"And the son of an Israelitish woman, whose father was an Egyptian, went out among the children of Israel: and this son of the Israelitish woman and a man of Israel strove together in the camp; (they fought) 11) And the Israelitish woman's son blasphemed the name of the LORD, and cursed. And they brought him unto Moses:... 12) And they put him in ward, that the mind of the LORD might be shewed them. 13) And the LORD spake unto Moses, saying, 14) Bring forth him that hath cursed without the camp; and let all that heard him lay their hands upon his head, and let all the congregation stone him. 15) And thou shalt speak unto the children of Israel, saying,* **Whosoever curseth his God shall bear his sin. 16) And he that blasphemeth the name of the LORD, he shall surely be put to death...".**

This scripture speaks of profanity being used in conjunction with taking the LORD'S name in vain. It's an offense punishable by death. However, we certainly can't go around stoning, or killing everyone that we hear profaning the LORD'S name at this day and time. But, if someone we know does it, we **MUST** call it out and warn them of God's wrath that can pour down on them.

God's fourth Commandment, found in Exodus 20, beginning with verse 8, states;

#4 *"Remember the sabbath day, to keep it holy. 9) Six days shalt thou labour, and do all thy work: 10) But the seventh day is the sabbath of the LORD thy God: in it thou shalt not do any work, thou, nor thy son, nor thy daughter, thy manservant, nor thy maidservant, nor thy cattle, nor thy stranger that is within thy gates: 11) For in six days the LORD made heaven and earth, the sea, and all that in them is, and rested the seventh day: wherefore the LORD blessed the sabbath day, and hallowed it."*

In **Book 2**, I have an entire chapter dedicated to keeping God's Sabbath, but the majority of that pertains to the physical aspect of keeping it. Let's look more closely at the literal intent.

On the Sabbath, the 7th day, He goes into great detail about who all is to rest... Everyone, including the animals!

Our thoughts should be spent on thinking about Him, and talking about Him with our family. Look at Deuteronomy 6:4-9. Verse 7 tell us, *"And thou shalt* **teach them diligently unto thy children, and shalt talk of them when thou sittest in thine house, and when thou walkest by the way, and when thou liest down, and when thou risest up."*

And that's how we should, as a family, spend our Sabbath, talking about God... all night until we **"liest down"**, and all day the following day after we **"risest up"**. When you truly have God in your heart, you never tire of talking about Him!

As for me, living alone, I **literally** rest most of the day on Saturday... napping and resting!

There was a time that resting and napping all day would have prevented me from being able to sleep that night. But not the case now! When God wants you to do something, He makes sure that things like that don't happen. He wants us to be well rested because *"Six days shalt thou labour, and do all thy work:"* (Exodus 20:9)

While researching information for this chapter, I once again opened my Artscroll Tanach (The Jewish Bible With Insights From Classic Rabbinic Thought). Unlike my first time using it, that I spoke of in **Book 2**, I was pleased with the information I found.

Under the **Commentary** section, regarding the **Fourth Commandment: The Sabbath**, (20:9-10), it states; "**The commandment of the Sabbath includes not only deed, but attitude, for when the Sabbath arrives, one should feel that all his work is finished, even though his desk or workbench is still piled high.** *Six days shall you work and accomplish all your work* **means that no matter what is left to be done, one should feel as much at ease as if everything were finished.**"

The **attitude** is crucial! If your heart is not in it, and you are reluctant or dreading it in any way, **it will seem like the longest 24 hours of your life**! Now, if you keep the Sabbath, and that's how your day seems... then maybe you should rethink your attitude. But if you think that your attitude is in check, then pray for guidance!

One thing about the physical aspect of keeping the Sabbath that I will stress, is the day on which it should be kept... The **Sabbath takes place on the seventh day of the week**, and any calendar will show you that the seventh day is Saturday.

Look also at Exodus 16, beginning with verse 22. It states; *"And it came to pass, that on the sixth day they gathered twice as much bread, two omers for one man: and all the rulers of the congregation came and told Moses. 23) And he said unto them, This is that which the LORD hath said, To morrow is the rest of the*

25

*holy sabbath unto the LORD: bake that which ye will bake to day, and seethe that ye will seethe; and that which remaineth over lay up for you to be kept until the morning... 25) And Moses said, **Eat that to day; for to day is a sabbath unto the LORD: to day ye shall not find it in the field. 26) Six days ye shall gather it; but on the seventh day, which is the sabbath, in it there shall be none.** 27) <u>**And it came to pass, that there went out some of the people on the seventh day for to gather, and they found none.**</u> 28) And the LORD said unto Moses, **How long refuse ye to keep my commandments and my laws?** 29) See, for that the LORD hath given you the sabbath, therefore he giveth you on the sixth day the bread of two days; <u>**abide ye every man in his place,**</u> <u>**let no man go out of his place on the seventh day**</u>."*

I felt it necessary to reiterate this, emphasizing that we all are to keep God's Sabbath **in our homes**... <u>***let no man go out of his place on the seventh day!***</u>

God's fifth Commandment, found in Exodus 20, verse 12, states;

#5 *"Honour thy father and thy mother: that thy days may be long upon the land which the LORD thy God giveth thee."*

Again, I'd like to provide a quote from the **Tanach** (also spelled Tanakh). Under the Commentary, **20:12. Fifth Commandment: Honouring parents**. It states; "**The Ten Commandments are inscribed on two tablets, five on each. <u>The first tablet contains laws regarding Man's relationship with God while the second refers to relationships among people.</u> This casts a revealing light on the significance God attaches to the honour He wants us to show parents. When people honour their parents, God regards it as if they honour Him.**"

Wow! I never knew that the tablets were broken down that way. In all of my years of going to Church and Sunday School, never has that information been stated! Not just that, but the fact that **honouring our parents** is found on the first tablet, and how **it is among the laws regarding Man's relationship with God.**

I knew that **honouring our parents** was extremely important to Him, based on the scriptures in which He speaks of death being the penalty for all manner of harm or disrespect to your parents. But the arrangement of the laws on the two tablets being done intentionally is something that I never would have considered.

Look at Exodus 21, beginning with verse 15. It states; *"And **he that smiteth his father, or his mother, shall be surely put to death... 17) And he that curseth his father, or his mother, shall surely be put to death.**"*

Now, Leviticus 20:9, *"For **every one that curseth his father or his mother shall be surely put to death: he hath cursed his father or his mother; his blood shall be upon him.**"*

Deuteronomy 5:16, *"**Honour thy father and thy mother**, as the LORD thy God hath commanded thee; **that thy days may be prolonged, and that it may go well with thee, in the land which the LORD thy God giveth thee.**"*

Proverbs 20:20, *"**Whoso curseth his father or his mother, his lamp shall be put out in obscure darkness.**"*

Proverbs 30:17, *"**The eye that mocketh at his father, and despiseth to obey his mother, the ravens of the valley shall pick it out, and the young eagles shall eat it.**"*

However, death is not always the penalty. Sometimes it's a curse! Just like that of Noah's son Ham. Genesis 9:20-25 tells of Noah passing out naked in his tent after drinking too much wine, and Ham making fun of his father to his brothers. Shem and Japheth went into his tent, and without looking upon their father's nakedness, covered him. When Noah awoke and found out what had happened, he cursed Ham's son Canaan. Which Canaan's land became part of the land that God gave to the Israelites.

Furthermore, those that have read **Book 2**, hopefully recall my statements regarding **generational curses**. And how our disrespect of parents can and does come back to plague us with our children. **We reap what we sow**!

If we do not listen to our parents, our children will not listen to us. If we disobey our parents, our children will disobey us. If we lie to our parents, our children will lie to us. And, if we steal from our parents, our children will steal from us. Whatever we do, or don't do, we can count on it being done, or not done, to us.

Just as the scripture states; *"...visiting the iniquity of the fathers upon the children unto the third and fourth generation..."*. (Exodus 20:5)

Lamentations 5:7, *"Our fathers have sinned, and are not; and we have borne their iniquities."*

Sadly, most cannot see these repercussions until we are older, and have walked a mile in our parent's shoes. We have to live it, to learn it!

God's sixth Commandment, found in Exodus 20, verse 13, states;

#6 *"Thou shalt not kill."*

This one is pretty tricky. These laws were originally created for God's chosen people, the Israelites. Then, they were expanded to include the **Stranger**, those that chose to sojourn with them, to be circumcised, and to keep the LORD God's Laws, Commandments, Testimonies, and Sabbaths.

It is my understanding that the law pertaining to killing applied only to the killing of those that were God's people. His people killing one another.

The following are verses which provides validation of God's viewpoint on this matter, the matter of lawful and unlawful killing, and His reasons for it.

Deuteronomy 7, beginning with verse 1; *"When the LORD thy God shall bring thee into the land whither thou goest to possess it, and hath cast out many nations before thee, the Hittites, and the Girgashites, and the Amorites, and the Canaanites, and the Perizzites, and the Hivites, and the Jebusites, seven nations greater and mightier than thou; 2) And when the LORD thy God shall deliver them before thee; thou shalt smite them, and utterly destroy them; thou shalt make no covenant with them, nor shew mercy unto them: 3) Neither shalt thou make marriages with them; thy daughter thou shalt not give unto his son, nor his daughter*

28

shalt thou take unto thy son. 4) For they will turn away thy son from following me, that they may serve other gods: so will the anger of the LORD be kindled against you, and destroy thee suddenly."

This scripture says everything that needs to be said, and I am certainly not saying that it's ok to go around killing people that are not Israelites! I'm speaking of God's people being unequally yoked with others that have different beliefs.

Look also at Deuteronomy 20, beginning with verse 16; **"But of the cities of these people, which the LORD thy God doth give thee for an inheritance, thou shalt save alive nothing that breatheth: 17) But thou shalt utterly destroy them** ... *as the LORD thy God hath commanded thee: 18)* **That they teach you not to do after all their abominations, which they have done unto their gods; so should ye sin against the LORD your God.**"

At the time that God gave His people these Commandments, they had just been freed from Egyptian slavery. Moses was leading them to the land that God had promised to their forefathers, and while enroute it became evident that laws were necessary to keep the people in check.

Furthermore, once they arrived at their destination, and God **delivered** the inhabitants of the **Promised Land** to them (the occupants that were being removed), He wanted to make certain that they eliminated any obstacles that might become stumbling blocks in the future. He wanted their loyalty and sworn allegiance forevermore.

But they refused to be obedient. Which, once again, disobedience has consequences.

Ezra 10, beginning with verse 2, states; *"And Shechaniah the son of Jehiel, one of the sons of Elam, answered and said unto Ezra,* **We have trespassed against our God, and have taken strange wives of the people of the land: yet now there is hope in Israel concerning this thing. 3) Now therefore let us make a covenant with our God to put away all the wives, and such as are born of them,** *according to the counsel of my lord, and of those that*

29

tremble at the commandment of our God; and let it be done according to the law."

According to Merriam-Webster, the definition of **put away** means;

1 a : DISCARD, RENOUNCE
  b : DIVORCE
2   : to eat or drink up : CONSUME
3 a : to confine especially in a mental institution
  b : BURY
  c : **KILL**

Based on God's strict instructions given in Deuteronomy 7:2, *"thou shalt smite them, and utterly destroy them; thou shalt make no covenant with them, nor shew mercy unto them",* I feel strongly that the men which had to **put away all the wives, and such as are born of them**, had to **kill** them. Otherwise, they would have lived the rest of their lives tempted to return to them, and stray from God.

I know that sounds harsh but read His words in Deuteronomy 7:2-4 and 20:16-18 again. Then, ask yourself what you think God would want them to do. Leave your opinions and emotions out of it. Look again, *"make no covenant with them, nor shew mercy unto them".*

Just in case you think that God would be more merciful than what I have given Him credit for, at least regarding this matter, look at Deuteronomy 21. Beginning with verse 18, it states; *"If a man have a stubborn and rebellious son, which will not obey the voice of his father, or the voice of his mother, and that, when they have chastened him, will not hearken unto them: 19)* **Then shall his father and his mother lay hold on him, and bring him out unto the elders of his city, and unto the gate of his place; 20) And they shall say unto the elders of his city, This our son is stubborn and rebellious, he will not obey our voice; he is a glutton, and a drunkard. 21) And all the men of his city shall stone him with stones, that he die; so shalt thou put evil away from among you; and all Israel shall hear, and fear.** *"*

I believe that this example confirms my understanding of how God would handle the matter of the **strange wives and their children.**

Please understand, **put away** doesn't always mean to **kill**. The books of Moses talk about divorce, even using the term **put away**, but that is speaking of marriages between people who are **evenly yolked**. Meaning that, all those who are God's people should only marry others within the same religious confines.

God is merciful! But there are certain things that He will not tolerate, or make exceptions for. He knows the bigger picture! Actually, I should say that He **knew** the bigger picture! He just tried to stave off the inevitable as long as possible.

Let's talk about killing as it relates to abortion, because I'm sure that many are curious about that. We all are aware that there was no such procedure at that time, the time during which God's Commandments were written.

I then Googled, **When did the first abortion occur?** I was quite surprised to see the first response that popped up. The Wikipedia states, "The first recorded evidence of induced abortion is from the Egyptian Ebers Papyrus in **1550 BCE**. Many of the methods employed in early cultures were non-surgical. Physical activities such as strenuous labor, climbing, paddling, weightlifting, or diving were a common technique."

The article also states, "Various methods have been used to perform or attempt abortion, including the administration of abortifacient herbs, the use of sharpened implements, the application of abdominal pressure, and other techniques."

Now, I'm not trying to write a chapter about the history of abortion, I am merely pointing out the fact that it has been going on for centuries... since ancient times!

And, there are numerous reasons as to **why** someone would want to terminate a pregnancy. Some involving rape, health risks, financial circumstances, unmarried, interference with career, interference with school, too young, parent's decision, too many children already... and the list goes on.

But the bottom line is, if we were all living by God's laws, we wouldn't need to have abortions, **for the most part**. If we eliminate all of the **casual sex, adultery, going to bars and nightclubs where drunkeness affects our judgment, or makes women vulnerable to attack, or rape by drunken males, or individuals that prey on drunken females. Or college students attending frat parties where, once again, drunkenness is a factor. Or females out late at night, walking alone or unescorted. If we just eliminated all of that, can you imagine how many less abortions would result?**

Furthermore, I realize that there are all kinds of birth control options. But, again... **Look at the bottom line stated above!**

As for rape, look at Deuteronomy 22, beginning with verse 25; *"But if a man find a betrothed damsel in the field, **and the man force her, and lie with her**: then the man only that lay with her shall die: 26) But unto the damsel thou shalt do nothing; **there is in the damsel no sin worthy of death**: for as when a man riseth against his neighbour, and slayeth him, even so is this matter: 27) **For he found her** in the field, **and the** betrothed **damsel cried, and there was none to save her.**"*

I realize that this scripture is speaking of a **damsel** that is **betrothed**, but focus on the parts which I've highlighted. Verses 28-30 speaks of a **damsel that is a virgin**, but it's worded a little differently. The scripture quoted above better serves the point I wish to make.

Look at verse 27, where it's highlighted. **For he found her**, **and the damsel cried, and there was none to save her.** And, because so, **there is in the damsel no sin**. Therefore, based on this scripture, **rape** is a crime that a woman is found to be without sin.

Does that mean that a pregnancy that may result could be terminated in God's eyes?

Well, we know how He feels about marrying those **that are of strange beliefs** and **bearing children with them**, could this be one of those situations? For a man to overpower a woman, and rape her makes me question his morals, and his relationship to God, or if he has one at all?

I'm not trying to judge anyone, it's not my place to. I, myself, am guilty! At least I was, when I was young and ignorant. When I was a teenager, during a time when sex was not discussed, one or both parents would have **the talk**! And, depending on how comfortable a parent was talking with their child about sex, could sway the pubescent teen's decision one way or the other. Too much said can really scare girls, and too little said can make them even more curious.

Regardless, parents haven't, and don't, **teach their children diligently**! And, sadly, the Church, having a less than honourable intent, discourages people from even reading the Old Testament, let alone preaching sermons about **parents teaching their children diligently**!

What is God's position on abortion? Stop having casual sex with numerous partners! Stop FORNICATING!

The definition of **fornication** means, "sexual intercourse between people not married to each other." (Oxford Languages)

Aside from that, if you have had an abortion, for whatever reason, I can only encourage you to pray about it. It's between you and God. And, **God is a merciful god**.

God's seventh Commandment, found in Exodus 20, verse 14. It states;

#7 "Thou shalt not commit adultery."

If you are married and have sexual relations with someone other than your spouse, then you are committing **adultery.**

Look at Leviticus 20:20, *"And **the man that committeth adultery with another man's wife, even he that committeth adultery with his neighbour's wife, the adulterer and the adulteress shall surely be put to death.**"*

Also, Deuteronomy 22:22, *"**If a man be found lying with a woman married to a husband, then they shall both of them die, both the man that lay with the woman, and the woman: so shalt thou put away evil** from Israel."*

What I find concerning, is that the Old Testament only speaks of adultery from the perspective of a man having sexual relations with a married woman. I have found nothing about a married man having sexual relations with someone other than his wife.

The New Testament provides many scriptures regarding divorce, which pertains to both men and women. But, once again the teachings of Jesus contradicts that of God's.

Looking at the Commentaries from the Tanach, regarding the **Seventh Commandment: Prohibition against adultery**, it states; "By definition, this term refers only to cohabitation with a married woman, which is a capital offense. **It is parallel to the second commandment, which forbids idolatry, for someone who betrays the marital relationship can be expected to betray God.**"

The **International Standard Bible Encyclopedia Online** explains the **Subordinate Position of Woman**, saying;

"Woman, among the Hebrews, as among most nations of antiquity, occupied a subordinate position. Though the Hebrew wife and mother was treated with more consideration than her sister in other Semitic countries, her position nevertheless was one of inferiority and subjection. The marriage relation from the standpoint of Hebrew legislation was looked upon very largely as a business affair, a mere question of property. A wife, nevertheless, was, indeed, in most homes in Israel, the husband's 'most valued possession.' And yet while this is true, the husband was unconditionally and unreservedly the head of the family in all domestic relations... Nowhere is this more evident than in the matter of divorce. **According to the laws of Moses a husband, under certain circumstances, might divorce his wife**; on the other hand, **if at all possible, it was certainly very difficult for a wife to put away her husband.**"

The **mechon-mamre.org** states; "According to the Torah, **only the husband can initiate a divorce, and the wife cannot prevent him from divorcing her.**"

Deuteronomy 24 tells us, beginning with verse 1; *"When a man hath taken a wife, and married her, and it come to pass that she*

34

find no favour in his eyes, because he hath found some uncleanness in her: then let him write her a bill of divorcement, and give it in her hand, and send her out of his house. 2) And when she is departed out of his house, she may go and be another man's wife. 3) And if the latter husband hate her, and write her a bill of divorcement, and giveth it in her hand, and sendeth her out of his house; or if the latter husband die, which took her to be his wife; 4) Her former husband, which sent her away, may not take her again to be his wife, after that she is defiled; for that is abomination before the LORD: and thou shalt not cause the land to sin, which the LORD thy God giveth thee for an inheritance."

So, this is saying... If for some reason the man is not happy with his wife, **she find no favour in his eyes**, or **he hath found some uncleanness in her**, that he can divorce her and she can marry another.

However, if husband #2 divorces her as well, or dies, she can never go back to husband #1 again. Once she has had sex with another man, she has become defiled in such a way that she can no longer return to her previous husband. But she can take another.

Look at Jeremiah 3, verse 1; *"They say, **If a man put away his wife, and she go from him, and become another man's, shall he return unto her again? shall not that land be greatly polluted?** but thou hast played the harlot with many lovers; yet return again to me, saith the LORD."*

As you can see, Jeremiah makes reference to the same scripture, but speaks of the wife as **land being greatly polluted.** Then, he continues by including the fact that regardless of our whoredom, our infidelity with other gods, God will take us back!

The example of divorce that Deuteronomy 24 provided, is acceptable in God's eyes. And even though this may seem to be somewhat one-sided, the truth of the matter is, **God created man first**. Then, as stated in Genesis 2:18, *"... the LORD God said, It is not good that the man should be alone; **I will make him a help meet for him.**"*

Divorce today is rampant, but no surprise given the lack of commitment between husband and wife. People jump in and out of marriage, having no regard for the vows that each have made.

Vanguardngr.com states; **"A true marriage is the joining together of a man and a woman to become one flesh"**. The premise of that statement is found in Genesis 2:24, which says; *"Therefore shall a man leave his father and his mother, and shall cleave unto his wife: and they shall be one flesh."*

From the beginning of creation, from the creation of woman, God made His intentions known... that **a man... shall cleave unto his wife: and they shall be one flesh.**

The sanctity of marriage is **a holy covenant between each husband and wife, and a covenant between that couple and the LORD God. And need I remind you, or anyone else, how important covenants are to God.**

Marriages are failing because God is no longer a part of them. In fact, God has been removed from most all aspects of life. But understand this... The majority of all these multiple marriages, or hopping from one relationship to another, is nothing more than adultery!

God's eighth Commandment, found in Exodus 20, verse 15. States;

#8 *"Thou shalt not steal."*

Quoting the Commentary from the Tanach, regarding the **Eighth Commandment: Prohibition against kidnapping. "Stealing'** refers to a kidnaper who forces his victim to work for him and sells him into slavery. He is liable to the death penalty (*Sanhedrin* 86a). **The commandment against ordinary theft is found in *Leviticus* 19:11.** *Mechilta* compares stealing to the third commandment because a thief may cover his tracks by swearing falsely."

I'm taken aback by this Commentary, mainly because of its primary focus being towards **kidnapping**. Before I say anything further, allow me to quote Leviticus 19:11, as directed.

It states; *"Ye shall not steal, neither deal falsely, neither lie one to another."*

Okay. The entire 19th chapter of Leviticus touches on every Commandment, but one, in a somewhat abbreviated fashion, with random Statutes mixed in.

Take a look at just the first four verses. Beginning with verse 1, it states; *"And the LORD spake unto Moses, saying, 2) Speak unto all the congregation of the children of Israel, and say unto them, **Ye shall be holy: for I the LORD your God am holy.** 3) **Ye shall fear every man his mother, and his father,** and **keep my sabbaths**: I am the LORD your God. 4) **Turn ye not unto idols, nor make to yourselves molten gods**: I am the LORD your God."*

*Verse 2 would be (**#1**) **I am the LORD thy God...** and **Ye shall be holy** is equivalent to **Thou shalt have no other gods before me.**

The definition of **holy** means; "dedicated **or consecrated to God** or a religious purpose; sacred."

*Just within verses 3 and 4, I see three different commands. (**#5**) To **honour your mother and father**, but the word **fear** is used in place of **honour**. (**#4**) To **keep the Sabbath** and (**#2**) **Not to worship idols**.

If verse 3 isn't clear enough about **keeping the Sabbath**, look at verse 30; *"Ye shall keep my sabbaths, and reverence my sanctuary: I am the LORD."*

*Once again, verse 11 states; *Ye shall not steal, neither deal falsely, neither lie one to another."*

Here we see (**#8**) To **not steal**. And (**#9**) To **not bear false witness**, ie., **lie**.

*Verse 12 states; *"And **ye shall not swear by my name falsely, neither shalt thou profane the name of thy God**: I am the LORD."*

That would be (**#3**) To **not take the LORD'S name in vain.**

*Verse 13 states; *"**Thou shalt not defraud thy neighbour, neither rob him**: the wages of him that is hired shall not abide with thee all night until the morning."*

This would be (**#10**) To **not covet.** The definition of **covet** means; "yearn to possess or have (something)." (Oxford Languages)

However, under **People also ask**, in the results displayed of a Google search, the question was asked; **What does the 10th commandment thou shalt not covet mean?**

The response provided by whig.com states; "The commandment refers to **desire to the point of seeking to take something that belongs to another individual.**"

Under the same section, but the question now asked was; **What is the biblical definition of defraud?**

The response, provided by studylight.org states; "To deprive of right, either by obtaining something by deception or artifice, or **by taking something wrongfully without the knowledge or consent of the owner**...".

Given that definition of **defraud**, I can definitely see where verse 13 would be (**#10**) **not to covet.**

*Verse 20 states; *"And **whosoever lieth carnally with a woman, that is a bondmaid, betrothed to a husband, and not at all redeemed, nor freedom given her**; she shall be scourged; they shall not be put to death, **because she was not free.**"*

This is (**#7**) To **not commit adultery.**

The only Commandment that is not present in chapter 19 is **#6**, Thou shalt not kill. But, despite that, all other nine are present. So, based on all that I have just pointed out, how is it that the Rabbi who provided the Commentary for **"Stealing"** explains that it "refers to a kidnaper who forces his victim to work for him and sells him into slavery..."?

The Commandment specifically states; "**Thou shalt not steal.**" And Leviticus 19:11 states; "**Ye shall not steal**...". So, how on earth could the Rabbi distinguish one verse from the other, saying "**The** commandment against ordinary theft is found in *Leviticus* **19:11**". The only difference between the two, other than location, is the first word being **Ye** instead of **Thou**!

Looking at the 8th Commandment in the Wikipedia, it states; "'Steal' in this commandment has traditionally been interpreted by Jewish commentaries to refer to the stealing of an actual human being, that is, to **kidnap**. With this understanding, a contextual translation of the commandment in Jewish tradition would more accurately be rendered as '**Thou shalt not kidnap**'. Kidnapping would then constitute a **capital offence** and thus merit its inclusion among the Ten Commandments."

Given that, **the difference is that only those laws, or commands, that, when violated, result in the penalty of death.**

After reading this, I went back and reread Exodus chapter 20, and found nothing said about any of these Commandments, that if not kept, would result in the death penalty. I also read from midway of chapter 19 to the end of it, looking for context. Looking for anything leading up to, and after, that provided further insight.

I will say that verse 1 of chapter 21 states; *"Now these are the **judgments** which thou shalt set before them."* Then, the scripture begins to speak of **buying a Hebrew servant,** and **six years he shall serve.** It continues to elaborate about the **judgments** pertaining to servants through verse 11, then verse 12 speaks of **smiting.**

Continuing, verse 16 states; *"**And he that stealeth a man, and selleth him, or if he be found in his hand, he shall surely be put to death.**"*

Well, isn't that interesting! **Why is this verse specifically addressing stealing a person, and yet it is not worded as such in the Ten Commandments? Why is this issue addressed separately if it, supposedly, means the same thing as what is stated in the Ten Commandments? Why are we being told that stealing means stealing a person, when clearly God knows how to be very specific?** Is it just me? Am I misunderstanding something here? I don't think so, but let's continue.

39

Then, I turned to Deuteronomy chapter 5, the second location where the Ten Commandments are found. And, to my surprise, verse 1 states; *"And Moses called all Israel, and said unto them, Hear, O Israel, **the statutes and judgments which I speak in your ears this day**, that ye may learn them, and keep, and do them."*

The scripture continues; *"The LORD our God made a covenant with us in Horeb. 3) The LORD made not this covenant with our fathers, but with us, even us, who are all of us here alive this day. 4) The LORD talked with you face to face in the mount out of the midst of the fire, 5) (I stood between the LORD and you at that time, to shew you the word of the LORD: for ye were afraid by reason of the fire, and went not up into the mount;) saying,"*

Beginning with verse 6, the Ten Commandments are restated, almost verbatim, as what is stated in Exodus 20.

Again, nothing is said about a penalty of death.

Backtracking now. The subtitle of chapter 4 is **Moses Exhorts the People to Observe God's Law,** and that's exactly what takes place. **Exhorts** means to "strongly encourage or urge (someone) to do something." (Oxford Languages)

Throughout chapter 4, keeping God's **statutes** and **judgments** are mentioned in; (verses 1, 5, 8, 14, 40, and 45), His **commandments** (verses 2, 13, and 40), and His **covenant** (verses 13, 23, and 31).

Of all the numerous times that these are mentioned, the only time that the scripture speaks of death as a punishment, is in verse 26. I quoted this passage earlier when discussing God's second Commandment, but please allow me to quote it once more. Verse 25, so you can see the reason for their destruction, and verse 26 which describes it.

Deuteronomy 4, verse 25 states; *"When thou shalt beget children, and children's children, and ye shall have remained long in the land, **and shall corrupt yourselves, and <u>make a graven image, or the likeness of any thing</u>, and shall do evil in the sight of the LORD thy God, to provoke him to anger: 26)** I call heaven and earth to witness against you this day, **that ye shall soon utterly perish from** *off the land whereunto ye go over Jordan to possess it; ye shall not prolong your days upon it, <u>but shall utterly be destroyed</u>."*

Prior to that, verses 16-19 elaborate in detail about **corrupting themselves with graven images and likenesses.** In searching the scriptures more carefully, I began to notice that people worshipping graven images and likenesses appears to be the primary offence to God. The repetition of this warning is stated with far more frequency than that of all others.

Then, chapter 6 pertains to **Blessings Promised on Condition of Obedience**. And, beginning with verse 4, the **Shema** starts.

I also went through the Tanach, checking each of these scriptures as well. And I found no evidence of there being a **death penalty associated with the Ten Commandments**.

Let me clarify, when various passages speak of the different transgressions and offences, there are many that do result in death. Especially in Leviticus where it discusses the Laws and Statutes in greater detail.

And, as I previously stated, God does address **stealing a person** in Exodus 21:16, for which the death penalty is stipulated. However, in my opinion, it is not a Commandment. At least not one of the **Ten Commandments.**

But, as far as scripture leading up to and following the Ten Commandments, which explicitly states that anyone breaking any of these commandments **is liable to the death penalty,** I have found nothing.

In fact, one scripture that I did find states; *"And **if a soul sin, and commit <u>any of these things which are forbidden to be done by the commandments of the LORD</u>; though he wist it not, yet is he guilty, and shall bear his iniquity**. 18) And he shall bring a ram without blemish out of the flock, with thy estimation, for a trespass offering, unto the priest: and the priest shall make an atonement for him concerning his ignorance wherein he erred and wist it not, and it shall be forgiven him."* (Leviticus 5:17-18)

I only included verse 18 so you could see that there is an offering that can be made for atonement.

One last statement. In checking the **Sanhedrin 86a** referenced, it is the **Babylonian Talmud: Tractate Sanhedrin, Folio 86a**. It states; The "thirteen principles whereby the Torah is interpreted. [one of which is that] a law is interpreted by its general context: of what does the text speak? of [crimes involving] capital punishment: **hence this too refers [to a crime involving] capital punishment**."

This Tractate focuses mainly on **stealing a person,** and other than it referencing the **law**, as stated above, it says nothing of the Ten Commandments. Furthermore, **stealing** should not be changed to **kidnapping** just because kidnapping appears to some as being a greater offence, worthy of **capital punishment**. Need I remind you of our previous discussion about **coveting** and the **biblical definition of defraud?**

It is my understanding that **stealing means just what it says, not what it doesn't say!** And, Yes! There are, without a doubt, certain cases of **stealing (theft)**, that would be worthy of **capital punishment**.

Punishment of crimes were much harsher in times of old. And, because so, the crime rate was considerably lower. It wasn't because populations were smaller, but due to laws being enforced, and people fearing the consequences.

"**Ancient Egypt** also had laws and courts to deal with thieves. Those convicted were subject to corporal punishment, such as mutilation, flogging, penal servitude or **death by staking**."

"**In the Roman Empire, too, stealing could be punishable by death**, but if the thief was not killed when caught in the act, he could instead be sentenced to reimburse the victim, often four or five times the value of the stolen goods."

"**In the Middle Ages**, fines were the most common punishment for theft, and one that was not considered dishonourable. **More severe cases** could be punishable by flogging, the cutting off of one or both ears or a hand, **or death by hanging**." (All 3 quotes from historicallocks.com)

If only people feared the consequences of God as much!

God's ninth Commandment, found in Exodus 20, verse 16. States;

#9 ***"Thou shalt not bear false witness against thy neighbour."***

What exactly does **bear false witness** mean? Dictionary.com states; "**knowingly state as fact that which is untrue**; begin or perpetuate a rumour by **lying** about a person, thing, or event."

Vocabulary.com states; "a person who deliberately gives a false testimony."

Bearing false witness and lying are two different things, but go hand in hand together, because someone cannot be a false witness without lying.

Look at Proverbs 6, beginning with verse 16; ***"These six things doth the LORD hate: yea, seven are an abomination unto him: 17) A proud look, a lying tongue, and hands that shed innocent blood, 18) A heart that deviseth wicked imaginations, feet that be swift in running to mischief, 19) A false witness that speaketh lies, and he that soweth discord among brethren."***

Count them, there are seven things... two of which are **a lying tongue** and **a false witness that speaketh lies**. All are an **abomination unto God**!

Exodus 23, beginning with verse 1. The English Standard Version (ESV) states; ***"You shall not spread a false report. You shall not join hands with a wicked man to be a malicious witness. 2) You shall not fall in with the many to do evil, nor shall you bear witness in a lawsuit, siding with the many, so as to pervert justice, 3) nor shall you be partial to a poor man in his lawsuit."***

Not often do I stray from the KJV, but the wording of these verses in the ESV made it so much easier to understand.

Psalm 58:3, *"The wicked are estranged from the womb: **they go astray as soon as they be born, speaking lies.**"*

43

Psalm 101:7, *"**He that worketh deceit shall not dwell within my house: he that telleth lies shall not tarry in my sight.**"*

Proverbs 19:9, *"A false witness shall not be unpunished, and **he that speaketh lies shall perish.**"*

Isaiah 59:4, *"None calleth for justice, **nor any pleadeth for truth**: they trust in vanity, and **speak lies**; they conceive mischief, **and bring forth iniquity.**"*

Revelation 21:8, *"But the fearful, and unbelieving, and the abominable, and murderers, and whoremongers, and sorcerers, and idolaters, **and all liars, shall have their part in the lake which burneth with fire and brimstone**: which is the second death."*

Revelation 22:15, *"**For without are dogs**, and sorcerers, and whoremongers, and murderers, and idolaters, **and whosoever loveth and maketh a lie.**"*

Why does God despise liars so much?

Because...*"**Ye are of your father the devil, and the lusts of your father ye will do**. He was a murderer from the beginning, **and abode not in the truth, because there is no truth in him. When he speaketh a lie, he speaketh of his own: for he is a liar, and the father of it.**"* (John 8:44)

2nd Thessalonians 2:9 *"**Even him, whose coming is after the working of Satan with all power and signs and lying wonders**, 10) And with all deceivableness of unrighteousness in them that perish; because **they received not the love of the truth**, that they might be saved. 11) And for this cause God shall send them strong delusion, that they should believe a lie: 12) **That they all might be damned who believed not the truth**, but had pleasure in unrighteousness."*

It's not just the **bearers of false witness** and the **liars** that God despises, but **all those who have not a love for the truth!**

God's tenth, and last Commandment, found in Exodus 20, verse 17. States;

#10 *"**Thou shalt not covet thy neighbour's house, thou shalt not covet thy neighbour's wife, nor his manservant, nor his**

maidservant, nor his ox, nor his ass, nor any thing that is thy neighbour's."

I mentioned this just moments ago when talking about the 19th chapter of Leviticus, and how it "touches on every Commandment, but one, in a somewhat abbreviated fashion, with random Statutes mixed in".

I quoted the 13th verse of chapter 19, showing how it would be equivalent to the 10th Commandment.

Again, verse 13 states; *"Thou shalt not defraud thy neighbour, neither rob him:..."* .

I cited the definition of **covet**, which means; **"yearn to possess or have** (something)." (Oxford Languages)

And even provided a response (given by whig.com) regarding the question; **What does the 10th commandment thou shalt not covet mean?**

The response stated; "The commandment refers to **desire to the point of seeking to take something that belongs to another individual.**"

All of this applies, but let's explore this Commandment a little further because God is very explicit about everything that our neighbour has that we should not **covet**.

His (speaking in a general sense) wife (husband), house, servants, and a breakdown of all his livestock. What it boils down to is all of his material possessions. And our **neighbour** is anyone that lives around us.

In today's terminology, that verse would read, **my neighbour's beautiful wife, his big house, his SUV, his swimming pool, his riding lawnmower, his great job and his perfect life!**

The definition of **envy** means, *noun;* **"a feeling of discontented or resentful longing aroused by someone else's possessions, qualities, or luck."** Or, *verb;* **"desire to have a quality, possession, or other desirable attribute belonging to** (someone else)." A *Similar* word is **jealousy.** (Oxford Languages)

Now that we have a better understanding of what coveting is, think about all of the times that you have said, **I wish I had...**

Our world today is designed to make us **covet.** Think about all of the ads in magazines, commercials on TV, and even ads on websites. Fashion magazines are filled with all sorts of pictures of the latest trends in wardrobe, hair styles and makeup.

Or, all of the shopping malls with mannequins displayed in store windows, sporting the latest styles in clothing, complete with all the accessories. Jewelry stores with all the **bling**... sparkling rings, necklaces, bracelets and earrings beautifully arrayed in glass cases.

Sporting goods stores with all of their wares, designed to lure in the athletes and outdoorsy types. Department stores with a multitude of TVs, stereos, computers, all of the latest and greatest in technology. And that's just one department. They have housewares, bathroom accessories, plumbing supplies, home improvement, lawn and garden, clothing, makeup and personal hygiene, cleaning equipment and supplies, automotive, toys, books, music, movies, and all sorts of gadgets, decorations, and anything else your heart desires.

Furniture showrooms all staged with living room groupings, dining room arrangements, and bedroom ensembles. All pre-staged with pictures, artificial plants, throw pillows, bed spreads, and any other accessories that would catch your attention.

Rarely have I ever went into a department store, that I left without buying something! And, what about the grocery store? Regardless of where we go, certain items are always strategically displayed to capture our attention, and that is no coincidence!

Our world is deliberately staged to encourage our tendencies to **covet**, to always want something that someone else has! And many are buried in credit card debt, or struggling with astronomical mortgage payments, or car payments, or student loans... all due to our desire to **keep up with the Jones'**!

How many of God's Commandments are you guilty of breaking? I'm not looking for an answer, and I'm certainly not passing judgment, because I'm guilty on all counts myself. Hopefully many that read this will be moved to take a closer look at their lives and make some changes, as I did. I would say that it's never too late, but the day will soon come that it is.

Evolution... More Pollution

For those that believe in the theory of evolution, I have some questions to ask. I, myself, am not looking for answers, but hopefully my questions will help some of those who believe in it, to think again.

My first question, if we all were a product of evolution, where did all of our different languages come from? How does something like that evolve? Not just human languages, but the languages of all species?

Lions roaring, birds chirping, dogs barking, whales singing, every species has a means of communicating amongst themselves. Even in ways that are not always audible to humans. How is that? How does something like that evolve?

I will say that God provides us with an explanation of man's different languages in the Bible, why and how they came to be. Which is more than I can say for the scientists who teach their theories of evolution.

Genesis chapter 11, beginning with verse 2, states; *"And the whole earth was of one language, and of one speech... 3) And they said one to another... let us make brick, and burn them thoroughly. And they had brick for stone, and slime had they for mortar. 4) And they said... let us build us a city and a tower, whose top may reach unto heaven... 5) And the LORD came down to see the city and the tower, which the children of men builded. 6) And the LORD said, Behold, the people is one, and they have all one language; and this they begin to do: and now nothing will be restrained from them, which they have imagined to do. 7) ... let us go down, and there confound their language, that they may not understand one another's speech... 8) So the LORD scattered them abroad from thence upon the face of all the earth: and they left off to build the city."* (stopped building it)

And lastly, verse 9 states; *"Therefore is the name of it called Babel; because the LORD did there confound the language of all the earth: and from thence did the LORD scatter them abroad upon the face of all the earth."*

Furthermore, if evolution did take place, how did that first human learn to communicate? Movies would have us to believe that the **"caveman"**, "Neanderthal", communicated through a series of grunts!

Oxford Languages tells us that a **Neanderthal** is "an extinct species of human that was widely distributed in ice-age Europe **between c. 120,000-35,000 years ago...**".

Ok, I'll stop right there because, if you have read **God, the Devil, and the Lie** (from this point on will be referred to as **Book 1**), then you know that I have created a timeline, using the lineage provided in the Old Testament, along with other significant events, proving that our earth is only nearing 6,000 years old.

Not just that, but the book of Genesis tells us how man learned to communicate. Look at chapter 2, beginning with verse 15. It states; *"And the LORD God took the man, and put him into the garden of Eden to dress it and to keep it. 16) And **the LORD God commanded the man, saying,** Of every tree of the garden thou mayest freely eat:"*

God created an intelligent being that he was able to communicate with immediately!

Look at verse 19; *"And **out of the ground the LORD God formed every beast of the field, and every fowl of the air; and brought them unto Adam to see what he would call them: and whatsoever Adam called every living creature, that was the name thereof. 20) And Adam gave names to all cattle, and to the fowl of the air, and to every beast of the field**; but for Adam there was not found a help meet for him."*

I don't know about you, but the names that Adam came up with sound as though they were thought of by someone with **intelligence**!

And we all know what came next... **Woman**!

Beginning with verse 21, the scripture states; *"And the LORD God caused a deep sleep to fall upon Adam, and he slept: and he took one of his ribs, and closed up the flesh instead thereof; 22) And the rib, which the LORD God had taken from man, made he a woman, and brought her unto the man. 23)* **And Adam said, This is now bone of my bones, and flesh of my flesh: she shall be called Woman, because she was taken out of Man.***"*

Does that sound like something a "**Neanderthal**" would say?

Why do people ignore what the Bible tells us, and instead, choose to believe in all of these scientific theories? Most of which don't even make sense!

Look at 2nd Timothy, chapter 4, beginning with verse 3; *"****For the time will come when they will not endure sound doctrine; but after their own lusts shall they heap to themselves teachers, having itching ears; 4) And they shall turn away their ears from the truth, and shall be turned unto fables.****"*

After God created woman, chapter 3 tells us that she had intelligence as well. Beginning with verse 1, it states; *"Now the* **serpent** *was more subtle than any beast of the field which the LORD God had made. And he said unto the woman, Yea, hath God said, Ye shall not eat of every tree of the garden? 2)* ***And the woman said unto the serpent, We may eat of the fruit of the trees of the garden: 3) But of the fruit of the tree which is in the midst of the garden, God hath said, Ye shall not eat of it, neither shall ye touch it, lest ye die.****"*

Yes, I realize what happens next. However, there is a difference in having intellect, and being **ignorant of the wiles of the Devil!** Look at verse 1 again... the **serpent** was more subtle than any beast!

One of the definitions of the word **subtle** means, "**making use of clever and indirect methods to achieve something.**" And what the **serpent** was trying to **achieve** was to manipulate Eve into defying God's explicit instructions, *"But of the tree of the knowledge of good and evil,* **thou shalt not eat of it***: for in the day that thou eatest thereof thou shalt surely die."* (Genesis 2:17)

And, yes! I am saying that the **serpent** in the garden was the **Devil**!

Need I remind you of Revelation, chapter 12? Beginning with verse 7, it states; *"And there was war in heaven: Michael and his angels fought against the dragon; and the dragon fought and his angels, 8) And prevailed not; neither was their place found any more in heaven. 9) And the great dragon was cast out, **that old serpent, called the Devil, and Satan,** which deceiveth the whole world: he was cast out into the earth, and his angels were cast out with him."*

Even if people have never made that connection to the **serpent being the Devil**, has no one ever even thought it strange that the **serpent could talk??**

Maybe that's not so strange at all. Maybe Adam and Eve could understand the animals. After all, Genesis 1:26 does tell us; *"And God said, Let us make man in our image, after our likeness: and let them* **have dominion over the fish of the sea, and over the fowl of the air, and over the cattle, and over all the earth, and over every creeping thing that creepeth upon the earth."**

God gave them **dominion** over all creatures. However, there is one group of animals that isn't included, **the beast of the earth.** I talk about that in **Book 1**, and those that are interested, can check it out.

The definition of **dominion** means; "sovereignty or control". So, given the definition, in order to control someone or something, you must be able to communicate with it on some level. Is it possible that the whole premise of **Dr. Doolittle** being able to speak to animals, originates from Adam and Eve's ability to communicate with them? Hmm!

Looking at verse 26 again, notice how I have underlined *"Let us make man in our image, after our likeness: **and let them**"*. At this point in the scripture, we are led to think that woman had not been created yet. But, look at the specific way it states, *"**and let them**"*. Who's the **them**?

I believe that it was God's plan to create woman all along, based on the statement; *"Let us make **man in our** image, after **our** likeness"*. He is speaking to His female counterpart, the **Spirit of God**.

Look at chapter 1, verse 2; *"And the earth was without form, and void; and darkness was upon the face of the deep. **And the Spirit of God moved upon the face of the waters.**"*

Again, I address this in **Book 1**, but real quick... If male and female both exist, not just in the human species, but with all species, then there would have to be a female counterpart to God. And, He makes that very clear by stating **in our image**, **in our likeness**.

With that said, even though man was created first, this verse tells me that it was His intention, all along, to create female as well.

Part of understanding God's word, is looking at all of His words. He is very specific because all of His words are significant. Always pay close attention to the details!

As I explain in **God Help Us All** (from this point on will be referred to as **Book 2**), **chapter 1**, the **serpent, called the Devil, and Satan** is one of the **four horsemen** that **walked to and fro through the earth**, that would report back to God with updates. And, Satan just loves to, not only tempt people into disobeying God, but accuse them of their wrong doing before God.

Look at Revelation 12:10, *"And I heard a loud voice saying in heaven, Now is come salvation, and strength, and the kingdom of our God, and the power of his Christ: **for the accuser of our brethren is cast down, which accused them before our God day and night.**"*

For centuries he would come and go, back and forth to heaven. The books of Job and Zechariah confirms this. And, as I state in **Book 2,** I strongly suspect that his **fall from heaven** possibly occurs during the reign of Hezekiah. My theory being primarily based on Isaiah 14's specific wording...

Verse 12 states; *"**How art thou fallen from heaven, O Lucifer, son of the morning! how art thou cut down to the ground, which didst weaken the nations!**"*

It always seemed very strange to me, how Isaiah just comes out of nowhere with it! Right in the midst of chapters and verses, leading up to, and following all of his talk about the **Assyrian**.

Another scripture that supports my conclusion is that of Ezekiel 31:2-18, regarding the **Assyrian**. In **chapter 7 of Book 2**, I provide my breakdown of this scripture, and trust me... It's not talking about trees!

Regardless, **that old serpent** was on the scene in the Garden of Eden, tempting Eve. And he succeeded! He has been undermining and corrupting God's creation since the beginning.

Getting back to my original point, human beings were created with intelligence! God clearly communicated with them from day one, and they communicated with each other. And I seriously doubt that it was through a series of grunts and groans!

The anatomy of the human body, or the anatomy of any species for that matter, is so complex, and functions with such precision, that for us to believe that these sophisticated structures evolved from single-celled organisms over time, is complete lunacy!

All of the organs, and their functions, interacting with each other... an intelligent networking system between the organs that is replicated within each individual organ as well.

For example, the brain... It's not just an organ. It's a system of nerves and neurotransmitters, the electrical panel of the body. The heart is a system of pumps, tubes and valves that transports and circulates blood. And the lungs are a system that generates, filtrates and transports oxygen.

All of which is then replicated throughout every creature, every habitat and every civilization that functions in the same manner... The "blueprint" that was designed and is present in all aspects of God's creation.

Just like a house... it requires electricity, water and air. The same systems that are found in God's blueprint.

An article found at jacksonsun.com, titled; **Your body is a temple**, dated June 19, 2015, states; "Our bodies are indeed amazing creations. Your nose has the capability of remembering 50,000 different scents. Your taste buds are replaced every 10 days. Your body sheds about 600,000 particles of skin every hour. There are 100,000 miles of blood vessels in an adult human body. Our ears and nose never stop growing."

"While awake, the human brain produces enough electricity to power a light bulb. Human bones are ounce for ounce stronger than steel, though they are composed of 31 percent water. The human eye can distinguish about 10 million different colors. If uncoiled, the DNA in all the cells in your body would stretch 10 billion miles."

"Your heart will pump nearly 1.5 million barrels of blood during your lifetime, enough to fill 200 train tank cars. When you take one step you are using up to 200 muscles. There are over 650 named skeletal muscles in the human body (some figures suggest as many as 840)."

One last quote, "Yes, your body is an amazing organism. **It was made by and belongs to God. Therefore, take good care of it and use it for God's purposes.**"

What a fascinating article, which was written by Dr. Ryan Fraser, an assistant professor of counselling at Freed-Hardeman University. And, despite the length of it, which was not quoted in its entirety, there was no way that I could not include that last quote!

Again, how would abilities, like those stated above, evolve?

Think about **Air, Earth, Water and Fire.** *"In the beginning God created the **heaven** and the **earth.** 2) And the earth was without form, and void; and darkness was upon the face of the deep. And the Spirit of God moved upon the face of the **waters.** 3) And God said, Let there be **light...".**

The **heaven** is indicative of **air.** Yes, there is **Heaven**, the place we all hope to end up in. But, another definition of the word

firmament, means **"the heavens or the sky, especially when regarded as a tangible thing."** (Oxford Languages)

So, again, **heaven** represents **air. Earth** represents **earth**, not just the planet on which we live, but also, the clay/dirt that God fashioned our bodies from. **Water** not only represents the **water** that is crucial for the survival of the human body, as well as all other aspects of creation, but also the blood... the fluid that runs throughout our bodies. And **fire** represents not only the **light** that God created, the sun (the big ball of fire in the sky), but the **intelligence** that God gave to man. All creatures!

Just as the Bible is written with the use of metaphors, enabling multiple meanings, so it is with His creation! You must understand that He is a being that is multi-faceted, with intelligence that functions the same way.

The definition of **multi-faceted** means, **"having a variety of different and important features or elements"**. (collins dictionary.com)

Oxford Languages states, **"having many facets"**. After which, the following example is provided... **"the play of light on the diamond's multifaceted surface"**.

Think about the example of that diamond for a moment. Depending on the surroundings, each of those facets reflects a different image!

The same is true of a fly's eye. **"Each eyeball has thousands of lenses, enabling them to see a wider field around them without turning their heads. The number of lenses per eye can range from 150 to 8,000."**

I am not saying that God has eyes like a fly. I'm referring to His ability to think about and process multiple things in a given instant. Talk about **multi-tasking!**

And furthermore, who knows what His vision is capable of. The concepts for these various characteristics that creatures have, had to have come from somewhere. Either His ability to see, as through multiple lenses (like flies), or to see multiple things through one lens. Whichever the case, matters not!

Think about the various scriptures that reference creatures or objects which have numerous eyes. Look at Ezekiel 10:12, ***"And their whole body, and their backs, and their hands, and their wings, and the wheels, <u>were full of eyes round about</u>, even the wheels that they four had."***

Zechariah 3:9, *"For **behold the stone that I have laid before Joshua; <u>upon one stone shall be seven eyes</u>**: behold, I will engrave the graving thereof, saith the LORD of hosts, and I will remove the iniquity of that land in one day."*

Revelation 4:6-8; *"And before the throne there was a sea of glass like unto crystal: and in the midst of the throne, and round about the throne, were **four beasts full of eyes before and behind**... 8) And the four beasts had each of them six wings about him; **and they were full of eyes within**: and they rest not day and night, saying, Holy, holy, holy, Lord God Almighty, which was, and is, and is to come."*

And, Revelation 5:6, *"And I beheld, and, and, lo, in the midst of the throne and of the four beasts, and in the midst of the elders, stood a Lamb as it had been slain, having seven horns and **seven eyes**, which are the seven Spirits of God sent forth into all the earth."*

Even though man was created in His image, we need to stop thinking that this verse has only one interpretation. We may be in His likeness, but what does that encompass?

He gave us a form, intelligence, and the ability to see, hear, and communicate. And these qualities may, very well be, the likeness that is spoken of.

The definition of **likeness** means, 1. "the fact or quality of being alike; **resemblance**." 2. "the **semblance**, guise, or outward appearance of." It then provides an example, "humans are described as being made in God's likeness." (Oxford Languages)

The definition of **image** means, "to copy or imitate". (vocabulary.com)

56

Is it possible that there is an **Immortal Pattern** that He used? Whereby all mortal creatures were fashioned in different aspects of His own image. An image that varies depending on what qualities, or characteristics He was copying of Himself at the time each species was created. Or, was it more of an **evolution** of His thought process?

I have alluded to this before in **Book 1**. In chapter 1, I stated; "Now, given God's unfathomable intellect, He has proven that His mind is capable of devising even the most complex organisms and species, and after creating a mental schematic (of sorts), all He has to do is **Speak it**, and there it is! When you think about it, many species have, if not the same, a very similar biological blueprint.

So, with that in mind, it's just a few minor adjustments to the exterior design, and then just **Speak it**! And *'God said'*. "

One thing leading to another! His imagination knows no bounds, no limitations! I can certainly understand how it could have been an **evolution** of His thought process... look at the results!! And, anyone who believes that all of these thousands of species are the result of evolution, which began with a single-celled organism, are seriously gullible... and I would have to question their intelligence, or at least their common sense.

And, for those that don't believe in the existence of God, then they must ascribe to the theory of evolution. And, if not, then exactly what are their thoughts about all of this... their existence and how it came about? And, if they have no thoughts at all on the matter, then they're worse off than the others!

For me, believing that a God exists who created all of this is much more rational than believing that it all evolved from a single-celled organism. But, when you believe their lies about the earth being billions of years old, then... I guess their theory of evolution becomes more plausible. And, as I have already proven in **Book 1**, this earth is only nearing 6,000 years old.

Before I continue, I must ask... So, did this single-celled organism evolve into some sort of tadpole type creature, that eventually slithered out of the sludge one day, and then sprouted arms and legs, and after another million years of crawling around, began to walk upright... then how long did this creature have to wait for another creature like himself, but this time a female, to evolve?

And, was it just a coincidence that the female just happened to evolve in the same sludge pool that the male came from? Because, after all, that is an amazing coincidence that both just happened to slither up in the same area... out of this great big world... How does that happen?

Or, was this a special sludge pool that just happened to contain a certain kind of sludge that was ideal for all of these single-celled organisms to form? You know... all the animals, insects, birds, fish... all of it! As unimaginable as this sounds, this is what scientists would have us believe.

An article, titled **The Microbial Eve: Our Oldest Ancestors Were Single-Celled Organisms**, dated January 31, 2018. By npr.org, which states; "We now know that all extant living creatures derive from a single common ancestor, called **LUCA**, the **Last Universal Common Ancestor. It's hard to think of a more unifying view of life**. All living creatures are linked to a single-celled creature, the root to the complex-branching tree of life."

So, the writer of this article **finds it hard to think of a more unifying view of life. Seriously? How could someone find that view of the beginning of life more unifying than a loving Creator who brought each species about through much thought and planning. I find that statement to be very denigrating, to think that coming into existence in this manner is unifying. God is the only unifying view of life!**

Also, regarding dinosaurs... The Bible speaks of **dragons**, numerous references. Look at...

Psalm 148:7, *"Praise the LORD from the earth, ye **dragons**, and all deeps:"*

Isaiah 13:22, *"And the wild beasts of the islands shall cry in their desolate houses, and **dragons** in their pleasant palaces...".*

Isaiah 27:1, *"In that day the LORD with his sore and great and strong sword shall punish **leviathan the piercing serpent**, even leviathan that crooked serpent; and **he shall slay the dragon that is in the sea.**"*

I highlighted the **piercing serpent** because it also is describing the **dragon, Leviathan.** Which ties into the next verse...

Isaiah 30:6, *"The burden of the beasts of the south: into the land of trouble and anguish, from whence come the young and old lion, the viper and **fiery flying serpent**, they will carry their riches upon the shoulders of young asses, and their treasures upon the bunches of camels, to a people that shall not profit them."*

Isaiah 14:29, *"Rejoice not thou, whole Palestina, because the rod of him that smote thee is broken: for out of the serpent's root shall come forth a cockatrice, and his fruit shall be a **fiery flying serpent.**"*

Isaiah 34:13, *"And thorns shall come up in her palaces, nettles and brambles in the fortresses thereof: and it shall be a habitation of **dragons**, and a court for owls."*

Isaiah 43:20, *"The beast of the field shall honour me, the **dragons** and the owls: because I give waters in the wilderness, and rivers in the desert, to give drink to my people, my chosen."*

Isaiah 51:9, *"Awake, awake, put on strength, O arm of the LORD; awake, as in the ancient days, in the generations of old. Art thou not it that hath cut Rahab, and wounded the **dragon**?"*

Jeremiah 9:11, *"And I will make Jerusalem heaps, and a den of **dragons**...".*

Ezekiel 29:3, *"Speak, and say, Thus saith the Lord GOD; Behold, I am against thee, Pharaoh king of Egypt, the great **dragon** that lieth in the midst of his rivers, which hath said, My river is mine own, and I have made it for myself."*

I realize that Ezekiel is referring to Pharaoh, the king of Egypt, as the **dragon**, but where do all of these references to **dragons** come from, and not just by Isaiah, but Jeremiah, Ezekiel, and Revelation.

Revelation 12, verses 3, 4, 7, 9, 13, 16 and 17, all of which are speaking of the Devil... *"And the **great dragon** was cast out, that old **serpent, called the Devil, and Satan, which deceiveth the whole world: he was cast out into the earth, and his angels were cast out with him."** (Revelation 12:9)

And numerous times the **dragon** is spoken of in other chapters throughout Revelation. But, if you read the other scriptures I referenced, most are not talking about the Devil, but speaking of **dragons** as very real creatures.

Also, what about other supposedly "mythical" creatures that Isaiah, and others speak of. Look at Isaiah 13:21, *"But wild beasts of the desert shall lie there; and their houses shall be full of doleful creatures; and owls shall dwell there, and **satyrs** shall dance there."*

And, Isaiah 34:14, *"The wild beasts of the desert shall also meet with the wild beasts of the island, and the **satyr** shall cry to his fellow; the screech owl also shall rest there, and find for herself a place of rest."*

A **Satyr**, as defined by Easton's Bible Dictionary, states; "hairy one. Mentioned in Greek mythology as **a creature composed of a man and a goat**, supposed to inhabit wild and desolate regions. The Hebrew word is rendered also **'goat' and 'devil'**, i.e., **an idol in the form of a goat**".

It sounds to me, like the origins of the **Baphomet** creature that I have spoken of and described in **Book 2.**

And, **Unicorns**. Look at Numbers 23:22, *"God brought them out of Egypt; he hath as it were the strength of a **unicorn**."*

Numbers 24:8, *"God brought him forth out of Egypt; he hath as it were the strength of a **unicorn**: he shall eat up the nations his enemies, and shall break their bones, and pierce them through with his arrows."*

Deuteronomy 33:17, *"His glory is like the firstling of his bullock, and his horns are like the horns of **unicorns**: with them he shall push the people together to the ends of the earth: and they are the ten thousands of Ephraim, and they are the thousands of Manasseh."*

Job 39, verses 9-11; *"Will the **unicorn** be willing to serve thee, or abide by thy crib? 10) Canst thou bind the **unicorn** with his band in the furrow? or will he harrow the valleys after thee? 11) Wilt thou trust him, because his strength is great? or wilt thou leave thy labour to him?"*

Psalm 22:21, *"Save me from the lion's mouth: for thou hast heard me from the horns of the **unicorns**."*

Psalm 29:6, *"He maketh them also to skip like a calf; Lebanon and Sirion like a young **unicorn**."*

Psalm 92:10, *"But my horn shalt thou exalt like the horn of a **unicorn**: I shall be anointed with fresh oil."*

And, lastly, Isaiah 34:7, *"And the **unicorns** shall come down with them, and the bullocks with the bulls; and their land shall be soaked with blood, and their dust made fat with fatness."*

How can creatures, some of which are spoken of as early as the book of Numbers, be considered as **"mythical"**? Especially given the numerous times they are referenced, and by different authors. I realize that **satyrs** are only mentioned twice, and just by Isaiah, but the fact that a **satyr's image is the same as the Baphomet** idol, gives validation to their existence.

Furthermore, as for Archaeological finds of Dinosaur skeletons, when I see movies like **Jurassic Park** and **Jurassic World,** some of those dinosaurs sure do remind me of **dragons**! **Put some wings on that T-Rex, and fire coming out of his mouth, and you've got yourself a dragon!**

One last thought about dragons, there is a reason that Lucifer is referred to as *"the **great dragon...** that old **serpent, called the Devil, and Satan"***, because he and his demons have the ability to **shape-shift**!

Getting back to God's creation...

At **Aish.com** it is stated; **"Earth, Wind, Fire & Water: The Four Elements of our Inner World".** Rabbi Shlomo Buxbaum writes; **"Jewish tradition compares the building blocks of *nefesh* (our** inner world) to the four fundamental elements of creation. These four elements reflect the four states that all matter exist in: Solid, Plasma, Gas, and Liquid."

Not only does God have a blueprint that He uses, but specific elements... building blocks... that are the materials which He utilizes in all creation.

Another aspect that is essential to His design, is having both male and female genders. One piece of validation is found in Isaiah 13:10. It states; *"For the stars of heaven and the constellations thereof shall not give their light: the **sun** shall be darkened in **his going forth**, and the **moon** shall not cause **her light** to shine."*

I had never noticed those portions highlighted before until my research for this book made me look more closely at it. Technically, God made me look more closely at it!

The **sun**, the larger of the two, is **male**, and the **moon**, the smaller, is **female!** I find that to be very significant!

After making this discovery, I went back to Genesis to see if I had overlooked this detail in my past studies, but was relieved to see I hadn't. But I did find something else.

It's interesting how one little oversight can hone your senses from henceforth, causing us to be more mindful of the details.

Genesis 1, beginning with verse 2 states, *"And the earth was without form, and void; **and darkness was upon the face of the deep**. And the Spirit of God moved upon the face of the waters. 3) And God said, **Let there be light: and there was light.**"*

However, the sun and the moon were not created until the 4th day! Look at the scripture. Verse 14, *"And God said, Let there be lights in the firmament of the heaven to divide the day from the night; and let them be for signs, and for seasons, and for days, and years: 15) And let them be for lights in the firmament of the heaven to give light upon the earth: and it was so. 16) And **God made two great lights; the greater light to rule the day, and <u>the lesser light to rule the night</u>**: he made the stars also. 17) And God set them in the firmament of the heaven to give light upon the earth, 18) And* *to rule over the day and over the night, and to divide the light from the darkness: and God saw that it was good. 19) And the evening and the morning were **the fourth day**."*

Looking at verses 2 and 3 again, there was **darkness** and God created **light** on the **first day**! So, since day one, **darkness** and **light** existed, but that **light was not generated by the sun or the moon.**

* A quick sidenote, looking at the scripture just quoted from Isaiah, and that portion of Genesis 1:16 which I've underlined, **the moon gives off her own light**. Look at Isaiah 13:10 again, "*... and the moon shall not cause her light to shine".*

Science has told us that the moon reflects the sun's light. However, when I look at a great big full moon, like a supermoon, one so close to the earth that it looks like it could be hit with a rock when thrown, how is it that the sun's light is reflecting off of it dead on??

Common sense tells me that the sun would have to be directly in front of the moon, and totally unobstructed, for it to cause the **full moon** appearance that we see.

A **supermoon** is "When a full Moon occurs **at the closest point to Earth during its orbit, it appears larger and brighter**". (nhm.ac.uk>discover)

So, when the moon is **at the closest point to Earth**, how is the sun's light hitting it dead on? Unobstructed? Impossible! Once again, more things that don't add up! More lies!!

According to the **Book of Enoch**, both the sun and the moon go through gates, which causes the different phases, or changes in the moon's appearance.

The next full supermoon we have, I want you to go outside and stand there, and just look at it. And, think to yourself, where would the sun's light be coming from that would enable it to hit, and reflect off the moon, dead on, directly in front of it, causing the **full, unobstructed view**!

Picking up where we let off with **darkness** and **light** on the first day... I realize that John 1:1 states, "In the beginning was the Word, and the Word was with God, and the Word was God." And preachers have been telling us for centuries that the **Word** spoken of is referring to Jesus. But, I beg to differ.

I have said in both of my previous books that **darkness** is a metaphor, and one of its interpretations means **ignorance**. And, just as I have said only moments ago, "**fire** represents not only the **light** that God created, the sun (the big ball of fire in the sky), but the **intelligence** that God gave to man, as well".

Light is a metaphor for **intelligence!** Day one, **darkness** existed, and in this case represents the absence of communication! Again, we're dealing with metaphors, enabling multiple meanings. So, stay with me.

The **light** represents communication... the **spoken word!** Just like John says... "In the beginning was the Word, and the Word was with God, **and <u>the Word was God</u>**." It was God's **spoken word!** The **spoken word** that enabled Him to create... **And God said!**

Look at Psalm 33:6-9, *"**By the word of the LORD** were the heavens made; and all the host of them by the breath of his mouth. 7) He gathereth the waters of the sea together as a heap: he layeth up the depth in storehouses. 8) **Let all the earth fear the LORD: let all the inhabitants of the world stand in awe of him. 9) <u>For he spake, and it was done; he commanded, and it stood fast</u>**."*

It has nothing to do with Jesus!! And John making it about Jesus just shows how deceived John was, by Jesus.

I think that **darkness,** as spoken of in Genesis chapter 1, refers to silence! **Silence** *was upon the face of the deep*! And then the **light** was created, the **spoken word!** Which, as we all know, language, or one's ability to communicate, is a sign of **intelligence**.

So, **darkness** is a metaphor that can mean **silence, ignorance,** and **stillness of mind**, or **absence of thought**. And, **light** is a metaphor that can mean **speech (word)**, or **communication, intelligence**, and **thought**.

The **spoken word** was the first thing that God created, and it enabled Him to create everything else from that moment on.

I am not saying that communication didn't exist. I believe it did, but mentally. There was no need for verbal communication. At least not until God made the decision to create, and His **spoken word** was how He accomplished it.

Have you ever heard it said, **be careful of what you say because our words have power**? Or, being told not **to speak something**, because in doing so, **we give life to it**. And now those warnings make perfect sense!

Is God's **word** an entity? I don't know. I do know, and have written in **Book 1**, about God sending **fire** and **brimstone** to destroy Sodom and Gomorrah. Which, I firmly believe that the two angels that spoke with Lot, were the actual entities themselves, but in the form of humans, while trying to persuade Lot to flee with his family before the city was destroyed.

Not just that, but think about **Death** and **Hell**. Revelation 6:8 even has both words capitalized, indicating that they are proper nouns, ie., names! And even though the names are not capitalized in Isaiah 28, verses 15 and 18, after reading Revelation 6:8, we now know that they should be.

Look again, Revelation 6:8, *"And I looked, and behold a pale horse:* ***and his name that sat on him was Death, and Hell followed with him.*** *And power was given unto them over the fourth part of the earth, to kill with sword, and with hunger, and with death, and with the beasts of the earth."*

Isaiah 28, verse 15; *"Because ye have said,* ***We have made a covenant with death, and with hell are we at agreement****; when the overflowing scourge shall pass through, it shall not come unto us: for we have made lies our refuge, and under falsehood have we hid ourselves:... 18) And* ***your covenant with death shall be disannulled, and your agreement with hell shall not stand****; when the overflowing scourge shall pass through, then ye shall be trodden down by it."*

Here's one more from Isaiah that we can add... Isaiah 25:8, *"****He will swallow up death in victory;*** *and the Lord GOD will wipe away* *tears from off all faces; and the rebuke of his people shall he take away from off all the earth: for the LORD hath spoken it."*

In reading the verses leading up to, and following this, I see nothing in the text that leads me to understand which **death** is being referenced. But this could very well be a metaphor symbolizing both. Because I can see where both, one's demise, and the physical entity (**Death/Lucifer**), will be **swallowed up in victory** by the LORD God.

And yes, it is my opinion that the possibility exists that the **spoken words** and **emotions** of God became living entities. Offspring that resulted from His **spoken words**. Keep in mind, His powers and abilities are incomprehensible to us!

Look at Isaiah 40:26, *"Lift up your eyes on high, and behold who hath created these things, that bringeth out their host by number: **he calleth them all by names by the greatness of his might**, for that he is strong in power; not one faileth."*

Furthermore, creation itself is proof of it... **And God said**! **And, there it all is!** Sadly, in a far less pristine state than what it all first started out as.

One way that God's **word** becomes an actual entity, is **whomever He chooses to speak His words on His behalf, becomes the Word of God!**

We'll touch more on the **emotions of God** as we continue, but for now let's discuss the emotions of humans. Not just our emotions, but our instincts as well. How could it be possible for our instincts to nurture and protect evolve? How does something like that come about?

Again, God provides us with the answer of how He brought that about. Genesis 2:15 states; *"And the LORD God took the man, and put him into the garden of Eden <u>to dress it and to keep it</u>."*

If Adam was to **dress it and keep it**, that means that he was supposed to **take care of it**! To **nurture** it, and **protect** it. Which, I feel pretty confident in saying that **God put it in him to know!**

Just like Genesis 2:25 tells us, *"And they were both naked, the man and his wife, **and were not ashamed.**"*

Then, after they ate of the fruit of the forbidden tree, chapter 3, verse 8 explains; *"And they heard the voice of the LORD God walking in the garden in the cool of the day: **and Adam and his wife hid themselves from the presence of the LORD God** amongst the trees of the garden. 9) And the LORD God called unto Adam, and said unto him, Where art thou? 10) And he said, I heard thy voice in the garden, and **I was afraid, because I was naked; and I hid myself.**"*

God put it in them to not only have **fear**, but **shame**! In fact, as you continue to read the first 4 chapters, you see that man was equipped with numerous emotions. Some that were learned, and some that were innate.

For example, in chapter 3, verses 14-19, God became angry because they disobeyed Him, and punishes them. So, we see **wrath** because of **defiance**. Which also resulted in **guilt**. And, led to a future of **toil, pain, suffering** and **hardship**.

In verses 23 & 24, God casts them out of the garden of Eden. Now we see **rejection.**

In chapter 4, beginning with verse 1, *"And **Adam knew Eve his wife**; and **she conceived, and bare** Cain, and said, **I have gotten a man from the LORD.**"*

Immediately I see many emotions that would be associated with sexual intercourse, especially between husband and wife. **Love, arousal, stimulation, passion, orgasmic ecstasy,** and **contentment**. Then, **excitement, hormonal moodiness,** all of those emotions relating to pregnancy. During childbirth, **contractions, extreme pain**... and we all know how often the Bible compares times of great distress to a woman **travailing** while giving birth. And finally... **Joy, thankfulness, gratitude,** and **appreciation**. A gamut of emotions which are experienced just within this one verse.

This doesn't even take into consideration those emotions and instincts that kick in, such as **nurturing** and **protecting**. But even though there is no scripture provided that speaks of it, those qualities exist! I have evidence of it, and plan to share it in just a moment.

Next, verse 4; *"And Abel, he also brought of the firstlings of his flock and of the fat thereof. **And the LORD had respect unto Abel and to his offering:**"*

Here we see God showing **respect** to Abel, which must have made Abel feel **happy,** possibly even gave him some **self confidence,** and maybe even a little **pride.**

In verse 5, the scripture states; *"**And Cain was very wroth, and his countenance fell.**"* Cain feels **disappointment, rejection, sadness** and **anger.**

The definition of **countenance** states, "a person's face or facial expression". (Oxford Languages)

Also, "The general appearance of a person's face, which often **reflects   spiritual   attitude   and   state   of   mind**". (site.churchofjesuschrist.org)

I really like that second definition based on its inclusion of that portion highlighted in bold type. I feel that it more accurately defines the biblical use of it.

Continuing on. Cain's initial reaction then led to **resentment, jealousy, vengeance, rage** and **murder**. Verse 8 states; *"And Cain talked with Abel his brother: and it came to pass, when they were in the field, that **Cain rose up against Abel his brother, and slew him.**"*

In verse 9, Cain **lies** to God, when asked, *"Where is Abel thy brother?"* Saying, **I know not,** Am I my brother's keeper?

* Another sidenote... Verse 10 states; *"And he said, What hast thou done? **the voice of thy brother's <u>blood crieth unto me from the ground</u>.**"*

And now... Numbers 35:33, *"So ye shall not pollute the land wherein ye are: **for blood it defileth the land: and <u>the land cannot</u>**"*

be cleansed of the blood that is shed therein, but by the blood of him that shed it."

Can you even imagine how defiled all of the land throughout this world is? Not to mention, all of it crying out to God!

Back on track. What about the emotions that Adam and Eve were now experiencing? **Grief, despair, loss...** And let's not forget the emotions they were feeling over their older son killing their younger son! **Heartache** and **suffering** like they had never experienced before.

Next, in verse 11 God **curses** Cain, and makes him a **fugitive and a vagabond.**

Beginning with verse 13, Cain tells God, *"My punishment is greater than I can bear. 14) Behold, thou hast driven me out this day from the face of the earth; and from thy face shall I be hid; and I shall be a fugitive and a vagabond in the earth; and it shall come to pass, that every one that findeth me shall slay me."*

I see a lot of emotions going on here... **remorse**, possibly feeling **abandonment**, **demoralized**, maybe **embarrassed**, fear of **persecution**, fear of **isolation**, fear of being **cut off from God**, and ultimately his own **death**.

I can keep going... but, it's pretty evident that these emotions are hardwired into each of us, and triggered by different events, interactions, and reactions. And, how does something like that evolve?

Furthermore, all of those emotions that I cited from the first 4 chapters of Genesis, took place in less than 129 years. I base that on the birth of Seth, which occurs in chapter 4, verse 25.

Then, validation of the 129 years is found just 3 verses away from that, in chapter 5, verse 3; *"And Adam lived a hundred and thirty years, and begat a son in his own likeness, after his image; and called his name Seth:"*

I feel certain that those emotions were realized much sooner than 129 years, but regardless of whether it was 1 year or the full 129...

It took God only a fraction of time to accomplish it, compared to the billions of years that it came about through evolution!

Also, if Adam was 130 years old when Seth was born, how old was he when Cain and Abel were born? We have to remember that Adam wasn't born, so his 130 years began the day that he was created as a man.

With that said, it's entirely possible that Adam and Eve began their family within the first 5-10 years after being created.

My point is, I find it interesting that God changed the number of man's years to 120. I know that 12 is significant, but could it be that 120 is also significant because that was possibly the age that Abel was when he died? I believe that its highly possible!

Understand, 120 was still practically a child compared to the ages that people lived to be at that time, with Methuselah being the known oldest at 969. Adam, himself, lived to be 930. For those interested, this information is available in Genesis, chapter 5.

However, Abel dying at age 120 would be equivalent to being the age of a 10-12 year old, given the number of man's years today being 120 compared to approximately 1,000 back then.

If my theory is true, Adam would have been no more than 9 years old (after his creation), when Abel was born. Probably less, depending on the amount of time that passed between Abel's death and Seth's birth. The math proves to me that man's years being changed to 120, is no coincidence. God changed man's years to that number for a reason, just as He always has a reason for everything that He does.

The evidence that I spoke of, regarding our **emotions** and **instincts,** is as follows;

An email that I received on December 1, 2004, of which the **Subject** stated: **Sermon from a Duck** proved to be not only heartbreaking, but amazing, as well. It contained an article that ran in the **National Geographic** several years prior. It states;

"After a forest fire in Yellowstone National Park, forest rangers began their trek up a mountain to assess the inferno's damage.

One ranger found a bird literally petrified in ashes, perched statuesquely on the ground at the base of a tree. Somewhat sickened by the eerie sight, he knocked over the bird with a stick.

When he gently struck it, three tiny chicks scurried from under their dead mother's wings. The loving mother, keenly aware of impending disaster, had carried her offspring to the base of the tree and had gathered them under her wings, instinctively knowing that the toxic smoke would rise. She could have flown to safety, but had refused to abandon her babies.

Then the blaze had arrived and the heat had scorched her small body, the mother had remained steadfast. Because she had been willing to die, so those under the cover of her wings would live."

At the bottom of the email it states;

"He will cover you with his feathers, and under his wings you will find refuge." (Psalm 91:4)

What an incredible story! **How does science explain these instincts? Please tell me how it was possible for these instincts to evolve?**

Also, a quote from the series **Taboo** (Season 1, Episode 7)...

"The lioness will fiercely protect her cubs, regardless of the consequences. Even if that means her certain death."

A mother's (parent's) willingness to protect their young is an innate quality that is found in most all, if not all, mammals.

Britannica.com explains a **mammal** as, **"any member of the group of vertebrate animals in which the young are nourished with milk from special mammary glands of the mother.** In addition to these characteristic milk glands, mammals are distinguished by several other unique features."

God not only equipped us with the emotions and instincts to nurture and protect our young, but designed the females of each species with the features necessary to nourish their young.

I must confess... I just had a conversation with my oldest daughter last night, during which she told me about the latest topic that was raging throughout Social Media. How one question in particular is being asked, that no one seems to have an answer for anymore. That question being...

What is a woman?

This stems from all of the transgendering taking place, and also, from those that are born of one sex, but choose to **identify** as the other.

And, as I was copying the above quote from **Britannica.com**, it suddenly occurred to me how it is, for the most part, the very essence of what a woman is. With one additional inclusion that I will add... **A woman also was born with a womb to grow and nourish her baby while carrying it, and a vagina through which to deliver it.**

If you weren't born with these body parts... a uterus, cervix, vagina, and special mammary glands to nourish your young, then, regardless of what you choose to identify as....

You are not a woman!! What is a Woman? Someone BORN with all of the above stated parts!

It truly amazes me how things have been sent to me, or notes that I've made throughout the years, and have held onto all of this stuff for reasons unknown. And conversations that occur at just the right time. You may think that this is nothing out of the ordinary at all, that **coincidences** happen all the time, to many people. But I have made it very clear, **there is no such thing as a coincidence!**

Getting back on track... Let's talk about our nature and temperament, because that's something that varies from one person to another as well.

I have struggled with a duality, of sorts, throughout my adult life. More so during my fall from grace, as I call it, which I elaborate about in **Book 2**. It's kind of like that cartoon where you see the little angel sitting on one shoulder, and the little devil sitting on the other.

What I have personally lived, and came to realize, is that we all have good and evil in each of us. And, depending on which of those natures that you steer yourself towards, determines your inclination to be either good or evil.

If you strive to be good, and do good... good will dominate. If you take pleasure in being bad, or participating in activities that are not good, then you will, slowly but surely be drawn to the **dark side. Just like Star Wars!**

Just as I've explained the various interpretations associated with **light** and **darkness**, there is yet another that exists. That is **light** representing **good**, and **darkness** representing **evil**.

For me, having walked in **light**, and then **darkness**, and then returning to **light**, I feel this struggle, at times, where **good** and **evil** are tugging on me from both sides. I keep praying for God to cast out the evil from me, and to put a hedge around me to protect me. But, what if evil is part of our nature? That **duality** that I spoke of. And, if that's the case, can evil be cast out?

Bear in mind that I am speaking of two different aspects of our nature, and that is totally different than being possessed by evil spirits.

An example of being possessed by evil spirits would be **inviting Jesus to come into your heart.** As I stated in **Book 1**, anyone that has ever watched a vampire show or movie, or have read books about them, knows that **they must be given an invitation to come in**, to enter your home, your domain.

Don't you find it strange that Jesus requires an invitation to come into your heart? God doesn't! And, if Jesus was the true son of God, and one in the same, he wouldn't require an invitation either!

Furthermore, if someone ever knocks at your door, and for whatever reason they ask if you will invite them in? A red flag should immediately go up in your mind. Evil always requires an invitation. And I don't care how nice they are, or if they're giving away free Bibles, if they ask to be invited in, always say **no**!

God's laws are in our hearts. Our heart is where God resides. Look at Jeremiah 31:33, *"But this shall be **the covenant** that I will make with the house of Israel; After those days, saith the LORD, **I will put my law in their inward parts, and write it in their hearts**; and will be their God, and they shall be my people."*

Not just that, but as the article by Dr. Fraser was titled, **Your body is a temple**, it is! Look at 1st Corinthians 3:16-17, *"**Know ye not that ye are the temple of God, and that the Spirit of God dwelleth in you? 17) If any man defile the temple of God, him shall God destroy; for the temple of God is holy, which temple ye are.**"*

Look also at Leviticus 20:7, *"**Sanctify yourselves therefore, and be ye holy: for I am the LORD your God.**"*

And, when we **invite Jesus (evil) in, we just evicted God**. Because God will not coexist with evil.

Look at Psalm 5:4, *"**For thou art not a God that hath pleasure in wickedness: <u>neither shall evil dwell with thee</u>. 5) The foolish shall not stand in thy sight**: thou hatest all workers of iniquity."*

With that said, my mind is what becomes tormented by unwanted thoughts. Think about that old adage, **an idle mind is the devil's playground**!

It's never in my heart that temptation tries to lead me astray, it's always in my mind that it occurs, when it happens. I commanded Jesus to get out of my heart years ago, but the devil watches for those idle moments that he can pop in and assault me. He usually tries to scare me, or make me feel unworthy, putting doubts in my mind about these things I write.

One thought that pops in quite often is, **What if I'm wrong about Jesus?** But no sooner than that thought pops in, the next one right behind it is, **All the world will worship the beast!** And the moment that I recognize what's going on, I say aloud, **Get out of my head!**

Another example that occurs quite often, are thoughts that keep buzzing around in my head while I'm trying to pray. It's as though my mind is its own separate domain that functions independently from the rest of me. And just today, as I was praying, this very thing happened. At which point, I stopped in mid-sentence and asked God, **How does that happen? How can my mind be thinking of other things while I am, at the same moment, speaking out loud to you?**

Then, I was filled with the answer... **My prayer was coming from my heart, not my mind! And yes... they do work independently of one another!**

Look again at Isaiah 44:18, *"They have not known nor understood: for he hath shut their eyes, that they cannot see; and **their hearts, that they cannot understand.**"*

Again, not only are God's laws in our hearts, but that is where He resides as well... His temple! He communicates from within our hearts, pulling at our heart strings to do what is right. And, it is between the heart and the mind that this duality struggles.

The heart being God's command center, and the mind being the Devil's, at least his playground anyway.

Many times we are plagued, haunted by movies and shows that we watch, or books we read. Depending on the content, scary genre can plant seeds in our minds, causing us to dwell on things that make us fearful. Or, the devil using those fears to torment us. The same goes for genre containing violence.

Also, content that is of a sexual nature, causing us to possibly daydream about love and passionate situations. What we take in, or subject our minds to, can come back to haunt us. The devil knows our weaknesses, and our desires. He knows what we're watching on TV, or websites that we're looking at. And that's what he uses against us.

And if our nature is inclined to be swayed by the **dark side**, and our heart has been darkened because so, then we are driven by our nature to act on this visual and verbal content, allowing it to come out. Speaking it and doing it!

Look at verse 21; *"**For from within, out of the heart of men, proceed evil thoughts, adulteries, fornications, murders, 22) Thefts, covetousness, wickedness, deceit, lasciviousness, an evil eye, blasphemy, pride, foolishness: 23) All these evil things come from within, and defile the man.**"*

Look also at Mark 7:18-20; *"Do ye not perceive, that **whatsoever thing from without entereth into the man, it cannot defile him;** 19) Because it entereth not into his heart, but into the belly, and goeth out into the draught, purging all meats? 20) And he said, **That which cometh out of the man, that defileth the man.**"*

Even though this scripture has been twisted to mean that Jesus **declared all foods clean**, that's not what he's saying!

It means that we can subject ourselves to all sorts of content, that which is heard and seen. And, it isn't what we take in that corrupts us, but what comes back out of us. When we act on that content that we have heard or seen, that's when we become corrupt. But if we never act on it, no harm done!

However, once again Jesus' teachings are in opposition to God's, because in reality, God doesn't even want us to subject ourselves to anything that is unholy, whether it be content that we hear or see!

Look at Isaiah 33:15, *"He that walketh righteously, and speaketh uprightly; he that despiseth the gain of oppressions, that shaketh his hands from holding of bribes, that stoppeth his ears from hearing of blood, **and shutteth his eyes from seeing evil;**"*

And even though we may not act on it, we can still be haunted by it. The devil is always looking for those opportunities to throw temptation in our path, and we give him the ammunition to use against us.

But, if we refrain from **seeing evil**, we diminish the devil's power over us. And, sadly, at this day and time, evil is everywhere we look! So, for the sake of our children, we need to discuss the snares that are being set for them, and that's coming up in the next chapter.

While doing some research, I came across a website, Jewfaq.org, which confirmed my suspicion of this dual nature. It stated, regarding an **"Evil Impulse - Humanity was created with a dual nature: an impulse to do what is right and a selfish (evil) impulse. Free will is the ability to choose which impulse to follow."**

Isn't that interesting! On that note, look at Isaiah 7:16, *"**For before the child shall know to refuse the evil, and choose the good,** the land that thou abhorrest shall be forsaken of both her kings."*

I agree completely that choosing good over evil is a choice that we make. That is the very epitome of exercising our free will.

Human nature, as stated by the Wikipedia, says; "As originally created, the Bible describes **'two elements' in human nature: 'the body and the breath or spirit of life breathed into it by God**'. By this was created a 'living soul', meaning a 'living person'."

An article titled **Duality of Human Nature**, found online at The Student Voice Network, states; "'Duality is a presence that constitutes many important parts of the world. It is, at its core, the idea that nothing is singular: **to have existence is to have contrast**, but in that contrast there is still connectivity (Cambridge Dictionary). When discussing the duality of human nature, it is broadly 'the intuitive and psychological confusing nature of mankind to be twofold' (Urban Dictionary)). **It suggests that all humans have opposing forces making up their personalities and this governs their way of life. More directly, the duality of human nature can be broken down to the intentions in which one starts an action: whether that action is rooted in benevolence, or in selfishness.**"

I must say, I do believe there is something to this. Because why would God want to create humans that were only obedient, and completely submissive at all times? **He wants us to choose to be** obedient and submissive. **Not by force, but by choice.** Which, again, **there's the free will!**

More evidence of the existence of this **duality of human nature** can be found in the scripture, not far from where we were previously when discussing the **emotions** of man, and the death of Abel.

Genesis 6:5, *"And **GOD saw that the wickedness of man was great in the earth, and that every imagination of the thoughts of his heart was only evil continually.** 6) And it repented the LORD that he had made man on the earth, and it grieved him at his heart."*

In verse 7 the LORD states; *"... **I will destroy man whom I have created from the face of the earth; both man, and beast, and the creeping thing, and the fowls of the air; for it repenteth me that I have made them.**"*

God was so troubled by the death of Abel, and the evil in Cain that had brought it about, that He made the decision to destroy all of it. Not excluding Adam and Eve's disobedience being a factor as well. So, clearly, things were not going according to His plan.

Then verse 8 tells us, *"**But Noah found grace in the eyes of the LORD.**"* And when God saw that one man was worthy enough for Him to salvage, He made the decision to start again.

Genesis 8:21, *"And the LORD smelled a sweet savour; and the LORD said in his heart, **I will not again curse the ground any more for man's sake; for the imagination of man's heart is evil from his youth; neither will I again smite any more every thing living, as I have done.**"*

An article found under **Judaism** at britannica.com states; "Rabbinic literature created a technical term, *ha-ra'* ('the **evil impulse**'), to denote the source within humans of their **disobedience**, and subsequently the counter-term *yetzer ha-tov* ('the **good impulse**') was used to indicate humans' **obedience**. These terms more clearly suggest the ethical quality of human duality, while their opposition and conflict point to **human freedom and the ethical choices humans must make.**"

Again, we see that free will is man's biggest stumbling block!

Here are some interesting quotes from different sites, regarding the heart and the brain.

"The silent, often subconscious conversation that is taking place inside us is one of the most vital communications we will ever find ourselves engaged in. **It's the dialogue of emotion-based signal... between our hearts and our brains, also known as the heart-brain connection.**" (ncbi.nlm.nih.gov>pmc)

"Most of your decisions are made at the heart level, and then you justify them with your logical thinking head brain". (vistage.com)

"In the realm of decision-making, the clash between the heart and mind is a perennial struggle that individuals face. **The heart, driven by emotions, instincts, and desires, often pulls us in one direction, while the mind, guided by logic, reasoning, and analysis, urges us to follow a different path.**"

The real struggle when it comes to any decision-making is **common sense, what God put in our hearts to know, verses education... what institutions have taught our brains to believe, many of which are lies**!

This battle that takes place between the heart versus the mind, goes beyond that. With me, it's not just my mind that I struggle with, but my whole body.

I've shared, in **Book 2**, my battles with artificial sweeteners and formaldehyde, as well as all of my other sensitivities I have.

For me it boils down to the **spirit battling against the flesh**, the **flesh** representing the entire body. These bodies are basically vessels in which our spirit, or essence resides. And, as long as our spirit is trapped in these bodies, conflict will exist.

Also, look at Ephesians 6:12, *"**For we wrestle not against flesh and blood, but against principalities, against powers, against the rulers of the darkness of this world, against spiritual wickedness in high places.**"*

The battle that humans have, spoken of in this verse, is a **spiritual battle**, against very real **spiritual entities**. Entities that are not bound, trapped in, physical bodies. The fact that humans are bound by flesh, makes our battle against these spirits even more difficult.

However, as humans, **we do wrestle against flesh and blood... our own!**

Another interesting discovery that I've recently made is, when I'm doing something that I shouldn't be doing, He lets those tormenting thoughts attack.

An example of this is, many times during the Sabbath I would keep my notebook handy and write down thoughts that came to mind. This happens a lot when I'm working on a book. And, without realizing what I was doing, I would grab my notebook and start making notes, so I wouldn't forget anything. But I then began to notice a pattern. It was after each of these occurrences that I became tormented. It's nothing that I would consider terrifying, but more so aggravating. And I would pray for God to put a hedge around my mind, but the assault would continue.

Then, upon noticing the pattern and connecting it to my activities, I finally realized that **I had been working**! And, it matters not that I was working for God, it only mattered to Him **that I was working on the Sabbath!**

Once I recognized that, and stopped... the assault stopped. And please don't ever think that He doesn't know, or that you can fool Him. Look at Numbers 32:23, *"... behold, ye have sinned against the LORD: **and be sure your sin will find you out.**"* He always knows!

I'd like to close this chapter with one of my poems, which I find very fitting based on these things that we've discussed regarding God's creation.

To See the World as Thee

Oh, for a closer look I pray
To see the world as Thee...
To marvel at Thy hand at work
In perfect splendor, as it be.

Most all men are distracted
by their job at work, or play...
They never stop, not even once
To notice life before it fades.

The leaves that change their pigment,
in the coolness of the fall.
The frozen filigree on trees,
before the winter's chill doth thaw.

The hint of green, so ever slight
when spring is on its way...
With daffodils and crocus blooms
in bright hues are all array.

The sandy beaches burn with heat
as the summer's sun bears down...
With white capped waves of foamy froth,
its beauty is profound!

The vivid colors of the sky
when the sunset's at its peak...
The beauty of its glory,
of which there are no words to speak.

The features of a new born babe
when it's only minutes old...
Are fully formed and perfect,
complete with tiny lashes, and itty bitty toes!

God's creation is full of detail,
if only we would stop and look.
The workings of His fingers
are too amazing to be forsook.

Our eyes which He has given us,
are instruments to detect...
To see the miracle of His creation
None of which we should neglect.

Written 10/11/22

All of the details of life are a testimony of His creation.

They're Coming for Our Children

For many years now our children have been the target of an assault put forth by the evil regime that secretly runs, not just this country, but the world. Those of my generation are probably much more aware of it than those of more recent times.

Born in 1957, I was fortunate enough to be raised in an era that was still somewhat wholesome and shielded. We had one television that started out with 2 channels, until a local broadcasting station joined the lineup shortly thereafter.

It was all censored, no profanity, no nudity, not even cleavage! When Elvis Presley first appeared on the Ed Sullivan show in 1956, they even censored his performance, refusing to show his gyrating hips below his waist.

I wonder how many reading this are questioning, Who in the heck is Ed Sullivan? And, some of those from this present generation may not even be aware of who Elvis Presley is??

Those of my generation know what I'm talking about! Shows like **Leave it to Beaver** personified the average families of our time. I say **average** because dysfunctionality was not as prevalent then, but it did exist.

I'm so thankful that I had a near perfect childhood, but many others were not as fortunate. Sadly, that has been a pretty consistent factor throughout time. There have always been levels of disparity, but that is totally different from the levels of immorality that I am attempting to speak of.

My childhood was very similar to that of **Leave it to Beaver**, the main difference being that my mom, unlike June, didn't wear dresses around the house every day. Children were, for the most part, disciplined and well mannered. Our parents, coming from a generation of children that were to be seen and not heard, were not quite as rigid. But they too, were supporters of obedience.

That statement is the perfect example of the changes that have taken place just within my mother's lifetime, who still lives. Going from children that were to be seen and not heard, to children who are unruly, loud, and not allowed to be disciplined. Talk about opposite ends of the spectrum!

God makes it very clear in the Old Testament that not only are we to discipline our children, but He will discipline us as well. Look at Deuteronomy 8:5, *"Thou shalt also consider in thine heart, that, as a man chasteneth his son, so the LORD thy God chasteneth thee."*

2nd Samuel 7:14, *"... If he commit iniquity, I will chasten him with the rod of men, and with the stripes of the children of men".*

Proverbs 3:11, *"My son, despise not the chastening of the LORD; neither be weary of his correction: 12) For whom the LORD loveth he correcteth; even as a father the son in whom he delighteth."*

Proverbs 13:24, *"He that spareth his rod hateth his son: but he that loveth him chasteneth him betimes."*

Proverbs 22:6, *"Train up a child in the way he should go: and when he is old, he will not depart from it."*

Proverbs 22:15, *"Foolishness is bound in the heart of a child; but the rod of correction shall drive it far from him."*

Proverbs 29:15, *"The rod and reproof give wisdom: but a child left to himself bringeth his mother to shame."*

Proverbs 29:17, *"Correct thy son, and he shall give thee rest; yea, he shall give delight unto thy soul."*

Psalm 89:30, *"If his children forsake my law, and walk not in my judgments... 32) Then will I visit their transgression with the rod, and their iniquity with stripes... ".*

The list is extensive if you factor in the Book of Leviticus, which discusses the punishments for the various laws that are broken.

God makes it very clear that discipline is required for all, regardless of the age.

If children are not disciplined, they will not only rule the roost, but can make your life a living hell! And, for quite some time now, parents have become lax about disciplining, adopting new ways of correcting bad behaviour. Punishments which include **time outs**, **suspension of privileges**, and other non-physical ramifications that are, in my opinion, more like compromises.

But there is a difference between discipline and child abuse. And, because of those that are abusive, society has pretty much tied our hands when it comes to disciplining our children. Which has forced us to utilize those less effective options, thus leading to the current state of chaos and upheaval that now exists.

Children acting out in classrooms and on buses, knowing that teachers and bus drivers are powerless to stand against them. Daring them to lay a finger on them! And, not just teachers and bus drivers being powerless, but parents as well.

My youngest daughter has a daughter from a previous relationship, and she started seeing a man that also had a daughter from a previous relationship. They became pregnant, got engaged, and moved in together.

Her daughter was 8 at the time, and his daughter was 6, or both were nearly those ages.

Backtracking for a moment, I was raised by a man that believed in discipline and spared not the rod! However, his rod was a thin belt. My sister and I, being only 16 months apart, were a handful at times... at least for my mother, anyway!

I can remember, like it was yesterday, her yelling, **You just wait until your father gets home!** Of course, when he came home, we became perfect angels. But he knew better. And it never mattered who was at fault, if one got it, we both did!

After our spanking, we were sent to our room where we would sob as though we would surely never walk again! And, within 5-10 minutes our dad would come in, without fail, and tell us how much he loved us.

If we smarted off, or talked back, he would pop us in the mouth. Not with his fist, but the back of his hand. Just a quick pop! Not busting the lip open, or knocking our teeth out, or even giving us a fat lip. Most of the time we didn't even cry, because he wasn't trying to pop us that hard, he just wanted to get our attention... to make a point that that behaviour was unacceptable.

It's a technique! A very controlled flicking of the hand, making contact, but with precision, so as not to hit too hard. It's more of a **shock and awe tactic**!

Which means, "a military strategy based on **the use of** overwhelming **power and** spectacular **displays of force to paralyze the enemy's perception** of the battlefield **and destroy their will to fight**."

Trust me, that technique coupled with just the right facial expression is very effective! And, at times, he would add a few choice words, such as... **You'd better watch it, or next time I'll knock your teeth down your throat!** Like I said... **Shock and awe!**

My dad had many quips, one for every occasion! Some of which includes; **You better knock that chip off your shoulder before I knock it off for you!** Or, **I'll yank your arm off and beat you half to death with it!** And, **You better straighten up or I'll put the fear of God in you!**

And those that have read **Book 2**, know that my dad was in the military. So, not only was he extremely disciplined, but he disciplined us as well.

I'm sitting here laughing as I write these expressions that he would use, but they weren't funny a bit back then! God love him! He was a good man, and a great dad!

One thing that I learned from my dad was the importance of being methodical. If you are consistent with discipline, you won't need to take action very often. Just the threat of action will keep a child in check if they know that you have a proven track record. So as bad

86

as it may sound, popping a child in their mouth, was not only very effective, but seldom used.

Please don't misunderstand, he never left a mark or a bruise, but we knew that when he said something, he meant it! He truly put the **fear of God** in us! And, as I said in **Book 2**, he was our God until we were old enough to know better! He was our role model for how we should honour, respect, fear, obey and love God, once we knew the difference.

Growing up with discipline taught me to discipline my children when I became a parent. And I cannot tell you how many times I wanted to say to my children, **You just wait until your father gets home!** But my husband was not one to discipline.

I remember on one occasion we were in the car, and you wouldn't think that there being 6 years difference between them, that they would carry on so. But the younger one always found some way of irritating the older one.

I kept calling them down, to no avail. And, finally I looked at my husband, who was driving, and said, **Will you please speak to them!** And, turning his head to the side, he said, **Now girls, don't you see that you are driving your mother crazy?** That was not at all what I was hoping for, and from that point on I just handled it myself.

Like my dad, I too popped my children in the mouth for being disrespectful, back talking, or using inappropriate language. And there have been occasions where spankings were necessary as well.

Which brings me back to my story about my youngest daughter. Being raised by a parent that was a proponent of discipline, and having her mouth popped on occasions, she too utilized the same technique with her daughter.

Before I continue, let me say that I share these stories because they serve a point in the different issues that I speak of. Even though I don't mind sharing stories, I prefer not to share the names of my children, grandchildren or other loved ones that I speak of. It may make my stories sound less personal, or even somewhat cold, but that's not the case. So please be understanding of my privacy. Back to my story...

I've seen her in action. And there's something about being a grandparent, where you want to step in and calm the situation, and save your sweet little granddaughter from her mother's wrath. But, in doing so, I would be undermining her authority, and diminishing her power in front of her child. And that's not good!

So, when my daughter and her boyfriend became engaged, he wanted her to love his daughter as her own, which included disciplining her as well. He had been a single parent, with full custody, living at his mom's, who would help him with child care when needed. And knowing that his daughter had lacked the love and nurturing that a mother provides, he wanted her to finally have that.

Now, understand that there are all sorts of factors involved, and it's not my intention to go into all of those details. However, I will provide the ones that are necessary for understanding.

Her daughter was more disciplined due to her being exposed to it from the beginning. His daughter wasn't. Her daughter rarely argued, or talked back because she knew the consequences... the technique I spoke of earlier. His daughter, being raised differently, would argue and talk back, making sure that she always had the last word, or tried anyway.

Initially, my daughter would withhold any physical discipline, trying to build a relationship with his child. But then the situation worsened because her daughter began to resent the fact that she was being disciplined, and the other one wasn't.

Not only that, his daughter was beginning to enjoy seeing the other one punished, and she was not!

My daughter would tell her fiance about the issues that had occurred, upon his return home from work. But many times, it was then too late for him to do anything about it. Especially given the fact that his daughter had her daddy wrapped around her little finger and could convince him of whatever she wanted.

I was not being, nor have I ever been, impartial. I was merely an outsider looking in, watching as all of this unfolded. Not just that, but I, personally, had a situation arise where the child manipulated her grandmother, leading her to believe that I had said something to her (the child) that I had not! In fact, I was blown away by how young this child was, and yet so proficient at the art of manipulation.

Shortly after they had all united under one roof, they held a family gathering. They had a fairly large living room that exited from both ends, which would ultimately circle back to the kitchen regardless of which direction you went.

I was setting up a card table in the living room when his daughter came in to help. I opened up the small child's table, and she placed the two chairs on each side. I, then moved one of the chairs that was blocking the aisle, and told her, **Let's put this one here so we don't block the walkway.**

At that very moment her grandmother came in, and she immediately turned on the tears, I mean crocodile tears! Her grandmother, trying to console her, quickly asked what the matter was? And she said, **I wanted to put the <u>table</u> over there, and she wouldn't let me!** And she continued on about it, as the tears poured from her eyes.

The table was never the issue!

I stood there watching as this 5 1/2-6 year old child was giving the performance of her life, to her grandmother, to get her way. At that point, I just turned and left the room. I'm sharing this, not because I have an issue with a child that is not of my blood, but because this was my first occurrence of seeing her in action. And this story is necessary to lay the ground work of my next one.

So, school had now started, and my daughter was trying to stress that she (his daughter) get ready. But she continued to be uncooperative and argue.

Then suddenly, my daughter popped her... the technique that I spoke of. It was more of a reflex, from the times that she had found it necessary to discipline her own child. And trying now to be a mother to his daughter, the time had come to take a stand against back talking. And, the tears came pouring out!

She was finally able to calm the child, and the child even began to cooperate and finished getting ready for school. My daughter hugged her, and told her that she loved her, but explained that she was not going to tolerate back talking any more.

Then, upon her arrival at school, she was looking somewhat forlorned, so her teacher asked if she was ok? I'm sure you can imagine what happened next!

The school contacted the CPS, Child Protection Services, who then contacted my daughter.

Long story short, the matter was explained, resolved, and no formal charges were made. But, after that, my daughter never attempted to discipline her again. In fact, she even stopped disciplining her own daughter. Because how can you discipline only one, and not the other?

My point with this story is how our hands are tied to prevent us from disciplining our children! CPS was notified immediately, based on the broken heart of a 6 year old, and they were ready to take action. And in some cases, that includes the removal of children from their parents.

My daughter never has been abusive to her children, or anyone else's. But, the child, not realizing the backlash that could result, exaggerated the details, causing the school to sound the alarm.

And this story isn't just about my daughter! It's about any parent that tries to discipline their children at this day and time. Society is preventing us from touching them. Not only preventing us, but causing us to be fearful of doing so. I know it really scared my daughter!

Sadly, things like this don't just scare the parents, but it also empowers the children! Showing them that they now have leverage to use against their parents, and can play that trump card any time, to get their way.

And this is just one aspect of what's taking place. The courts continue to empower the children, not just regarding discipline, but by preventing parents from making decisions for their minor children in matters that affects their health and well-being. Decisions pertaining to the physical and psychological altering of their bodies!

Even schools are now being forced to, not only accept, but to make the necessary changes to accommodate students that are of one sex orientation, but identify as a different one.

And, for those students (children) that wish to become a different sex, through hormone altering drugs and surgical procedures, but are being prevented by their parents, are now being supported by the courts!

The headline reads, **"Court Upholds Removal of Child From Parents, Related to Child's Transgender Identity"**. The article is dated 10/21/2022 and written by Eugene Volokh (reason.com).

According to the article, the "Mother was verbally and emotionally abusing then-**sixteen-year-old** Child by using rude and demeaning language toward Child regarding Child's transgender identity".

In the 1st chapter of Numbers alone, God refers to the adults as those *"from twenty years old and upward"*, 15 times! Numbers 1:3, 1:18, 1:20, 1:22, 1:24, 1:26, 1:28, 1:30, 1:32, 1:34, 1:36, 1:38, 1:40, 1:42 and 1:45.

Also, Exodus 30, where God first tells Moses, in verse 12, "... *takest the sum of the children of Israel after their number, then shall they give every man a ransom for his soul unto the LORD... 14) Every one that passeth among them that are numbered, **from twenty years old and above**"*. Clearly, in God's eyes a person is considered to be a child until they reach the age of 20.

Another article, titled, **"Judge upholds Chico school district's protection of student's gender identity from parents"**. Dated 7/13/23 by Stephen Hobbs (The Sacramento Bee). A quote from the article states, **U.S. District Court Judge John Mendez said in a ruling that the authority of the district to safeguard the information overrode parental rights."**

Also, **"Chico staff were not forcing students to adopt a different identity or telling them to keep it secret from their parents, the judge wrote. Instead, school officials were just allowing students to choose who they wanted to share their identities with."**

Evidently, we now have a **Gender Identity Law** that "allows a person to modify their personal data in the National Registry and to change their registered name, image, and sex by submitting a letter."

The Wikipedia states, **"In addition, <u>it orders that all medical treatments for transitioning be included in the Compulsory Medical Program</u>, which guarantees coverage by practices throughout the health system, both public and private. Approved by the Senate on <u>9 May 2012</u> and promulgated on 24 May, it has been lauded by the United Nations as a pioneering step for transgender rights in the region."**

Regarding **Gender Identity**, the Wikipedia states, "Essentialists argue that gender identity is determined at birth by biological and genetic factors, while social constructivists argue that gender identity and the way it is expressed are socially constructed, instead determined by cultural and social influences."

Now, here's another opinion on its origins. An article by Abby Turner and Andrew Kaczynski, CNN, dated 7/13/2023. Headline states; **"Robert F. Kennedy Jr. repeatedly suggested that chemicals in water are impacting sexuality of children".**

As those who have read **Book 2**, already know, I discuss the evils of chemicals at length, not just in the water, but the food we eat, and the air we breathe. This article is a must read!

Kennedy, not only an environmental lawyer and anti-vaccine activist, is a Democratic presidential candidate in this upcoming 2024 election.

The article states that "Endocrine disruptors are chemicals that interfere with the body's hormones and endocrine system, according to the Environmental Protection Agency. Such chemicals are commonly found in pesticides and plastic, and can affect reproductive functions and increase the risk of obesity."

Dr. Andrea Gore, professor of pharmacology and toxicology at University of Texas at Austin, said the sex of humans is determined at the moment of conception, and cannot later be altered by endocrine-disrupting chemicals."

Kennedy isn't saying that these chemicals alter the physical characteristics, such as changing a penis into a vagina, or vice versa, but they alter the psychological and emotional characteristics instead... the hormones!

The **Functions of Hormones:**

- Food metabolism.
- Growth and development.
- Controlling thirst and hunger.
- Maintaining body temperature.
- Regulating mood and cognitive functions.
- **Initiating and maintaining sexual development and reproduction.**

This information was found at **byjus.com**, but numerous other sources supply basically the same as what is stated above.

Our bodies are under a constant attack from chemicals. The air we breathe through toxins that are being pumped into and/or released into the atmosphere, intentionally and accidentally?? Our food, by chemical preservatives, sweeteners, seed modifications (GMO's), growth hormones and herbicides. Our water, by chemicals that supposedly decontaminate or purify, not to mention the chemicals that are deliberately and/or accidentally released into our rivers and oceans. Detergents that we bathe in, and clean with. Prescription medications, chemical concoctions which they create to control all of our body's reactions to the numerous chemicals that we are subjected to daily... Read **Book 2!**

If all of these chemicals can cause, or mimic, the numerous diseases and illnesses that have resulted, because of our constant exposure, then I have no doubt, whatsoever, that these chemicals can interfere with the functions of all our internal systems as well. Corrupting them, altering them, modifying them, word it however you want! It's the same thing! Stop thinking that our world (those that run it) would never do this to us!

I have to ask, what else could be causing this worldwide leap of our young people questioning their sexuality? If this was a Sci Fi movie, the plot would involve **something being put into the water!** Like I stated in **Book 1**, there's a lot of truth to movies, and they love to put it right in our faces!

I will say this, I believe that Kennedy is on to something. And, I'm glad to see that someone in his position is speaking out about these things. Is he an upright man? Only he, and his entourage know the answer to that.

I do know that he is also a member of the **Solari Group**, along with Catherine Austin Fitts, that I spoke of in **Book 1.** The Group responsible for putting out the **Solari Report**, which my quote regarding the ingredients of the vaccine was taken from. The **"2nd Quarter Wrap Up: The Injection Fraud, A Sane Person's Guidebook to the Global Pandemic"**.

Please understand, I am not trying to drum up political support for any candidate, I'm leery of all of them. I'm not saying that he's good or bad, I'm just sharing information that involves his opinion. But I do know that even bad people can pretend to be good! So, we all must exercise caution and pray for guidance.

You must understand that there is an agenda in place. Look at the events of Revelation. It's basically an outline of what to expect.

And, even though most people refuse to see it, or believe it... we are in the **End Times**! Look at the degradation of this world.

Examples of **degradation** includes; "Deforestation, falling levels of ground water, soil erosion, water pollution, burning of fossil fuels, the hole in the ozone layer and combustion from automobiles causing extreme air pollution." (byjus.com)

According to the Journal of Ecosystem & Ecography, there are three types of Environmental Degradation... "Soil degradation, water degradation, and air degradation." And, if you've read **Book 2**, you know that we meet the criteria for all three.

However, in my opinion, there is **Social Degradation**, as well! The erosion of human morality! And it's only getting worse.

At one time I thought that our young people becoming **Furries** was an outrage! But I'll gladly settle for the **Furries** any day over the transgendering.

For those that are unaware of what **Furries** are, they are a "subculture interested in anthropomorphic animal characters." (Wikipedia). In other words, they dress up like their favourite animals.

WebMD explains, "Furries are people who have an interest in anthropomorphic animals, or animals with human qualities. Many furries create their own animal character, known as a fursona, which functions as their avatar within furry communities."

The Wikipedia also states that, "In their 2007 survey, Gerbasi et al. examined what it meant to be furry... they also identified furries who saw themselves as **'other than human'**...".

An article from Education Week (edweek.org), dated 11/29/22, states; "In late October, Don Bolduc, the Republican U.S. Senate nominee in New Hampshire, claimed schools were offering litter boxes for students who identified as cats and are part of the furries subculture."

"We have furries and fuzzies in classrooms,' Bolduc said at an Oct. 27 campaign event in North Hampton, N.H. 'They lick themselves, they're cats. When they don't like something, they hiss... and get this... they're putting litter boxes [in schools] for them."

This ended up being a hoax, supposedly, that spread like wildfire all over Facebook and the Internet, involving different schools and various people. But I can remember videos that my oldest daughter sent me, about these kids being allowed to attend school dressed as furries, and how, just like with everything else, we had to be accepting and tolerant of their behaviour. Where does it end?

"Documented media and online incidents have stigmatized furries and made it difficult for them to 'come out' or socialize for fear of negative repercussions, abuse, and ostracism. Many furries have faced emotional, physical, and bullying due to ignorance and intentional misrepresentations." (furscience.com>stigma)

Heaven forbid that we be allowed to, as parents, put our foot down and say... **This is not acceptable!**

It's no longer just costumes, but some people are having their faces permanently tattooed with their character's features instead of wearing masks. Google it... search it on YouTube, it's easy to find. My 6 year old grandson finds it, and thinks it's pretty neat! I have plenty more to say about that, it's coming soon!

We've all been brainwashed and bullied into accepting all of these unacceptable behaviours. Being told that we are prejudice in our treatment of others by not tolerating their **right to be different**.

The definition of **prejudice** states; "an unfair feeling of dislike for a person or group because of race, sex, religion, **etc.**" (britannica.com)

And there's the category they fall into, "**etc.**"!

The definition of the same word, by Oxford Languages, states; (noun) "preconceived opinion that is not based on reason or actual experience."

If my opinion was formulated based on a functioning society, where people were disciplined, mannerly, respectful, considerate and morally upright, and this was my actual experience that I lived with for the majority of my life, then who has the right to tell me that my opinion no longer matters? That everything I was raised to believe regarding morals, and hygiene, and respect, and manners doesn't matter anymore.

If that is my belief, and people are not respecting my beliefs, then **I am being discriminated against!**

It is my right not to accept those things that go against my beliefs! And it's not my opinion, it's God's!

I'll tell you this, I have tried to be accepting. Accepting of everyone's right to do as they please. As long as it didn't affect me, they could do whatever they wanted.

Then, in May of 2023 my oldest daughter sent me a video that changed my outlook.

The video is titled **"A Message From the Gay Community"**, Performed by the San Francisco Gay Men's Chorus. The song is 4:05 minutes long, and I encourage everyone to pull it up and listen to it. The lyrics are as follows:

You think we're sinful, you fight against our rights
You say we all live lives you can't respect.
But you're just frightened, you think that we'll corrupt your kids
If our agenda goes unchecked.
Funny, just this once... you're correct!
We'll convert your children, happens bit by bit
Quietly and subtly, and you will barely notice it.
After another stanza, the refrain begins, which says...
We're coming for them, we're coming for your children
We're coming for them, we're coming for your children
The gay agenda is coming home, the gay agenda is here

I was outraged when I heard this! This, to me, is a threat! It's one thing to have to be accepting of their choices, but for them to boldly tell me that they are **Coming for** my **Children!**

They can mince their words all they want, to make it sound as though they are trying to win our children over to acceptance of them, but there were just too many portions that made their

agenda very clear... They are coming for our children! Just like they said... Quietly and subtly... bit by bit!

I can't stress enough how important it is to watch it, because the lead singer's facial expressions are almost wicked. He's definitely smirking, especially when he says, **"Funny, just this once... you're correct"**!

I will tell you right now, **Evil is coming after our children. Evil in all shapes and forms**. And, as we continue, you will see what I'm talking about! However, I must advise you that some of the things that I will be touching on, are dark and even disturbing. But are necessary to create an awareness.

I realize that I just quoted Isaiah 35:15, which speaks of **shutting our eyes from seeing evil**. But sometimes we cannot avoid it. And, in an effort to protect our children, we must see it so we can recognize it, and know what we must do to prevent them from being caught in a snare.

As I previously stated, we aren't even allowed to discipline our children anymore. And the whole time that we are being prevented, they (the system) are allowing the television programming, social media, and all other avenues of media, to be littered with profanity, nudity, violence, crime, drugs and evil. No censorship whatsoever!

I know that many of these venues provide **Parental Controls**, but what about the ones that don't? What about the cartoons that are riddled with it, but in an animated version? Does that make it appear to be less violent? Does Devil horns on a cartoon character make it any less evil? And this is what our young children are being subjected to daily! Entertaining our children by **making evil look cute!!**

During the summer break from school, I watched my 6 year old grandson 3, sometimes 4 days a week while my daughter worked. It proved to be quite an eye opening experience.

One of the cartoons that he liked to watch was **Sonic the Hedgehog.** It seemed fairly innocent, at first. But, as time passed, and I paid closer attention, I began to notice some problems.

One of the problems, as I just stated, is the fact that despite the characters being animated, the plot is the same as most TV shows out there. Good versus evil, the good guy having an evil doppelganger, mind control, brainwashing, bullying, power struggles, evil trying to take over the world, violence, and the list goes on!

Why is it that a lot of people never question the impact that these cartoons are having on our children? Just because they have animated characters acting out these bad behaviours, does not lessen the examples being set. Kids not only watch these characters, but love and admire, and even emulate them.

Again, **just because they have made evil look cute, doesn't make it any less evil.**

Another cartoon that he would watch, was **My Little Pony**, which has been around for decades! And, remembering how it was when my daughters watched it, how could it not be safe? But trust me, it's nothing like it used to be.

One episode, S9E8, in the **"My Little Pony: Friendship is Magic"** series, there is a half man-goat, half horse character named Lord Tirek. His man-goat (upper body) is red, and he has horns. His horns are not goat horns, but more like devil horns. And fire spews from his mouth. Hmm!

It also features a wicked black pony (fairy-like), with a jagged/crooked black horn that illuminates with green energy (like a lightning bolt) when she's angry. Her name is Queen Chrysalis. She has pointed/jagged teeth, and she can shape-shift.

There's also this sweet looking little pony, Cozy Glow, that has a really bad mean streak. She can be very conniving and evil, always plotting and scheming.

The plot of this episode states; "Grogar sends his legion of doom on a mission to become allies, but his plan works too well and they almost become friends."

The 3 characters mentioned above sing a song, titled **"Better Way To Be Bad"**.

Is this what we want our children watching, and imitating? Not to mention, singing along! They are basically desensitizing our children to evil. Modeling their behaviour, **bit by bit**!

Another episode, S9E9, has more evil characters that consists of a **red dragon with pointed teeth**, and other dragons in different sizes and colors.

In S9E2, all of the ponies are under king Sombra's **mind control. And with his army of mind-controlled ponies, he lays siege upon Canterlot.**

That's something right out of the Book of Revelation!

I shut it down! No more **My Little Pony** for my grandson at my house! But the sad truth of the matter is that most cartoons are filled with these subjects that I previously listed.

An article titled **Cartoons and Mind Control** from **WordPress.com**, dated Nov 4, 2010, written by Al Bayyinah, states; "Besides music, Illuminati has used cartoons for brain programming of children in order to destroy their intellectual capabilities. The American Academy of Pediatrics (AAP) and the American Academy of Child and Adolescent Psychiatry (AACAP) both feel that TV does influence the behavior of children."

The article talks about the "evidence that 6-10 Hz ELF magnetic waves can affect brain waves and control the mind of any person. It is important to realize that when a person watches TV, they go into an **alpha brain wave state**, in which they are more suggestible than normal. In fact, a LOT of Illuminati programming is done in alpha state, since the person is relaxed and highly suggestible. Most cartoons have a subtle message as well as subliminal ones meant to influence the next generation of children, destroy their intelligence, family values and morality."

As stated, this article is from 2010... it is now 2023. And their **subtle messages** are not so **subtle** any longer!

If you have small children, I encourage you to watch cartoons with your child. This medium can no longer be relied upon as a suitable means of entertainment to occupy your children unsupervised.

Also, on several occasions, we would pull up YouTube on the TV and watch **LankyBox.** I must say, I'm not a **LankyBox** fan, due to the content of some of their programs. For those that are not familiar with the show, it is centered around these two guys, Justin Kroma and Adam McArthur, playing, what I would call video games.

Wikitubia explains that **LankyBox** created a show where Justin and Adam test different products". Which means, they play the games that were created by **Roblox** players/designers, and share advice with others watching on how to beat the game, and the traps to watch out for.

Roblox itself, is an "**app that allows users to play a wide variety of games, create games, and chat with others online. It combines gaming, social media, and social commerce."**

One of the questions asked regarding **Roblox** was; **Is Roblox safe for kids?** Commonsensemedia.org responded, "Such an open approach can pose some risks to kids, especially younger ones. **And though Roblox has some safety precautions in place, it remains a target for people with less-than-good intentions**."

During each episode, they play a different game while conversing back and forth about it, which is loud and, at times, obnoxious. Laughing, almost continuously, very much like Beavis and Butt-head.

Even though they act like teenagers, in reality, they are in their mid to late twenties. Kroma, from what I have seen, usually has purple colored hair, and they have toys that are, sometimes featured in their games, and are sold in stores and online. Target offers their merchandise and shows that it is **appropriate for ages 5-7**. And there's the snare!

Here's my problem. These different games that they play, usually have evil characters. For example...

Huggy Wuggy - "Poppy Playtime is a PC **horror game** that involves an unnamed protagonist investigating a mystery in an abandoned toy factory. As the player, you roam around the factory and collect VHS tapes to solve the mystery of what happened... 'Huggy Wuggy' is one of the game's most popular - and visually disturbing - characters. It's a giant, horrifying blue creature with bulging eyes, wide red lips, and long limbs who actively follows you around as you try to complete the game. He appears in the dark unexpectedly to try and catch you. If you get caught, Huggy Wuggy bears his wide and sinister grin and eats you." (saferschoolsni.co.uk)

They failed to mention that contained within his **wide red lips** are numerous white, pointed, razor sharp teeth!

Choo-Choo Charles - A "2022 **indie horror** video **game**... The player controls a monster-hunting archivist with the goal of upgrading their train's defenses in order to fight and defeat the titular character, **Charles, an evil spider-train hybrid monster that wonders the landscape looking for people to eat.**" (Wikipedia)

The front of the engine is the face of the evil spider, who has multiple rows of razor sharp teeth. The legs of the spider project outwards from the engine, with four on each side. These are very scary images, especially for younger kids.

Monsters (Garten of Banban) - Again, more monsters. Some are more evil looking than others.

Piggy - "Roblox's new hit, Roblox Piggy is a **unique horror game inspired by the children's character Peppa Pig** and the horror game Granny."

The character is a pig that walks upright, with one red eye and one black. She wears a dress that's soiled at the bottom, and carries a baseball bat.

All of these **Roblox** games, featuring these evil characters, and more, are what's being played on the **LankyBox** YouTube channel.

And, children are watching this show on YouTube, and parents are buying up all of this merchandise of these evil characters for their children. Backpacks, clothing, dolls, posters... You name it! What's wrong with people?

And worse than that, we wonder what's wrong with our kids??

Sadly, YouTube is flooded with these videos. Another one of which is this other twosome that, in my opinion, are just "LankyBox wannabes". They're called **Sunny and Melon**. They do the same thing, playing different **Roblox** games, with many of the same characters and more. Characters that are **monsters made to look cute**, which chase you about, and when they catch you, you're dead!

Doodle and Arkey, another site that contains **Roblox** content. Which, I only make mention of them due to their subject matter regarding the **Rainbow Friends**.

There's a big push lately, regarding the gay agenda, which involves **rainbows**! Headlines from an **Associated Press** article states, "**Rainbows around the world as LGBTQ+ Pride is celebrated throughout June**", in honour of June being **Pride Month**. The article states, "These days, Pride celebrations and events - teeming with images of rainbows, a symbol of hope, unity and diversity for LGBTQ+ people - can be found all over the world."

The article contains 34 photographs in which rainbow colored attire, rainbow colored hair, and all sorts of rainbow colored posters and fanfare is displayed throughout the world, all in honour of **Gay Pride Month.**

Not just that, but every department store that I shopped at during June, and the weeks leading up to it, had their **Rainbow Pride Month** fanfare displayed in center aisleways for all to see!

I am not one to discriminate, but I am not one to be accepting of something that is an abomination to God. The proof of that statement is found in Leviticus 20:13. It states; *"If a man also lie with mankind, as he lieth with a woman, both of them have committed an abomination: they shall surely be put to death; their blood shall be upon them."*

Please understand that the same is true for women lying with other women as well.

Again, I'm not trying to point fingers at the gay community, but I strongly oppose their use of rainbows. Something that is significant to God, and to our children as well.

In Genesis 9:9-17 is where God makes a covenant with Noah and the earth, that He will never again destroy the earth by water. Beginning with verse 13, it states; *"I do set my bow in the cloud, and it shall be for a token of a covenant between me and the earth. 14) And it shall come to pass, when I bring a cloud over the earth, that the bow shall be seen in the cloud: 15) And I will remember my covenant, which is between me and you and every living creature of all flesh; and the waters shall no more become a flood to destroy all flesh. 16) And the bow shall be in the cloud; and I will look upon it, that I may remember the everlasting covenant between God and every living creature of all flesh that is upon the earth. 17) And God said unto Noah, This is the token of the covenant, which I have established between me and all flesh that is upon the earth."*

Again, the **rainbow** is very significant to God, and they are using it as their symbol. And, luring our children to them with it.

Getting back on track... I downloaded a couple of games on my phone for my grandson to play, **Jump Bros** and **Car Out**. How evil could that be? And it was fine! Until I heard conversations coming from my phone, where there shouldn't have been!

I asked him, **What are you watching?** Knowing that his mom lets him play on her phone, watching **LankyBox**, and other **Roblox** videos, I agreed to allow it. After all, being familiar with the content, and knowing what our other options were, I felt that this was the lesser of two evils.

So, I began to let him play with my phone, but I would limit the amount of time that he could use it. I never had any reason to question what he was watching, and just assumed that he was continuing to watch the same YouTube **Roblox** videos he had been.

But then I reached the **Age of Knowing**!! I finally sat down one day and started going through my **History**. Clicking on each video, one by one... and I was sickened by it. I thank God that He moved me to investigate. And I thank Him that what I found was fairly tame compared to what it could have been. But, even at that, it certainly wasn't stuff that a 6 year old should be watching!

I will say that it started out fairly innocent, with Furries, and slime making, and silliness in general. Some things were even pretty interesting, and some even quite clever! And, given your continued participation in watching, it will keep feeding you more videos of similar content.

However, as it continued, it grew darker and darker - the use of profanity, acting out in class, being disrespectful to parents... And then, it continued to regress until it was nothing but pure evil! With black leather and chains, face piercings and tattoos, spiked hair in a variety of colors, but mostly black. Black leather chokers with spikes. Black fingernail polish and black eye makeup. Images of the devil, or skulls on their shirts, and giving hand gestures displaying the devil horns. Talking about killing people, hurting animals, bullying, pranks that were mean, and even harmful.

The style used to be called **Goth**, or **Gothic**, and still is. But now many have branched off, being called **Emo's.** "This fashion has at times been characterized as a fad. Early on, emo fashion was associated with a clean cut look but as the style spread to younger teens, the style has become darker, with long bangs and emphasis on the colour black replacing sweater vest. In recent years the popular media have associated **emo** with a stereotype that includes being **emo**tional, sensitive, shy, introverted, or angst-ridden. **It is also associated with depression, self-injury, and suicide.**" (acidcow.com)

A couple of more noteworthy videos includes;

@b.hensha **Murder On My Mind**. It shows the dad laying on the floor, working on the kitchen sink. And his toddler, maybe 2 years old, standing behind him holding a screwdriver, but she is holding it like someone would that was going to stab someone. It's very innocent on the child's part, she's still a baby! But, all the while, it keeps flashing over to this evil looking man who sings, "**She woke up in the morning with murder on her mind. She went and grabbed a screwdriver to stab him in his spine. He didn't even see it coming, it caught him by surprise. Her mom tried to stop her, she said bit** you're next in line**".

Why would someone make up a song like that and use it in a video about their toddler killing her dad? People are sick!

One more, @JakeFell **Among Us in HD (Part 53) Third Grade**. It shows these four beings, dressed in some type of space suits, all four were different colors, purple, blue, green and pink. Three were large, human size, and one was tiny... maybe a foot tall, sitting on a crate. And the little one was saying, "**I was in the 3rd grade, people treated me like a criminal, because I killed somebody...**".

One of the problems with these videos, **Shorts** as they are called on **YouTube** and **TikTok**, is the presentation! Just like the one that I last mentioned, colorful space suits, one extremely tiny... or videos containing other children, or young people dressed up in animal costumes, or teens doing outrageous things, having painted faces and colorful hair. All of which are very appealing to our children. And these are the snares that are being used to lure our children in.

Then, add some catchy tunes, and even though they may not be listening to the words, they're minds are still taking it in. And, as I stated, these sites continue to feed you more of the same type videos, similar in content or nature, that you have been watching, but the content matter continues to worsen. Little by little, until they're watching nothing but evil!

It sickens me that my 6 year old grandson saw this stuff, and that I, unknowingly, allowed it. But not anymore! Every parent, grandparent, and care provider of children should always make it their business to know what a child is looking at. Never assume anything! And, be diligent about it, checking frequently. Because, it may seem harmless at first, but that will more than likely change.

This very thing is discussed at length in the 2020 movie, **The Social Dilemma.** It is a documentary in which "Tech experts from Silicon Valley sound the alarm on the dangerous impact of social networking, which Big Tech use in an attempt to manipulate and influence."

Those sounding the alarm talk about the design of these systems and search engines, using algorithms and other techniques to monitor what sites we look at, what we watch, the amount of time we spend watching each, and how they use that information to continually feed us with more of the same, or even making suggestions of other content that is similar.

I stated in **Book 1** that the computer, in my opinion, is the **beast, the image that they created.** Revelation 13, beginning with verse 14, states; *"And deceiveth them that dwell on the earth by the means of those miracles which he had power to do in the sight of the beast; saying to them that dwell on the earth, **that they should make an image to the beast**, which had the wound by a sword, and did live. 15) And **he had power to give life unto the image of the beast, that the image of the beast should both speak,** and cause that as many as would not worship the image of the beast should be killed."*

Think about the computers of today. They **speak**, they even **think**! And, this documentary brings to light this very thing, talking about the intelligence that these computers not only possess, but how they continue to evolve! **They are sounding the alarm because it scares them!!**

I encourage everyone who reads this to watch **The Social Dilemma.** It's a real eye-opener!!

Getting back to my statement about the **computer being the image.** When you think about the technology that will be used to create the **chip** (the **mark of the beast**), or the **chip** itself being a computer... a **microcomputer**, then Revelation 13:16 & 17 makes perfect sense.

It states; *"And he causeth all, both small and great, rich and poor, free and bond, **to receive a mark in their right hand, or in their foreheads: 17) And that no man might buy or sell, save he that had the mark**, or the name of the beast, or the number of his name."*

I'm not sure how up to date most people are with current events, but **govtech.com** states, "A headline from **The Hill** in January 2023 proclaimed '**Human microchip implants take center stage**'."

"**Today, more than 50,000 people have elected to have a subdermal chip surgically inserted between the thumb and index finger, serve as their new swipe key, or credit card.**" (Article by Dan Lohrmann, written 2/5/23)

Another article, dated 4/11/2022, titled; **The microchip implants that let you pay with your hand**, by Katherine Latham @ BBC NEWS. She talks about the design of the chip, size and weight, how it operates, and its manufacturer. But the statement that I feel is most noteworthy, is; "For many of us, the idea of having such a chip implanted in our body is an appalling one, **but a 2021 survey of more than 4,000 people across the UK and the European Union found that <u>51% would consider it</u>**".

What I find more disturbing than that, is the fact that the time will come when we won't have a choice in the matter. Which, if my suspicions are correct, many of us may already be chipped. I say that based on the Covid vaccinations that were forced on people, and the technology that was included in it. My theories and supporting evidence are found in **Book 1**, some of which was taken from the Solari Report's **"2nd Quarter Wrap Up: The Injection Fraud, A Sane Person's Guidebook to the Global Pandemic"**.

Please understand that they (the **establishment**) are going to hide their intentions every way they can. After all, if a hunter seeks a prey, he's certainly not going to make his presence known! He's going to sneak up on it, and trap it! And there's the **snare** that the Bible speaks of, because many will fall victim unknowingly.

We have to be diligent in, not only being aware of the snares that we face, but of those that our children face as well.

Deuteronomy 6, beginning with verse 5 states, *"And thou shalt love the LORD thy God with all thine heart, and with all thy soul, and with all thy might. 6) And these words, which I command thee this day, shall be in thine heart: 7)* **And thou shalt teach them diligently unto thy children, and shalt talk of them when thou sittest in thine house, and when thou walkest by the way, and when thou liest down, and when thou risest up.** *"*

I regret that I was ignorant of my duties as a parent, the duty to teach my children diligently. But now that I am awake, I am trying to make up for lost time. And we all must **teach our children diligently**, or we will lose them.

Evil is coming at our children in all sorts of disguises, shapes and forms. And we must educate ourselves about it, so we can recognize it and stop it. Trust me, I don't like it one bit, delving into, and talking about evil. But, if that's what I have to do to protect my grandchildren, and anyone else's, then so be it! Better me walk into it with my eyes open, than them stumble into it blindly!

Just think about all of the cartoons... making **evil look cute**. The **TikTok** videos, **YouTube** videos, and **Social Media**. Think about **Facebook**, and all of the photographs and selfies that kids are posting of themselves. And, all of the **Friend Requests**, and **Friend Suggestions**... exactly what kind of predators are they making friends with?

Think about the TV shows they watch, their movie stars and music idols, the music they listen to, or concerts that they are allowed to attend.

Speaking of which, let's talk for a minute about the **Reality Show** featuring the **Kardashian's**. Everybody's always **Keeping Up With** them. And just look at the examples they're setting!

An article titled, **Kardashian's Choices of Beauty: Complete List of Family Members' Plastic Surgeries** by **Flymedi.com** states "All the members of the Kardashian-Jenner family are always the key figures for social media, public press, and TV shows. **Everything they do, say, and wear is carefully followed by people from all over the world.**"

This article provides a list of all the plastic surgeries, which includes breast augmentations, butt implants, liposuction, fat transfer, facelifts, Botox, and nose jobs for each family member. All are recipients, with the exception of Kendall. She "is the only member of the family that has a natural, non-touched look."

And let's not forget Bruce Jenner, who is now a woman, Caitlyn!

Again, "**Everything they do, say, and wear is carefully followed by people from all over the world.**" And just to give you some idea of what that involves...

Kylie Jenner... **Instagram followers over 399.1m people.**
Kim Kardashian... **Instagram followers over 364m people.**
Khloe' Kardashian... **Instagram followers over 311m people.**
Kendall Jenner... **Instagram followers over 294.6m people.**
Kourtney Kardashian... **Instagram followers over 223m people.**
Chris Jenner... **Instagram followers over 52.7m people.**
Bruce (Caitlyn) Jenner... **Instagram followers over 13.5m people.**

This family is a perfect example of the celebrities that our young people are modelling themselves after at this day and time. They are the trendsetters for style, including wardrobe, hair, body and behaviour. Is this really what we want our young people imitating?

Speaking of wardrobe... I watched another YouTube video that my oldest daughter sent me. She and I lived together for several years, back during the 2003-2008 time frame. She saw first hand the nightmare I was living that was caused by artificial sweeteners. I have an entire chapter devoted to it in **Book 2**, called **A Spoonful of Sugar.**

We were awakened at the same time, and God has always used us together, but in different ways. My entire focus was on God, the Bible, and biblical corruption. And she was on the Internet, looking at all sorts of other corruption. Truly, they're all just pieces of one big puzzle, with the God factor being the center of it.

Back to wardrobe, let's talk about **Balenciaga!** As I was saying, she sent me a YouTube video by **DailyWire+**, an excellent source with well investigated topics. This one is titled; **I fell down the Balenciaga rabbit hole. Here's what I found.**

It opens with a female singer saying, "daddy, daddy, if you want it drop the addy. Give me love, give me Fendi, my Balenciaga daddy, my Balenciaga daddy", at which point Brett Cooper (one of the host's along with Ben Shapiro) cuts in with, "Hold up, pause, Balenciaga, the same Balenciaga tied to Satan worshipping insta-photos, and child pornography court documents? And weren't they recently involved in a scandal with sexualizing kids in their ads?"

And, the whole time she is talking, pictures are being displayed, one after another. One of a devil figure on a stage. A demonic Baphomet head inside a pentagram as the backdrop to a runway stage. Pictures of children holding teddy bears wearing bondage outfits, and other appalling and inappropriate poses and stage props.

"Why advertise with a cocktail of extreme sex, Satanism and children?" she asks.

As she continues to share the findings of her research, movie clips of models walking the runways, wearing black leather outfits, with spikes. Some even having their entire faces covered in black leather masks. Many of which reminded me of the

Goths and **Emo's** that I spoke of just moments ago, except much darker. More so **evil**, than anything else.

She directs your attention to various bazaar stage props, as photos of children in their ads are displayed with teddy bears. But not your ordinary child's stuffed animal!

One plush purple colored bear was wearing a black thong and a black leather harness. Another bear, blue in color, with blackened eyes, wearing a studded harness.

Then, a photo is shown with a young boy standing in a bedroom, amidst a sea of clutter. But not just any clutter. On the floor is a white bear with one purple eye, and one blue one, which led me to think that it symbolized bruising. The bear was wearing black fishnet stockings and a padlock around its neck. Behind the boy is a "child's drawing of the devil" taped on a bookcase. The picture also shows a role of caution tape lying on the floor, with **Baalenciaga** written on the tape, "**a play on the name of the brand and the name of a demonic Old Testament Canaanite god, who demanded child sacrifice**."

Picture after picture, as she continues to point out every prop that was purposely staged. Such as papers tied to an actual Supreme Court case "that debates the legality of promoting child pornography", that one of the designer's purses was sitting on top of. "There's no way these documents made it into the photo shoot by accident. Everything on a fashion set is meticulously curated and staged."

Another picture shows a stack of books on the desktop where the model is posed. The title displayed on the spine says, Michael Borreman's, **As Sweet As It Gets**. She explains that upon doing a search, she found that he's a Belgian painter with some "incredibly disturbing work". And, how many of his paintings contain naked children soaked in blood.

She even names name's of many stars who wear the label, one of which was Kim Kardashian, showing pictures of Kim dressed in a black (leather possibly?) full-bodied suit of sorts, wearing the black face mask as well.

I've said enough! My point being, take a closer look at those who are creating these fashion trends. And are they even trends? Or are they really advertising the latest evening wear for all those who worship the Devil, that may be planning to attend parties in his honour?

It's so disturbing! This is what our world has come to! And, I fear that things are only going to get much worse.

As for the Kardashian's, an article in People, titled, **Kim Kardashian Starts Quietly Wearing Balenciaga Again Following Ad Campaign Controversy**, dated April 5, 2023.

"After taking a short break from rocking Balenciago threads after a heated controversy last year involving the brand, it appears Kim Kardashian is back to regularly wearing the fashion house's looks." (people.com)

And, on a slightly different note, Kylie Jenner's once boyfriend, and father of her two children, rapper Travis Scott, performed at the 2021 Astroworld Festival, that took place on November 5th, and resulted in at least 8 deaths.

An article titled, **Kylie Jenner 'devastated' over deadly tragedy at boyfriend Travis Scott's concert** in **CNA LIFESTYLE** states, "Kylie Jenner on Saturday (Nov 6) said she is 'broken' and 'devastated' over the deadly events that took place at the Astroworld music festival in Houston, Texas, where her boyfriend, rapper Travis Scott, was performing. Eight people were killed and numerous others injured after a stampede of fans surged to the stage during the performance on Friday night."

The **official** story states that over 50,000 people attended, and people were so restricted for space that most were unable to move, and some unable to even breathe.

However, numerous videos surfaced on YouTube made by people who actually attended, saying that all sorts of demonic activity were taking place. Some even witnessing shadow type entities descending into the crowds.

Another article, **Satanic Theories, Conspiracy Talk Booms on TikTok Following Astroworld** from **Rolling Stone**, dated November 8, 2021, states; "On TikTok, where some videos have gained millions of views... People have said the stage was shaped like an inverted cross leading to a portal to Hell, which they believe was represented by the arch-shaped set onstage. They also point to a shirt Scott wore at the show that depicts human figures walking through a door and emerging with what look like horns as further evidence that was leading fans to hell and sacrificing people's lives intentionally."

The article also mentioned that "one person Tweeted with a video of a fiery winged creature above Scott's stage." It sounds pretty demonic to me!

And sadly, even though unconscious people were being lifted into the air, and carried out over the tops of people's heads, the concert continued!

It was stated on TikTok, "typing 'Astroworld' into the search bar generates 'astroworld festival demonic' as one of the top suggestions." I just did a Google search typing **tiktok astroworld tragedy** and it pulled up numerous clips.

This is just one example of the things that are taking place at concerts today. I know that we can't protect our children from everything, but we can communicate with them about the evil that is rapidly spreading throughout the world. Just like cockroaches... squeezing in between the cracks. And people, I fear that we have a full-blown infestation!

As for our young children, and even our teens, we should always use discretion about the videos and movies they watch.

Because, once you see something, and are disturbed by it, there is no unseeing it.

According to Safer Schools, "There are multiple risks that can arise from children and young people being exposed to frightening content before they are prepared."

Some of the risks include;

* **Added anxiety and stress**
* **Intrusive thoughts**
* **New fears**

Looking at those **risks**, it reminds me of being 17 years old again. The movie **The Exorcist** was released in December of 1973, but I didn't see it until it made its television debut. I was 17 years old, and that movie changed my life! It still disturbs me to this day if I allow myself to even think about it. And to be perfectly honest, as I am sitting here writing this, at night, by myself, I can feel my anxiety level rise.
I can only imagine how some of these demonic images, and characters in video games, are affecting some of our children. Some are not bothered by it at all. Some may even be enthralled by it. But some may become terrified in the dark, or awakened by nightmares because of it.

Again, once the image is there, it's permanently embedded. That's how **The Exorcist** was for me! Why would we even want to subject our children to such things? But sometimes, we don't even know about it, until it's too late.

One last area of concern is that of our children that we are losing to drugs. The best way for me to address this issue, is by sharing the story of my nephew, and how we almost lost him.

By the time he was 15 years old, he was already drinking heavily. His dad, a war veteran from Vietnam, had struggled horribly with Post Traumatic Stress Disorder. And because so, was an alcoholic and substance abuser.

It wasn't long after my nephew graduated high school that he became addicted to pain pills, mixing his newly acquired addiction together with his old one. He continued with this combo until it no longer gave him the high, the head change, that he had come to require.

He got clean for a while, which, sadly, his circumstances prevented him for remaining that way.

My sister and her husband lived away from the city in a more rural area, having a couple of acres with a spacious three bedroom trailer. The entire subdivision consisted of mobile homes, which were, for the most part, well maintained. But as the years had passed, the "hood" as they called it, became overrun, more and more, with less desirables. People cooking meth, selling drugs, you name it. The "hood" had fallen victim to a bad element, and my nephew became one of those victims.

His new drug of choice was now heroin. And he was arrested numerous times for theft, to support his new habit. My sister, knowing how severe her son's addiction had become, would plead with his attorney to get rehab for him. But rehab isn't an option available with theft related charges.

So, in and out of correctional facilities became his new life. And, I must admit, we all breathed easier when he was incarcerated, because, at least while he was there, we didn't have to worry about him overdosing. Which he had done, numerous times!

My sister said, **"There is nothing like pulling your son up off the bathroom floor, wondering if he was still alive"**.

This pattern continued for many years. Using, stealing, lying, overdosing, and prison. In fact, his downward spiral began in 2002, when he was 15 years old, and reached its climax in 2021... **19 years later!** More than half of his life he had suffered with this horrible existence of alcohol abuse and drugs.

And, understand this, it's not just him that suffered, but his entire family! My sister more so than the rest, because she would protect him, keeping these things to herself, not wanting to bring shame upon him by sharing it with her family. Divulging his secret life to others that are incapable of understanding because they have never experienced anything like it themselves. So, she anguished in silence.

She would confide in me on occasions. But if you recall, my life was very questionable to others at that time, as well. However, as I continued my journey, walking away from all of my addictions, and proving my soundness of mind, I did everything in my power to help my nephew. I put money on his commissary at prison, and his phone account. I wrote inspirational letters and cards every week and a half to two weeks. But, more than anything else, **I prayed, begging God for His help. Asking Him to please bring my nephew out of this terrible addiction.**

Then finally, everything did come to a horrible climax, which proved to be a blessing in disguise.

In 2021, while in his attorney's office, he asked to use the bathroom. After several minutes had passed, his attorney stepped into the restroom and told him to hurry it up! My nephew returned to his office, and took his seat across from his attorney's desk. **And, immediately, after being seated, he slumped over dead!** It sends chills through my body just typing these words.

They called 911 and performed CPR, and by the grace of God, his life was spared. But, the real blessing of this story is the determination that his attorney was filled with, to get my nephew the help that he needed, once and for all!

Based on my nephew's overdose in his office, he was finally able to petition for rehabilitation, and got it! Furthermore, his attorney waived all legal fees that my nephew owed him. This man went above and beyond to make certain that this would never happen again!

My nephew has now made a full recovery and has been clean since that day. He has a great job, being recently promoted to a supervisor position. He has his own apartment, his driver's license has been reinstated, and above all else... **he sponsors other recovering addicts at the same facility that he, himself, had** attended. Giving back!! Truly God's Hand is all over this! So many answered prayers! Not only does my nephew credit God for all of his recovery, but for the countless blessings that continues to pour down upon him!

God is so Great! I thank Him and praise Him every day!

Sadly, there are many out there who were not so fortunate. Our children are in jeopardy. They are the target. Because the best way to get to the people, is through the children. Most of us would do practically anything for our children, and evil knows that.

I implore every parent and grandparent to **teach your children diligently,** and pray for God to put His laws into their hearts and a hedge of protection around them.

And then, as parents, be diligent about knowing what they're watching, where they're going, who their friends are, and always keep the line of communication open.

This truly is one big puzzle. And as each piece is assembled, the bigger picture becomes clear. That picture being one of worldwide corruption, on many levels! We are truly living in evil times!

Statutes, Testimonies & Judgments

"Because that Abraham obeyed my voice, and kept my charge, my <u>commandments</u>, my <u>statutes</u>, and my <u>laws</u>." (Genesis 26:5)

We can see from the way that Genesis 26:5 is specifically worded, that **commandments, statutes,** and **laws** are three entirely different things to God.

Take a look at Deuteronomy 6:17, *"Ye shall diligently keep the <u>commandments</u> of the LORD your God, and his <u>testimonies</u>, and his <u>statutes</u>, which he hath commanded thee."*

Here, again, we see **commandments** and **statutes** listed, but this time with **testimonies.**

So, what is the difference between God's **Laws, Commands, Statutes, Testimonies & Precepts?** In **Book 2,** I provide a brief definition of each, but even state that **these are man's definitions, not God's**. And I need you to keep that in mind as we continue, because many of the definitions of these terms tie various ones together, making it difficult to figure out which is which.

Let's start with **what is a command?** The Old Testament is full of verses where God gives **commandments** to His people.

The definition of the word **command** means; "give an **authoritative order**." (Oxford Languages)

Now look at the definition of **commandment**, "An **order** or injunction given by authority; a command; a **precept**; a mandate. ... **The act of commanding; exercise of authority**." (Wordnik.com)

Genesis, chapter 1 is full of verses where God is giving commandments, they are not called as such, but regardless, that's still the case.

Look at Genesis 1:3, *"And God said, Let there be light: and there was light."*

That was His very first commandment! Commanding, by speaking it, that it come into being. And, from that point on, every time that

119

Genesis states, **and God said**, He just gave another commandment, **order**, for something that He said to be done.

In verse 6, **And God said, Let there be a firmament... and it was so.** (verse 7)

Verse 9, **And God said, Let the waters under the heaven be gathered... and it was so.**

Verses 11, **And God said, Let the earth bring forth grass... and it was so.**

And, every time He said it, **it was so. Because He commanded it to come about.**

The first time that the word **commanded** actually appears in the scripture, is in chapter 2, verse 16. It states; *"**And the LORD God commanded the man,** saying, **Of every tree of the garden thou mayest freely eat: 17) But of the tree of the knowledge of good and evil, thou shalt not eat of it: for in the day that thou eatest thereof thou shalt surely die.**"*

Based on the specific wording of verse 17, I would say that this was God's first actual **commandment**, or **law** given. It was a specific **order commanding something that should, or should not be done.**

There is a difference in **commanding**, giving an instruction, and **making a commandment**, making it a **permanent law** to do, or never to do something.

Look at Genesis 6:13, *"And **God said unto Noah,** The end of all flesh is come before me; for the earth is filled with violence through them; and, behold, I will destroy them with the earth. 14) **Make thee an ark** of gopher wood; rooms shalt thou make in the ark, and shalt pitch it within and without with pitch... 22) **Thus did Noah; according to all that God <u>commanded</u> him, so did he.**"*

God gave Noah **instructions**, He **commanded** him.

There is also a difference between **laws** and **the Law.**

The **Law** - *Halakha* (Hebrew), "is the collective body of **Jewish religious laws** that are derived from the **written** and **oral Torah.**

Halakha is based on biblical commandments (***mitzvot***), subsequent **Talmudic** and **rabbinic laws**, and the customs and traditions which were compiled in the many books such as the ***Shulchan Aruch***. Halakha is often translated as 'Jewish law', although a more literal translation of it might be '**the way to behave**' or '**the way of walking**'." (Wikipedia)

Other definitions include:

* The first five books of the Old Testament; the Torah; the Pentateuch. (Nelson's NKJV Study Bible)

* The word **law** is defined as a rule or set of rules which prescribe or prohibit our actions to conform to a certain order or pattern of behaviour. (Kingdom Dynamics)

Scriptures pertaining to **Law**;

Deuteronomy 31:26, *"**Take this book of the law, and put it in the side of the ark of the covenant of the LORD your God,** <u>that it may be there for a witness against thee</u>."*

It was used as a **witness against them**, because it was **written in stone**, and there was no denying it. That's where that old adage comes from... **It is written in stone**... **legally binding!**

Psalm 19:7-8, *"**The law of the LORD is perfect, converting the soul**: the testimony of the LORD is sure, making wise the simple."*

Psalm 119:34, *"**Give me understanding, and I shall keep thy law; yea, I shall observe it with my whole heart.**"*

Ezra 7:26, *"And **whosoever will not do the law of thy God,** and the law of the king, **let judgment be executed speedily upon him, whether it be unto death, or to banishment, or to confiscation of goods, or to imprisonment.**"*

Commandments - *Mitzvah* (Hebrew, same as ***mitzvot***, stated above), "refers to a commandment **commanded by God** to be performed as a religious duty. Jewish law (***halakha***) in large part consists of discussion of these commandments. According to religious tradition, there are **613 such commandments.**" (Wikipedia)

The same source continues, "The commandments have been divided also into three general categories: **mishpatim**; **edot**; and **chukim**. **Mishpatim** ('laws') include commandments that are deemed to be self-evident, such as not to murder and not to steal. **Edot** ('testimonies') commemorate important events in Jewish history. For example, the **Shabbat** is said to testify to the story that **Hashem** created the world in six days and rested on the seventh day and declared it holy. **Chukim** ('decrees') are commandments with no known rationale, and are perceived as pure manifestations of the Divine will."

So, bear in mind that they are all part of God's **law**, the first five books of the Old Testament. And, they are all **commandments**, something that God **commanded** us to do. And, given the fact that there are **613 such commandments**, makes it even harder to determine what term applies to each. I phrase that as such, because, even though there are **three general categories**, as stated above, there are several terms involved as well.

Meaning, **ordinances, statutes, precepts, judgments, decrees,** and **testimonies.**

What makes it even more complicated, is the definitions provided for each oftentimes intermingle. Like that of **statute**. Its definitions include; **decree, law**, and **precept.**

In fact, someone asked; **How many statutes are there in the Bible?** Wikipedia responded... **613**! The same number of commandments! Evidently, whoever wrote the articles for **Commandments** and **Statutes** in the Wikipedia, must believe that they are one in the same. But they're not. If they were, there wouldn't be Bible verses that reference both at the same time.

Look at Deuteronomy 6:1, *"Now these are the **commandments**, the **statutes**, and the **judgments**, which the LORD your God commanded to teach you, that ye might do them in the land whither ye go to possess it:"*

Furthermore, in researching the definition of **precept**, it includes **rule, law, ordinance, statute** and **commandment. Decrees** includes

orders and **commands.** Every term that I have checked overlaps with one or two others.

I have searched through Biblical definitions, Hebrew interpretations, various dictionary definitions, and numerous religious sites, and I have become overwhelmed by trying to make sense of it. The conclusion that I have reached, just as I have said before, **God's definitions are not like that of man's!**

With that said, **only God knows, with certainty, what each of these terms mean.** And, at this point, using all of this information that I've found, I will just let Him guide me in assembling it.

The commands (mitzvot) "are the ordinances or commands related to the terms of the covenant; a commandment is an authoritative rule for action in which the obligation is set forth; are prescriptions or directions of God concerning matters". (Kingdom Dynamics)

Scriptures pertaining to **Commandments**;

Of course, we all are familiar with the **Ten Commandments**, which can be found in Exodus chapter 20, as well as Deuteronomy chapter 5. And clearly, they were extremely important to God for them to be brought together on two tablets of stone.

Look at Exodus 24:12, *"And the LORD said unto Moses, Come up to me into the mount, and be there: and **I will give thee tables of stone, and a law, and commandments which I have written; that thou mayest teach them**."*

Deuteronomy 5:22, *"**These words the LORD spake unto all your assembly** in the mount out of the midst of the fire, of the cloud, and of the thick darkness, with a great voice: **and he added no more. And he wrote them in two tables of stone, and delivered them unto me**."*

Furthermore, Deuteronomy 9:9-10 tells us, *"**When I was gone up into the mount to receive the tables of stone, even the tables of the covenant which the LORD made with you,** then I abode in the mount forty days and forty nights, I neither did eat bread nor drink water: 10) **And the LORD delivered unto me two tables of stone written with the finger of God**; and on them was written according* *to all the words, which the LORD spake with you in the mount out of the midst of the fire in the day of the assembly."*

Here Moses refers to them as the **tables of the covenant which the LORD made with you... written with the finger of God.** That's noteworthy!

I think that it's also worth pointing out, that Moses spent **forty days and forty nights in the mount with God, without any food or drink! God, and God only, sustained him.**

When I think about the Israelites murmuring for water and food in the wilderness, I believe that God would have sustained them as well, had they trusted God as Moses did.

For me, a commandment is like an **instruction. And sometimes those **instructions have repercussions if not followed.** As you read the scriptures provided, replace the word commandment(s) with instruction(s), and see if that seems accurate to you.

Numbers 9:18-23, *"**At the commandment of the LORD the children of Israel journeyed, and at the commandment of the LORD they pitched:** as long as the cloud abode upon the tabernacle they rested in their tents... 20) And so it was, when the cloud was a few days upon the tabernacle; **according to the commandment of the LORD they abode in their tents, and according to the commandment of the LORD they journeyed... 23) ... they kept the charge of the LORD, at the commandment of the LORD by the hand of Moses."***

He is instructing them!

Numbers 23:20, *"Behold, **I have received commandment** to bless: and he hath blessed; **and I cannot reverse it."***

Deuteronomy 4:13-14, *"And **he declared unto you his covenant, which he commanded you to perform, even ten commandments;** and he wrote them upon two tables of stone. 14) And **the LORD commanded me at that time to teach you statutes and judgments,** that ye might do them in the land whither ye go over to possess it."*

Deuteronomy 6:5-7, *"And **thou shalt love the LORD thy God with all thine heart, and with all thy soul, and with all thy might. 6) And these words, which I command thee this day, shall be in thine heart: 7) And thou shalt teach them diligently unto thy children, and shalt talk of them when thou sittest in thine house, and when thou walkest by the way, and when thou liest down, and when thou risest up.*"

Deuteronomy 11:26-28, *"Behold, I set before you this day a blessing and a curse; 27) **A blessing, if ye obey the commandments of the LORD your God**, which I command you this day: 28) And **a curse, if ye will not obey the commandments of the LORD your God, but turn aside out of the way which I command you this day,** to go after other gods, which ye have not known.*"

Psalm 19:8, *" ... **the commandment of the LORD is pure, enlightening the eyes.**"*

Psalm 119:21, *"**Thou hast rebuked the proud that are cursed, which do err from thy commandments.**"*

Psalm 119:66, *"**Teach me good judgment and knowledge: for I have believed thy commandments.**"*

The Old Testament is full of **commandments (instructions)**, from God! However, only 613 of them are **laws**!

~

Statute - ***Choq*** (Hebrew), is a "**civil decree or enactment from our Creator, something prescribed for us to do, or a boundary set**. As an example of what this means, we are instructed not to kindle a fire on the Sabbath. This is **a boundary, or limit set on what we cannot do**. Other examples would include what we cannot do while unclean or what a woman can or cannot do during her menstrual cycle. These are specific decrees." (119ministries.com)

* "Statute, 'prescription, rule, law, regulation' and can refer to **laws of nature** or **what is allocated, rationed, or appointed to someone**". (gotquestions.org)

* "Things inscribed; enacted laws." (Nelson's NKJV Study Bible)

* "(in Biblical use) a law or decree made by a sovereign, or by God." (Oxford Languages)

* "The Statute is the precepts or regulations for health care and hygiene...". (Kingdom Dynamics)

Scriptures pertaining to **Statutes**;

Nehemiah 10:28-32, *"And the rest of the people, the priests, the Levites, the porters, the singers, the Nethinims, and **all they that had separated themselves from the people of the lands unto the law of God, their wives, their sons, and their daughters, every one having knowledge, and having understanding**; 29) They clave to their brethren, their nobles, **and <u>entered into a curse, and into an oath, to walk in God's law, which was given by Moses the servant of God, and to observe and do all the commandments of the LORD our Lord, and his judgments and his statutes</u>; 30) And that we would not give our daughters unto the people of the land, nor take their daughters for our sons: 31) And if the people of the land bring ware or any victuals on the sabbath day to sell, that we would not buy it of them on the sabbath, or on the holy day: and that we would leave the seventh year, and the exaction of every debt. 32) Also we made ordinances for us, to charge ourselves yearly with the third part of a shekel for the service of the house of our God;"***

These are definite examples of enacted laws given by our Creator. In fact, Nehemiah 10:29 sends a strong message in saying that they have **entered into a curse, and into an oath!** Because that's exactly what it is.

Look at Deuteronomy 28, beginning with verse 15, *"But it shall come to pass, **if thou wilt not hearken unto the voice of the LORD thy God, to observe to do all his commandments and his statutes which I command thee this day; that all these curses shall come upon thee, and overtake thee:...** 45) **Moreover all these curses shall come upon thee, and shall pursue thee, and overtake thee, till thou be destroyed; because thou hearkenedst not unto the voice of the LORD thy God, to keep his commandments and his statutes which he commanded thee: 46) And they shall be upon thee for a sign and for a wonder, and upon thy seed for ever...** 58)*

If thou wilt not observe to do all the words of this law that are written in this book, that thou mayest fear this glorious and fearful name, THE LORD THY GOD; 59) Then the LORD will make thy plagues wonderful, and the plagues of thy seed, even great plagues, and of long continuance, and sore sicknesses, and of long continuance."

That's how serious God is about His commandments and statutes being kept! The curses can be found in chapters 27 and 28.

I realize that, given the curses involved, these could be considered **judgments.** But there is a big difference between being **cursed** and being **punished.**

Leviticus 6:9-23, *"Command Aaron and his sons, saying, **This is the law of the burnt offering: It is the burnt offering, because of the burning upon the altar all night unto the morning, and the fire of the altar shall be burning in it...** 13) <u>**The fire shall ever be burning upon the altar; it shall never go out.**</u> **14) And this is the law of the meat offering**: the sons of Aaron shall offer it before the LORD, before the altar... 16) <u>And the remainder thereof shall Aaron and his sons eat: with unleavened bread shall it be eaten in the holy place; in the court of the tabernacle of the congregation they shall eat it... 18) All the males among the children of Aaron shall eat of it.</u> **It shall be a <u>statute for ever in your generations</u> concerning the offerings of the LORD made by fire**: every one that toucheth them shall be holy."*

Leviticus 7:34-36, *"For **the wave breast and the heave shoulder have I taken of the children of Israel from off the sacrifices of their peace offerings, and have given them unto Aaron the priest and unto his sons by a statute for ever from among the children of Israel. 35) This is the portion of the anointing of Aaron, and of the anointing of his sons, out of the offerings of the LORD made by fire**, in the day when he presented them to minister unto the LORD in the priest's office; 36) Which the LORD commanded to be given them of the children of Israel, **in the day that he anointed them, by a <u>statute for ever throughout their generations</u>.**"*

Exodus 29:27-28, *"And thou shalt sanctify the **breast of the wave offering, and the shoulder of the heave offering,** which is waved,* and which is heaved up, of the ram of the consecration, even of that which is for Aaron, and of that which is for his sons: 28) And **it shall be Aaron's and his sons' by a statute for ever from the children of Israel: for it is an heave offering: and it shall be an heave offering from the children of Israel of the sacrifice of their peace offerings, even their heave offering unto the LORD.**"

Leviticus 10:15, "The **heave shoulder and the wave breast** shall they bring with the offerings made by fire of the fat, to wave it for a wave offering before the LORD; and **it shall be thine, and thy sons' with thee, by a statute for ever; as the LORD hath commanded.**"

Numbers 18:19, "**All the heave offerings of the holy things, which the children of Israel offer unto the LORD, have I given thee, and thy sons and thy daughters with thee, by <u>a statute for ever: it is a covenant of salt for ever before the LORD unto thee and to thy seed with thee</u>.**"

All three of these scriptures pertain to the **same Statute**, just being reiterated in three different books. I included all three quotes just so you could see that some **Statutes** are repetitive, but necessary to stress the importance of them. Aside from that, here we see examples of **allocation**.

Leviticus 7:23-27, "*Speak unto the children of Israel, saying,* **Ye shall eat no manner of fat,** *of ox, or of sheep, or of goat. 24) And* **the fat of the beast that dieth of itself, and the fat of that which is torn with beasts, may be used in any other use: but ye shall in no wise eat of it**. *25) For whosoever eateth the fat of the beast, of which men offer an offering made by fire unto the LORD,* **even the soul that eateth it shall be cut off from his people. 26) <u>Moreover ye shall eat no manner of blood</u>,** *whether it be of fowl or of beast, in any of your dwellings. 27)* **Whatsoever soul it be that eateth any manner of blood, even that soul shall be cut off from his people.**"

Leviticus 3:17, "**It shall be a <u>perpetual statute</u> for your generations throughout all your dwellings, <u>that ye eat neither fat nor blood</u>.**"

Anyone that has read either of my previous books knows how I've spoken out against Jesus for having everyone to symbolically (any manner) drink his blood, and wash in it.

Leviticus 17:10-16 elaborates further about eating blood, and *"he shall both wash his clothes, and bathe himself in water, and be unclean until the even: then shall he be clean."*

Touching blood makes us **unclean!**

Regarding the priests, Leviticus 10:9, *"Do not drink wine nor strong drink, thou, nor thy sons with thee, when ye go into the tabernacle of the congregation, lest ye die: it shall be a statute for ever throughout your generations:"*

Leviticus, chapter 11, laws pertaining to animals, insects, sea creatures, and birds that are considered unclean, some of which God states that *"they shall be an abomination to you"*, i.e., pork and all seafood other than fish with **both fins and scales!**

Leviticus chapter 15 are laws pertaining to what is considered unclean, such as; **a man having a running issue out of his flesh, everything that he has touched, sat on, or anyone that has touched him. If a man's seed of copulation go out from him..., including the woman that he laid with. A woman having her monthly issue, everything she sits on, lays on, or lays with, and her clothing.**

All of these are examples of what is **clean or unclean**, are *health care and hygiene* related as stated by Kingdom Dynamics.

Look at Exodus 15:24-26, *"And the people murmured against Moses, saying, What shall we drink? 25) And he cried unto the LORD; and the LORD shewed him a tree, which when he had cast into the waters, the waters were made sweet: **there he made for them a statute and an ordinance**, and there he proved them, 26) And said, **If thou wilt diligently hearken to the voice of the LORD thy God, and wilt do** that which is right in his sight, and wilt **give ear to his commandments**, and keep all his statutes, **I will put none of these diseases upon thee**, which I have brought upon the Egyptians: for I am the LORD that healeth thee."*

I questioned which category this one should be placed in, but two different times it says **statute**. It does fall within the descriptions provided. Also, I find it interesting that the specific wording says, *"give ear to his commandments"*. Not to obey, but to listen, heed. This lends validation to my statement about the commandments being **instructions**.

The next 9 scriptures pertain to **God commanding the laws of nature.**

Genesis 8:1-2, *"And God remembered Noah, and every living thing, and all the cattle that was with him in the ark: and **God made a wind to pass over the earth, and the waters asswaged; 2) The fountains also of the deep and the windows of heaven were stopped, and the rain from heaven was restrained;"***

Exodus 14:21-22, *"And Moses stretched out his hand over the sea; and **the LORD caused the sea to go back by a strong east wind all that night, and made the sea dry land, and the waters were divided**. 22) And the children of Israel went into the midst of the sea upon the dry ground: and the waters were a wall unto them on their right hand, and on their left."*

This was such an incomprehensible feat that scientists have tried to downplay it for decades, saying that it occurred in the Sea of Reeds, at a shallower crossing! Look at the scripture... *"the waters were a wall unto them on their right hand, and on their left"*.

Jeremiah 5:22, *"Fear ye not me? saith the LORD: **will ye not tremble at my presence, which have placed the sand for the bound of the sea by a perpetual decree, that it cannot pass it: and though the waves thereof toss themselves, yet can they not prevail; though they roar, yet can they not pass over it?"***

Job 28:26, *"**When he made a decree for the rain, and a way for the lightning of the thunder**:"*

Psalm 8:3, *"When I consider thy heavens, the work of thy fingers, **the moon and the stars, which thou hast ordained**;"*

Proverbs 8:29, *"**When he gave to the sea his decree, that the waters should not pass his commandment: when he appointed the foundations of the earth**:"*

Psalm 147:15-18, *"He sendeth forth his commandment upon earth: his word runneth very swiftly. 16) He giveth snow like wool: he scattereth the hoarfrost like ashes. 17) He casteth forth his ice like morsels: who can stand before his cold? 18) He sendeth out his word, and melteth them: he causeth his wind to blow, and the waters flow."*

Psalm 148:8, *"Fire, and hail; snow, and vapour; stormy wind fulfilling his word:"*

Isaiah 45:12, *"I have made the earth, and created man upon it: I, even my hands, have stretched out the heavens, and all their host have I commanded."*

I have one last scripture to include, which I'm not exactly certain which category it falls under. However, based on its content, it certainly applies to many. It's a Statute that pertains to our keeping of His Laws, Statutes and Commands, that has Judgments attached.

Leviticus chapter 26 starts off by stressing three things. The first of which is found in verse 1, which states; *"Ye shall make you no idols nor graven image, neither rear you up a standing image, neither shall ye set up any image of stone in your land, to bow down unto it: for I am the LORD your God."* The second is found in verse 2; *"Ye shall keep my sabbaths, and reverence my sanctuary: I am the LORD."* And the third begins in verse 3, or at least the first portion of it does. It states; *"If ye walk in my statutes, and keep my commandments, and do them;".*

The scripture then begins to elaborate about the blessings that God bestows upon those who do so. However, the second portion begins with verse 14, and speaks of God's punishments if we are not compliant.

Beginning with verse 14, it states; *"But if ye will not hearken unto me, and will not do all these commandments; 15) And if ye shall despise my statutes, or if your soul abhor my judgments, so that ye will not do all my commandments, but that ye break my covenant: 16) I also will do this unto you; I will even appoint over you terror, consumption, and the burning ague, that shall consume the eyes, and cause sorrow of heart: and ye shall sow your seed in vain, for your enemies shall eat it."*

The Biblical definition of **ague** means "**an inflammatory or burning fever**". (biblestudytools.com).

Allow me to highlight portions of the next 23 verses due in part to the length, but also the wording which speaks to the people of that time. Even though we would likely not find ourselves in a position where **our land shall not yield her increase** or **wild beasts shall rob us of our children**, that doesn't mean that God wouldn't find other ways of inflicting these punishments. Like possibly taking away our income which would lead to our starvation, or afflicting our children with some disease that would **rob us of them**.

So, as you read the following, just try to imagine what that would equate to in today's world.

Verse 17*; "And I will set my face against you, and ye shall be slain before your enemies: they that hate you shall reign over you; and ye shall flee when none pursueth you."* None will respect you. You'll be paranoid, thinking that everyone's out to get you.

Verse 18; *"And if ye will not yet for all this hearken unto me, then I will punish you seven times more for your sins. 19) And I will break the pride of your power... 20) And your strength shall be spent in vain... 21) And if ye walk contrary unto me, and will not hearken unto me; I will bring seven times more plagues upon you according to your sins. 22) ... rob you of your children... 23) And if ye will not be reformed by me by these things, but will walk contrary unto me; 24) Then will I also walk contrary unto you, and will punish you yet seven times for your sins. 25) And I will bring a sword upon you, that shall avenge the quarrel of my covenant: and when ye are gathered together within your cities, I will send the pestilence among you; and ye shall be delivered into the hand of the enemy. 26) ... ye shall eat, and not be satisfied. 27) And if ye will not for all this hearken unto me, but walk contrary unto me; 28) Then I will walk contrary unto you also in fury; and I, even I, will chastise you seven times for your sins. 29) And ye shall eat the flesh of your sons, and the flesh of your daughters shall ye eat.* (That sounds like zombie apocalypse stuff right there!)

And it continues! This is very real stuff! God's power to do these things is supernatural, and something that would make you believe that you were living in a horror movie.

I had a taste of it myself just recently, while writing this book. Back when I was working on **Book 2**, after I had been keeping the Sabbath for several months, I had kept my notebook close at hand while reading my Bible during the Sabbath, to make notes on various passages that I could use. And all the while I was plagued with nightmares and restless sleep, scary thoughts that would pop into my mind out of nowhere.

I kept praying about it, asking God to please put a hedge around my mind, to protect me. But then He finally made me realize that I was bringing it on myself, by working on the Sabbath. Even though I was reading my Bible, my taking notes of scriptures to use in my book was still considered work.

Upon making that realization I stopped, and the torment stopped as well. Then, while working on this book, I began to do it again, but modified it. Meaning, I would only jot down the Book, chapter and verse number so I could follow up on it after the Sabbath.

I, again, was plagued by strange dreams, usually involving searching for scripture or counting. At that same time, I started having all sorts of problems with Amazon, not being able to upload revised manuscripts. I remember precisely the day that this began, September 13, 2023, because my last revision was just the day prior on the 12th. I kept going around in circles with different people every day, trying to explain the issues that I was experiencing, but never was able to get the help necessary to remedy to the problem.

I ended up having to purchase a new laptop, which that expense was preceded by a trip that I had planned to Myrtle Beach SC, that I had to postpone due to 3 hurricanes sitting in the Atlantic at the same time. Which ended up costing me another $99 to reschedule my flight. And, after all of this, I discovered that both of my front tires on my car kept losing air! Hmm!

During this same time period, the day immediately following the Sabbath I would wake up feeling sick at my stomach, and somewhat feverish. Even though I felt nauseous for about 3 days, I never once actually had any vomiting. And this happened three weeks in a row, always occurring on the Sunday following the Sabbath. And... I, not once, was ever exposed to anyone with sickness. I live alone, and I had not been anywhere or seen anyone that would have caused it!

I also became plagued with these black beetle type insects, with a few spiders mixed in! It wasn't an infestation, but it was making me crazy! I'm not a bug person! And, definitely not a spider person!

Once I was finally back on track with Amazon, and able to upload revisions, all activity came to an abrupt stop on all four books for 7 solid days. I mean not the first order! Which is extremely unusual for **Book 1**. Everything seemed as though it was spiralling out of control!

Finally, on October 7, 2023, during the Sabbath, I once again opened my Bible to read. And, this scripture is what God led me to. In fact, I had started rereading the Old Testament only a couple months prior, on the Sabbath. And my reading for that night began with Leviticus 24. Then, as I began to read chapter 26, I quickly realized that I had been living this very scripture!

God wanted me to understand that me breaking His Sabbath, even ever so slightly, was no longer acceptable and would not be tolerated anymore. And, trust me when I say, I didn't want to find out how much worse it could have gotten if I had continued to violate it. Because, as frustrating as all of this was, I know that He was going easy on me. And, message received!! I know that I've said that before, but the consequences were much harsher this time.

Many would think that God is punishing me for these horrible things that I say about Jesus, but please don't be fooled by that. This is very real stuff, with very serious consequences for all who He has made a covenant with. He has proven it to me on more than just one occasion. His Laws are real. His Statutes are expected to be followed, and His Judgments are certain!

**Update 4/28/24

While writing **Book 4, God's Passover** (Published 3/8/24), I was, once again, discussing the God's Feasts. And, as I was writing about the Day of Atonement and the Feast of Tabernacles (Sukkot), God made me realize that I had failed to, not only keep, but even remember both of these commemorative occasions last year.

With that said, when you look at the time frames, that I spoke of, regarding my hardships that I was dealing with, I feel certain that my failure to recognize, and honor, both of these events were factors in God's wake-up call.

Even though keeping these Feasts were new to me, I certainly can no longer claim ignorance after God has made it known to me in the scripture, and even had me write about them. I should have been more vigilant, paying close attention to the calendar so I would be aware of any upcoming events.

When chaos comes upon you, God is trying to tell you something. And we all, myself included, must do a better job of paying attention.

Once again, after you reach the **Age of Knowing** about a given matter, you will be held accountable. And using ignorance as your excuse will no longer be acceptable!

~

Testimonies - *Edot* (Hebrew), "**commemorate important events in Jewish history**. For example, the **Shabbat** is said to testify to the story that **Hashem** created the world in six days and rested on the seventh day and declared it holy." (Wikipedia)

*   "Ordinances; God's standard of conduct according to the Ten Commandments." (Nelson's NKJV Study Bible)

* "A solemn protest or declaration." (Oxford Languages)

Scriptures pertaining to **Testimonies**;

Exodus 23, beginning with verse 14 states; *"**Three times thou shalt keep a feast unto me in the year. 15) Thou shalt keep the <u>feast of unleavened bread</u>:** ... **16) And the <u>feast of harvest, the firstfruits of thy labours, which thou hast sown in the field</u>:** and the <u>feast of ingathering, which is in the end of the year, when thou hast gathered in thy labours out of the field</u>."*

Which, looking at Leviticus 23, beginning with verse 10, it states; *"Speak unto the children of Israel, and say unto them, When ye be come into the land which I give unto you, and **shall reap the harvest thereof, then ye shall bring a sheaf of the firstfruits of your harvest unto the priest**: 11) And he shall wave the sheaf before the LORD, to be accepted for you: on the morrow after the sabbath the priest shall wave it. ... 14) And **ye shall eat neither bread, nor parched corn, nor green ears, until the selfsame day that ye have brought an offering unto your God: <u>it shall be a statute for ever throughout your generations in all your dwellings</u>.**"*

This is called the **Feast of Firstfruits** and takes place during the time of **Passover and the Feast of Unleavened Bread**. It is the **first fruits that were harvested, which "coincided with the barley harvest"**. (titus2homemaker.com)

Then, Leviticus 23, beginning with verse 15 tells us when the next feast was to take place. It states, *"And **ye shall count unto you from the morrow after the sabbath, from the day that ye brought the sheaf of the wave offering; seven sabbaths shall be complete: 16) Even unto the morrow after the seventh sabbath shall ye number fifty days; and ye shall offer a new meat offering unto the LORD.** 17) Ye shall bring out of your habitations two wave loaves of two tenth deals: they shall be of fine flour; they shall be baken with leaven; **they are the firstfruits unto the LORD**... 20) And the priest shall wave them with the bread of the firstfruits for a wave offering before the LORD, with the two lambs: they shall be holy to the LORD for the priest. 21) **And ye shall proclaim on the selfsame day, that it may be a holy convocation unto you: ye shall do no servile work therein: <u>it shall be a statute for ever in all your dwellings throughout your generations</u>.**"*

This is the **Feast of Weeks**, the second feast that God spoke of, also called **Shavuot**. It also speaks of the firstfruits because God always wanted them to provide an offering of the **firstfruits** that were harvested, before anyone could eat of it themselves. This feast was celebrated "**at the time of the wheat harvest**". (titus2homemaker.com)

And, the third feast, the **Feast of Ingathering**, is found in Leviticus 23, beginning with verse 34. It states; *"Speak unto the children of Israel, saying, The fifteenth day of this seventh month shall be the **feast of tabernacles** for seven days unto the LORD... 39) Also in the fifteenth day of the seventh month, **when ye have gathered in the fruit of the land**, ye shall keep a feast unto the LORD seven days: on the first day shall be a sabbath, and on the eighth day shall be a sabbath... 41) And ye shall keep it a feast unto the LORD seven days in the year. **It shall be a <u>statute for ever in your generations</u>: ye shall celebrate it in the seventh month.**"*

Not only does God tell us when this feast is held, the **Feast of Ingathering**, also known as the **Feast of Tabernacles,** but provides instructions on how it is to be celebrated, and the exact days it should begin and end on. Just as He also does with the other two as well. All three **must be celebrated every year and are statutes** *"for ever in your generations"*.

Leviticus 23:27-31, *"Also **on the tenth day of this seventh month there shall be a day of atonement**: it shall be a holy convocation unto you; **and ye shall afflict your souls**, and offer an offering made by fire unto the LORD. 28) And **ye shall do no work in that same day: for it is a day of atonement, to make an atonement for you before the LORD your God. 29) For whatsoever soul it be that shall not be afflicted in that same day, he shall be cut off from among his people.** 30) And whatsoever soul it be that doeth any work in that same day, the same soul will I destroy from among his people. 31) Ye shall do no manner of work: **it shall be a statute for ever throughout your generations in all your dwellings.**"*

Even though the scripture states that it is a **Statute**, it also falls under the category of being a **Testimony** as well, due to its requirement of annual recognition... To "**commemorate important events in Jewish history**".

Exodus 30, verse 10 also speaks of the command by God for this. It states; *"And Aaron shall make **an atonement upon the horns of it once in a year with the blood of the sin offering of atonements: once in the year shall he make atonement upon it throughout your generations: it is most holy unto the LORD.***"

This is what the Jewish people call **Yom Kippur**. The Day of Atonement "is considered the most important holiday in the Jewish faith". (history.com)

The article states, "According to tradition, it is on Yom Kippur that God decides each person's fate, so Jews are encouraged to make amends and ask forgiveness for sins committed during the past year."

One thing that I came to understand, and wrote about in **Book 2**, was that a **holy convocation not only applies to a Sabbath, but it also pertains to other events that are holy and are required to be commemorated.**

As I explain in **Book 2**, at the time that all of God's Feasts and Sabbaths were implemented by God, everything was established based on 13 months, with each month having 28 days, for a total of 364 days per year.

In doing so, this allows for every Sabbath and Feast to fall on the proper day, year after year. A calendar with this exact layout would be the only way that these Feasts would begin on, and end on the exact day that God had stipulated.

The Day of Atonement provides proof of my understanding.

Look once again at Leviticus 23:27, *"Also **on the tenth day of this seventh month there shall be a day of atonement**: it shall be a holy convocation unto you; **and ye shall afflict your souls**...".*

God is very specific about this event taking place on the **tenth day of this seventh month**. The scripture even states that it should be a

holy convocation. But... the key to understanding when exactly this event should be held, is found in verse 32 of chapter 23.

It states; *"**It shall be unto you a sabbath of rest**, and ye shall afflict your souls: **in the ninth day of the month at even, from even unto even, shall ye celebrate your sabbath.**"*

This verse tells us that the event **shall be unto you a sabbath of rest**, but then it goes on to explain that the actual Sabbath was to begin on the **ninth day**!

Furthermore, look at Leviticus 23, verse 24, which states; *"Speak unto the children of Israel, saying, **In the seventh month, in the first day of the month, shall ye have a sabbath**, a <u>memorial of blowing of trumpets</u>, **a holy convocation.**"*

This verse tells us that the **first day of the seventh month shall be a sabbath.** In order for the date to align with the **ninth**, the **first day of the month would have to take place on a Friday, and the 2nd of the month would begin at sundown, which would start the Sabbath.**

In looking at a calendar, the first of the month taking place on a Friday would display the technical date that the Sabbath would begin on. Therefore, the wording of the verse is accurate.

But, at sundown the new day would begin, which would then become the 2nd. **This, now, aligns with the 9th being a Sabbath**, as well.

This also confirms my statement regarding a **holy convocation pertaining to other events that are holy and are to be commemorated.** Because the 10th would take place on the day following the Sabbath, or at sundown when the Sabbath would end, and the Day of Atonement would then begin. And it is to be conducted just as a Sabbath would be, only we would be required to afflict ourselves.

According to the Holman Bible Dictionary (studylight.org), regarding **"What are afflictions in Hebrew"**, states; "Old Testament, The two primary Hebrew words used for affliction mean **'to lower, humble, or deny'.**"

Even though I count 3 words, and believe that all apply, I think the term "**deny**" really stands out above the rest. **We afflict ourselves by denying ourselves of all the things that give us pleasure.**

And, given the fact that it is to be held on a Sabbath, activities are already limited. But you can still deny yourself by fasting, or eating foods that are less desirable.

One more point before we continue... Did you notice verse 24 where I had it underlined? It, again, states; *"... In the seventh month, in the first day of the month, shall ye have a sabbath, **a memorial of blowing of trumpets**, a holy convocation."*

According to the Wikipedia, the Jewish people call this event **Rosh Hashanah**. It "is a two-day observance and celebration that begins on the first day of Tishrei, which is the seventh month of the ecclesiastical year... the beginning of the civil year, according to the teachings of Judaism, and is the traditional anniversary of the creation of Adam and Eve...".

The same source continues, "Rosh Hashanah customs include sounding the **shofar** (a hollowed-out ram's horn), as prescribed in the Torah, following the prescription of the Hebrew Bible to 'raise a noise' on **Yom Teruah**".

Now researching **Yom Teruah**, nehemiaswall.com states; "While the Torah does not explicitly tell us the purpose of Yom Teruah, its name may indicate that it is intended as **a day of public prayer. The verb form of Teruah often refers to the noise made by a gathering of the faithful calling out to the Almighty in unison.**"

The same source continues, "**The transformation of Yom Teruah (Day of Shouting) into Rosh Hashanah (New Years) is the result of pagan Babylonian influence upon the Jewish nation. The first stage in the transformation was the adoption of the Babylonian month names.**"

Why am I not surprised?? It appears that the only thing regarding this event that is being conducted properly, is the **blowing of the shofar** (ram's horn). However, in the Book of Numbers there appears to be several occasions for which trumpets are to be blown.

Chapter 10 elaborates about the blowing of trumpets for assembly of the people, for sounding an alarm, and recognition of the beginning of a new month, as well as other occasions.

Numbers 10, beginning with verse 8 states; *"And the sons of Aaron,* ***the priests, shall blow with the trumpets; and they shall be to you for an ordinance for ever throughout your generations.*** *9) And if ye go to war in your land against the enemy that oppresseth you, then ye shall blow an alarm with the trumpets; and ye shall be remembered before the LORD your God, and ye shall be saved from your enemies. 10) Also in the day of your gladness, and in your solemn days, and in the beginnings of your months, ye shall blow with the trumpets over your burnt offerings, and over the sacrifices of your peace offerings;* ***that they may be to you for a memorial before your God: I am the LORD your God.****"*

Here we see numerous occasions for which trumpets should be blown, but are they? I can't answer that because I've never had the privilege of attending a Jewish Feast for which it would be.

Moving on. Other events in Jewish history that could be regarded as **Testimonies**, includes...

Psalm 89:3-4, *"**I have made a covenant with my chosen, I have sworn unto David** my servant, 4) Thy seed will I establish for ever, and build up thy throne to all generations. Selah."*

Also, Psalm 89:34-37, *"**My covenant will I not break, nor alter the thing that is gone out of my lips. 35) Once have I sworn by my holiness that I will not lie unto David.** 36) His seed shall endure for ever, and his throne as the sun before me. 37) **It shall be established for ever as the moon, and as a faithful witness in heaven...**".*

I believe this to be a perfect example of a **solemn protest or declaration, made by God Himself!**

Jeremiah 31:33-36, *"But **this shall be the covenant that I will make with the house of Israel; After those days, saith the LORD, I will***

141

put my law in their inward parts, and write it in their hearts; and will be their God, and they shall be my people. *34) And they shall teach no more every man his neighbour, and every man his brother, saying, Know the LORD: for they shall all know me, from the least of them unto the greatest of them, saith the LORD: for I will forgive their iniquity, and I will remember their sin no more. 35)* **Thus saith the LORD, which giveth the sun for a light by day, and the ordinances of the moon and of the stars for a light by night, which divideth the sea when the waves thereof roar;** *The LORD of hosts is his name: 36)* **If those ordinances depart from before me, saith the LORD, then the seed of Israel also shall cease from being a nation before me for ever.**"

~

Decrees - "**Chukim** (Hebrew, 'decrees'), are **commandments with no known rationale, and are perceived as pure manifestations of the Divine wil**l." (Wikipedia)

* "Decrees issued by rulers, written commands having the effect of law, and the metaphor of God as King of the world provide the imagery behind the Bible's reference to God's 'decrees'." (biblestudytools.com)

Based on my understanding of that stated above, one example of this is found in Exodus 7, beginning with verse 1. It states; *"And the LORD said unto Moses, See, I have made thee a god to Pharaoh: and Aaron thy brother shall be thy prophet. 2) Thou shalt speak all that I command thee: and Aaron thy brother shall speak unto Pharaoh, that he send the children of Israel out of his land. 3)* **And I will harden Pharaoh's heart, and multiply my signs and my wonders in the land of Egypt.**"

God **hardening Pharaoh's heart** would be a perfect example of God's **Divine will** at work! Even though Exodus 7:3 only makes God's intentions known, He does it, not just once, but I count **11 times**!

Look at Exodus 7:13, *"And **he hardened Pharaoh's heart**, that he hearkened not unto them; as the LORD had said."*

142

7:22, *"And the magicians of Egypt did so with their enchantments:* **and Pharaoh's heart was hardened**, *neither did he hearken unto them; as the LORD had said."*

8:15, *"But when Pharaoh saw that there was respite,* **he hardened his heart**, *and hearkened not unto them; as the LORD had said."*

* Many say that Pharaoh hardened his own heart here, but you must remember that this was God's intention all along. Pharaoh was insolent, so God put it in him to be hardened, more and more.

8:19, *"Then the magicians said unto Pharaoh, This is the finger of God:* **and Pharaoh's heart was hardened**, *and he hearkened not unto them; as the LORD had said."*

8:32, *"****And Pharaoh hardened his heart*** *at this time also, neither would he let the people go."*

* Same as before... God's Hand at work!

9:7, *"And Pharaoh sent, and, behold, there was not one of the cattle of the Israelites dead.* **And the heart of Pharaoh was hardened**, *and he did not let the people go."*

9:12, *"And* **the LORD hardened the heart of Pharaoh,** *and he hearkened not unto them; as the LORD had spoken unto Moses."*

9:34, *"And when Pharaoh saw that the rain and the hail and the thunders were ceased, he sinned yet more,* **and hardened his heart**, *he and his servants."*

* God's Hand still at work!

10:20, *"****But the LORD hardened Pharaoh's heart***, *so that he would not let the children of Israel go."*

10:27, *"****But the LORD hardened Pharaoh's heart***, *and he would not let them go."*

And 14:8, *"****And the LORD hardened the heart of Pharaoh*** *king of Egypt, and he pursued after the children of Israel: and the children of Israel went out with a high hand."*

All of this, in my opinion, is a pure manifestation of the Divine will of God. By His Will, He was bending the will of Pharaoh to accomplish His ultimate goal... proving that He, alone, is God!

In Numbers 24:13 Moses states, " ... *I cannot go beyond the commandment of the LORD, <u>to do either good or bad of mine own mind; but what the LORD saith, that will I speak</u>?*"

Look also at Ezra 1:1, *"Now in the first year of Cyrus king of Persia, that the word of the LORD by the mouth of Jeremiah might be fulfilled,* **the LORD <u>stirred up the spirit</u> of Cyrus king of Persia, <u>that he made a proclamation</u> throughout all his kingdom, and put it also in writing,** *saying,"*

Same thing! God **stirred up the spirit** in Cyrus, which lead to Cyrus making a proclamation, a **decree**.

Ezra 5:13, *"But in the first year of* **Cyrus the king of Babylon** *the same king Cyrus* **made a decree to build this house of God.**"

Ezra 6:1-3, *"Then* **Darius the king made a decree, and search was made in the house of the rolls,** *where the treasures were laid up in Babylon. 2) And there was found at Achmetha, in the palace that is in the province of the Medes, a roll, and therein was a record thus written: 3) In the first year of Cyrus the king the same Cyrus the king made a decree concerning the house of God at Jerusalem, Let the house be builded, the place where they offered sacrifices, ...".*

Ezra 6:14, " ... **And they builded, and finished it, according to the commandment of the God of Israel, and according to the commandment of Cyrus, and Darius, and Artaxerxes king of Persia.**"

All of these verses from Ezra contain **decrees issued by rulers that were inspired by or prompted by God.**

Daniel 3:12-25, *"**There are certain Jews whom thou hast set over the affairs of the province of Babylon, Shadrach, Meshach, and Abednego; these men, O king, have not regarded thee: they serve not thy gods, nor worship the golden image which thou hast set up. 13) Then Nebuchadnezzar in his rage and fury commanded to bring Shadrach, Meshach, and Abednego... 14) Nebuchadnezzar** spake and said unto them, Is it true... do not ye serve my gods, nor worship the golden image which I have set up? 15) Now if ye be ready that at what time ye hear ... all kinds of musick, ye fall down and worship the image which I have made; well: but **if ye worship not, ye shall be cast the same hour into the midst of a burning fiery furnace; and who is that God that shall deliver you out of my hands?** 16) Shadrach, Meshach, and Abednego, answered and said to the king, O Nebuchadnezzar, ... 17) If it be so, **our God whom we serve is able to deliver us from the burning fiery furnace, and he will deliver us out of thine hand, O king**. 18) But if not, be it known unto thee, O king, that we will not serve thy gods, nor worship the golden image which thou hast set up. 19) Then was **Nebuchadnezzar full of fury**, and ... he spake, **and commanded that they should heat the furnace one seven times more than it was wont to be heated...** 24) Then Nebuchadnezzar the king was astonied, and rose up in haste, and spake, and said unto his counsellors, **Did not we cast three men bound into the midst of the fire?** They answered and said unto the king, True, O king. 25) He answered and said, Lo, **I see four men loose, walking in the midst of the fire, and they have no hurt; and the form of the fourth is like the Son of God.**"

And, verse 28, "Then Nebuchadnezzar spake, and said, **Blessed be the God of Shadrach, Meshach, and Abednego,** who hath sent his angel, and delivered his servants that trusted in him, and have changed the king's word, and yielded their bodies, that they might not serve nor worship any god, except their own God. 29) **Therefore I make a decree, That every people, nation, and language, which speak any thing amiss against the God of Shadrach, Meshach, and Abednego, shall be cut in pieces, and their houses shall be made a dunghill: because there is no other God that can deliver after this sort.**"

I tried to shorten the story where possible, but much of it was necessary to prove God's miraculous Hand at work. Not only that, but the **decree that was made by the king, as a result.**

Look also at Daniel 6:16-22, "Then **the king commanded, and they brought Daniel, and cast him into the den of lions.** Now the king spake and said unto Daniel, **Thy God whom thou servest** *continually, he will deliver thee. 17) And **a stone was brought, and laid upon the mouth of the den; and the king sealed it with his own signet**, and with the signet of his lords; that the purpose might not be changed concerning Daniel... 19) Then the king arose very early in the morning, and went in haste unto the den of lions. 20) And when he came to the den, he cried with a lamentable voice unto Daniel: and **the king spake and said to Daniel, O Daniel, servant of the living God, is thy God, whom thou servest continually, able to deliver thee from the lions?** ... 22) **My God hath sent his angel, and hath shut the lions' mouths, that they have not hurt me**: forasmuch as before him innocency was found in me; and also before thee, O king, have I done no hurt."*

Then, verse 25 states, "Then **king Darius wrote unto all people,** *nations, and languages, that dwell in all the earth; Peace be multiplied unto you. 26)* **I make a decree, That in every dominion of my kingdom men tremble and fear before the God of Daniel: for he is the living God, and stedfast for ever, and his kingdom that which shall not be destroyed, and his dominion shall be even unto the end.**"

Here, again, we see God's Hand mysteriously at work! And it too, ended in a **decree for all of the kingdom to tremble, fear, and honour the LORD God.**

In chapter 4, Daniel interprets another dream for Nebuchadnezzar, involving a tree cut down. Verse 24 states; *This is the interpretation, O king, and* **this is the decree of the most High,** *which is come upon my lord the king: 25) That* **they shall drive thee from men, and thy dwelling shall be with the beasts of the field, and they shall make thee to eat grass as oxen, and they shall wet thee with the dew of heaven, and seven times shall pass over thee, till thou know that the most High ruleth in the kingdom of men, and giveth it to whomsoever he will.** *26) And whereas* **they commanded to leave the stump of the tree roots; thy kingdom shall be sure unto thee, after that thou shalt have known that the heavens do rule.** *27) Wherefore, O king,* **let my counsel be acceptable unto thee, and break off thy sins by righteousness, and thine iniquities by shewing mercy to the poor; if it may be a lengthening of thy tranquillity...** *30) The king spake, and said, Is* not this great Babylon, that I have built for the house of the kingdom by the might of my power, and for the honour of my majesty? *31) **While the word was in the king's mouth, <u>there fell a voice from heaven, saying, O king Nebuchadnezzar, to thee it is spoken; The kingdom is departed from thee</u>... 33) <u>The same hour was the thing fulfilled upon Nebuchadnezzar: and he was driven from men, and did eat grass as oxen, and his body was wet with the dew of heaven, till his hairs were grown like eagles' feathers, and his nails like birds' claws</u>. 34) And at the end of the days I Nebuchadnezzar lifted up mine eyes unto heaven, and mine understanding returned unto me, and I blessed the most High, and I praised and honoured him that liveth for ever, whose dominion is an everlasting dominion, and his kingdom is from generation to generation: 35) And all the inhabitants of the earth are reputed as nothing: <u>and he doeth according to his will in the army of heaven, and among the inhabitants of the earth: and none can stay his hand, or say unto him, What doest thou</u>?"*

Now, I'm not sure what is meant by **commandments with no known rationale, and are perceived as pure manifestations of the Divine will**, but in my understanding, all three of these stories are centered around **pure manifestations of the Divine will**. And, in my opinion, the **rationale** was to turn people to Him, **by making examples of others, good and bad**!

1st Samuel 16:10-14, "*Again, Jesse made seven of his sons to pass before Samuel. And Samuel said unto Jesse, **The LORD hath not chosen these**. 11) And Samuel said unto Jesse, **Are here all thy children?** And he said, **There remaineth yet the youngest, and, behold, he keepeth the sheep. And Samuel said unto Jesse, Send and fetch him**: for we will not sit down till he come hither. 12) And he sent, and brought him in. Now he was ruddy, and withal of a beautiful countenance, and goodly to look to. **And the LORD said, Arise, anoint him: for this is he. 13)** Then Samuel took the horn of oil, and anointed him in the midst of his brethren: <u>and the Spirit of the LORD came upon David from that day forward</u>. So Samuel rose up, and went to Ramah. 14) **But <u>the Spirit of the LORD departed from Saul, and an evil spirit from the LORD troubled him</u>**.*"

Look now at 1st Samuel 16:1, *"And the LORD said unto Samuel, How long wilt thou mourn for Saul, seeing I have rejected him from reigning over Israel? fill thine horn with oil, and go, I will send thee to Jesse the Bethlehemite: for I have provided me a king among his sons."*

God knew who he was looking for when He and Samuel went to Jesse's home. God had planned David, and made his conception come about. All of this is explained in **Book 2.** And the moment He saw David, He told Samuel **arise and anoint him.** And the **Spirit of the LORD came upon David from that day.** But, as a result, God's Spirit left Saul, and an evil spirit from the LORD troubled him.

Going back to 1st Samuel 9:17, *"**And when Samuel saw Saul, the LORD said unto him, Behold the man whom I spake to thee of! this same shall reign over my people.**"*

These are all examples of God's Hand at work, whether it be **providing Himself a king** by bringing about the birth of a specific person or guiding a prophet to locations where chosen ones are to be found. Sending His Spirit into someone, or even sending an evil spirit into someone, **it all comes about by His Divine will**.

Look at 2nd Kings 20:5-11, *"Turn again, and tell Hezekiah the captain of my people, Thus saith the LORD, the God of David thy father, **I have heard thy prayer, I have seen thy tears: behold, I will heal thee**: on the third day thou shalt go up unto the house of the LORD. 6) And **I will add unto thy days fifteen years; and I will deliver thee and this city out of the hand of the king of Assyria; and I will defend this city for mine own sake, and for my servant David's sake**... 8) And Hezekiah said unto Isaiah, **What shall be the sign that the LORD will heal me**, and that I shall go up into the house of the LORD the third day? 9) And Isaiah said, **This sign shalt thou have of the LORD**, that the LORD will do the thing that he hath spoken: **shall the shadow go forward ten degrees, or go back ten degrees? 10) And Hezekiah answered, It is a light thing for the shadow to go down ten degrees: nay, but let the shadow return backward ten degrees. 11) And Isaiah the prophet cried unto the LORD: and he brought the shadow ten degrees backward, by which it had gone down in the dial of Ahaz."*

Another example of **God's Divine will** at work, both in healing someone, and commanding the forces of nature to prove that He had, in fact, healed the person.

Some other examples of things, that in my opinion, **have no known rationale**, but are indeed rational to Him, are as follows...

Look at Deuteronomy 22:9, *"Thou shalt not sow thy vineyard with divers seeds: lest the fruit of thy seed which thou hast sown, and the fruit of thy vineyard, be defiled."*

22:10, *"Thou shalt not plow with an ox and an ass together."*

22:11, *"Thou shalt not wear a garment of divers sorts, as of woollen and linen together."*

He doesn't like things, regardless of what they are, mingled together. Why? It doesn't matter. Whatever His reasons for it, which He certainly has them, it isn't for us to question, just obey!

Leviticus 19:19 adds further validation. It states; *"Ye shall keep my statutes. **Thou shalt not let thy cattle gender with a diverse kind: thou shalt not sow thy field with mingled seed: neither shall a garment mingled of linen and woollen come upon thee.**"*

Which, regarding the garments with diverse threads mingled, once you become aware of His commandment pertaining to this, and you begin to check the labels in your clothing, its alarming to see that most everything we wear has mixed threads. 60% Cotton, 35% Polyester and 5% Spandex. Or, 95% Cotton and 5% Spandex. I even found one garment that was 99% Cotton and 1% Spandex!! Why?? I believe it to be intentional, to force everyone into breaking God's laws, just as it is with everything else! Check your labels!

All of these are **manifestations of God's Divine will**! And I've yet to find any **commandments with no known rationale**, because I look for God's Hand at work in all things. And once you see it, you see it all the time!

~

Precepts - "**Any commandment, instruction, or order intended as a rule of action or conduct**; especially, **a practical rule guiding**

149

behaviour, technique, etc. In the scriptures the word which is translated 'Precept' is a general term for the responsibility God places upon His people. Precepts are guiding truths which have the good of the individual in mind... **Precepts encourage responsibility, promote truth, are beneficial and acknowledge dependence.**" (Higher Ground Ministry)

* "In a general sense, any commandment or order intended as an authoritative rule of action; but applied particularly to commands respecting **moral conduct.**" (KJV Dictionary)

* "**A general rule intended to regulate behaviour or thought.**" (Oxford Languages)

* "**Guiding principles or rules used to control, influence, or regulate conduct**. Precepts also are commands or principles intended primarily as a general rule of action." (Kingdom Dynamics)

Scriptures pertaining to **Precepts**;

Exodus 20:12, *"**Honour thy father and thy mother**: that thy days may be long upon the land which the LORD thy God giveth thee."*

Exodus 20:13, *"**Thou shalt not kill.**"*

Exodus 20:14, *"**Thou shalt not commit adultery.**"*

Exodus 20:15, *"**Thou shalt not steal.**"*

Exodus 20:16, *"**Thou shalt not bear false witness against thy neighbour.**"*

Exodus 20:17, *"**Thou shalt not covet thy neighbour's house, thou shalt not covet thy neighbour's wife, nor his manservant, nor his maidservant, nor his ox, nor his ass, nor any thing that is thy neighbour's.**"*

All of these are **laws that regulate behaviour.**

Deuteronomy 6:5-7, *"And **thou shalt love the LORD thy God with all thine heart, and with all thy soul, and with all thy might. 6) And these words, which I command thee this day, shall be in thine*** *heart: 7) And thou shalt teach them diligently unto thy children, and shalt talk of them when thou sittest in thine house, and when thou walkest by the way, and when thou liest down, and when thou risest up."*

This is definitely a **rule of action encouraging our responsibility** to teach our children diligently about God's words.

Exodus 21:22-25, *"If men strive, and hurt a woman with child, so that her fruit depart from her, and yet no mischief follow: he shall be surely punished, according as the woman's husband will lay upon him; and he shall pay as the judges determine. 23) And if any mischief follow, then thou shalt give life for life, 24) Eye for eye, tooth for tooth, hand for hand, foot for foot, 25) Burning for burning, wound for wound, stripe for stripe."*

Leviticus 19:14, *"Thou shalt not curse the deaf, nor put a stumblingblock before the blind, but shalt fear thy God: I am the LORD."*

Leviticus 19:32, *"Thou shalt rise up before the hoary head, and honour the face of the old man, and fear thy God: I am the LORD."*

The **hoary head** means someone with grey hair. This verse is teaching us to show respect for our elders.

Leviticus 19:35-36, *"Ye shall do no unrighteousness in judgment, in meteyard, in weight, or in measure. 36) Just balances, just weights, a just ephah, and a just hin, shall ye have: I am the LORD your God, which brought you out of the land of Egypt."*

Deuteronomy 22:5, *"The woman shall not wear that which pertaineth unto a man, neither shall a man put on a woman's garment: for all that do so are abomination unto the LORD thy God."*

This one is a little tricky. Are pants (trousers) considered clothing that *"pertaineth unto a man"?* If so, the majority of most women are in violation! I won't lie, I am! But, I believe that God is convicting me of it as I speak. Which is why I feel compelled to even discuss it further. In fact, He's been working on me about this for a week now, along with the scriptures which pertain to **wearing diverse threads**.

I'm pretty certain that I'll be cleaning out my closet and revamping my wardrobe within the next couple of weeks. Once He convicts me of something, He wants it handled right away!

As for everyone else, this is your heads up! All women wearing pants and men wearing dresses, you have now reached the **Age of Knowing!**

Also, look at Numbers 15, beginning with verse 38. It states; *"Speak unto the children of Israel, and bid them that they **make them fringes in the borders of their garments throughout their generations, and that they put upon the fringe of the borders a ribband of blue**: 39) And it shall be unto you for a fringe, **that ye may look upon it, and remember all the commandments of the LORD, and do them**; and that ye seek not after your own heart and your own eyes, after which ye use to go a whoring: 40) **That ye may remember, and do all my commandments, and be holy unto your God."***

All of this falls under **practical rules guiding behaviour.**

Leviticus 23:22, *"And when ye reap the harvest of your land, **thou shalt not make clean riddance of the corners of thy field when thou reapest, neither shalt thou gather any gleaning of thy harvest: thou shalt leave them unto the poor, and to the stranger**: I am the LORD your God."*

Deuteronomy 15:1-3, *"**At the end of every seven years thou shalt make a release.** 2) And this is the manner of the release: **Every creditor that lendeth ought unto his neighbour shall release it; he shall not exact it of his neighbour, or of his brother; because it is called the LORD'S release.** 3) **Of a foreigner thou mayest exact it again: but that which is thine with thy brother thine hand shall release;"***

Isaiah 33:15-16, *"**He that walketh righteously, and speaketh uprightly; he that despiseth the gain of oppressions, that shaketh his hands from holding of bribes, that stoppeth his ears from*** *hearing of blood, and shutteth his eyes from seeing evil; 16) He shall dwell on high: his place of defence shall be the munitions of rocks: bread shall be given him; his waters shall be sure."*

All are good examples of moral conduct.

Isaiah 11:3-4, *"And shall **make him of quick understanding in the fear of the LORD: and he shall not judge after the sight of his eyes, neither reprove after the hearing of his ears: 4) But with righteousness shall he judge the poor, and reprove with equity for the meek of the earth: and he shall smite the earth with the rod of his mouth, and with the breath of his lips shall he slay the wicked."***

Even guiding kings, giving them the understanding necessary to **control, influence, or regulate the conduct** of others.

Ezekiel 18:5-9, *"But **if a man be just, and do that which is lawful and right,** 6) And hath not eaten upon the mountains, **neither hath lifted up his eyes to the idols** of the house of Israel, **neither hath defiled his neighbour's wife, neither hath come near to a menstruous woman,** 7) And **hath not oppressed any, but hath restored to the debtor his pledge, hath spoiled none by violence, hath given his bread to the hungry, and hath covered the naked with a garment; 8) He that hath not given forth upon usury, neither hath taken any increase, that hath withdrawn his hand from iniquity, hath executed true judgment between man and man, 9) Hath walked in my statutes, and hath kept my judgments, to deal truly; he is just,** he shall surely live, saith the Lord GOD."*

~

Judgments - *Mishpatim* (Hebrew), "Mishpatim is usually translated as judgments. It more accurately means **right-rulings.** Mishpatim represents **those moral and ethical commandments that need no explanation, neither is explanation needed for the punishment that will be rendered.**" (ourancientpaths.org)

Even though this website explains that *Mishpatim* is translated as **judgments**, if you recall the definition provided at the beginning of this chapter, "**Mishpatim** ('laws') include commandments that are

153

deemed to be self-evident, such as not to murder and not to steal". (Wikipedia)

Which, as I have stated, they're all laws! And, looking at the definition of **Mishpatim** provided by the Wikipedia, it includes such things as murdering and stealing, which are offences that are **moral and ethical in nature.**

Again, we see **terms overlapping**, but applicably so.

* "A binding law; judicial decision." (Nelson's NKJV Study Bible)

* "A misfortune or calamity viewed as a divine punishment." (Oxford Languages)

What I'm understanding here, is the definition of **Judgments** is two-fold. One pertaining to the **judicial decision**, and the other being the outcome of that decision, or punishment.

The Old Testament is full of examples of God's **divine punishments**, but there are only a few scriptures that His **judicial decisions** are mentioned. I'm referring to the use of **Urim** and **Thummim**.

Take a look at Exodus 28:30, *"**And thou shalt put in the breastplate of judgment the Urim and the Thummim**; and they shall be upon Aaron's heart, when he goeth in before the LORD: and Aaron shall bear the judgment of the children of Israel upon his heart before the LORD continually."*

Also, Numbers 27:21, *"**And he shall stand before Eleazar the priest, who shall ask counsel for him after the judgment of Urim before the LORD**: at his word shall they go out, and at his word they shall come in, both he, and all the children of Israel with him, even all the congregation."*

The jewishvirtuallibrary.org states; "The Urim and Thummim (Heb. םי .רוא םי .מ .ת .) was a priestly device for obtaining oracles. **On the high priest's ephod (an apron-like garment) lay a breastpiece (ן .ש ́n) – a pouch inlaid with 12 precious stones engraved with the names of the 12 tribes of Israel – that held the Urim and Thummim** (Ex. 28:15-30; Lev.8:8). **By means of the Urim, the priest inquired of YHWH** on behalf of the ruler (Num. 27:21; cf.

Yoma 7:5, 'only for the king, the high court, or someone serving a need of the community'); they were one of the three legitimate means of obtaining oracles in early Israel (Urim, dreams, prophets; I Sam. 28:6). Owing to the oracular character of the Urim, the breastpiece is called "the breastpiece of decision" (ח ש ̣ |
ט ̣ פ ̣ ש ̣ מ ̣ ה ̣".)

More is said, but this quote provides the information needed. I ask you to focus mainly on that portion highlighted in bold type because based on its limited description in the Books of Moses, the priest used them to determine one's guilt or innocence as judged by God, and wasn't restricted to just the king or high court.

Another quote, from the Wikipedia, states; "According to classical rabbinical literature, in order for the Urim and Thummim to give an answer, it was first necessary for the individual to stand facing the fully dressed high priest, and vocalise the question briefly and in a simple way, though it was not necessary for it to be loud enough for anyone else to hear it. Maimonides explains that the High Priest would stand facing the Ark of the Covenant with the inquirer behind him, facing the Priest's back. After the inquirer asked his question, the Holy Spirit would immediately overcome the Priest and he would see the letters protruding in a prophetic vision."

The Wikipedia continues, "The Talmudic rabbis argued that *Urim and Thummim* were words written on the sacred breastplate. Most of the Talmudic rabbis, and Josephus, following the belief that *Urim* meant 'lights', argued that the rituals involving Urim and Thummim involved questions being answered by great rays of light shining out of certain jewels on the breastplate; each jewel was taken to represent different letters, and the sequence of lighting thus would spell out an answer (though there were 22 letters in the Hebrew alphabet, and only 12 jewels on the breastplate); two Talmudic rabbis, however, argued that the jewels themselves moved in a way that made them stand out from the rest, or even moved themselves into groups to form words."

As you can see, there is a great deal of speculation about what exactly **Urim** and **Thummim** were, and how they worked. But, in the back of my 1945 King James Bible, A New and Practical Plan of Self-Pronunciation section, it states that **Thummim** means "**truth**".

Surprisingly, **Urim** isn't listed. But, given the fact that **Thummim** means **truth**, is it possible that **Urim** means the opposite?

There are numerous sites online, with all sorts of thoughts on the matter. So, as always, I encourage everyone to seek additional information for yourselves.

Moving on, let's look now at scriptures that pertain to God's **Judgments**, as it relates to punishments.

Genesis 2:16-17, *"And the LORD **God commanded the man, saying, Of every tree of the garden thou mayest freely eat: 17) But of the tree of the knowledge of good and evil, thou shalt not eat of it: for in the day that thou eatest thereof thou shalt surely die.**"*

Genesis 3:14, *"And the LORD **God said unto the serpent, Because thou hast done this, <u>thou art cursed above all cattle, and above every beast of the field; upon thy belly shalt thou go, and dust shalt thou eat all the days of thy life</u>; ... 16) Unto the woman he said, <u>I will greatly multiply thy sorrow and thy conception; in sorrow thou shalt bring forth children; and thy desire shall be to thy husband, and he shall rule over thee</u>. 17) And unto Adam he said, Because thou hast hearkened unto the voice of thy wife, and hast eaten of the tree, of which I commanded thee, saying, Thou shalt not eat of it: <u>cursed is the ground for thy sake; in sorrow shalt thou eat of it all the days of thy life</u>; ... 23) Therefore the LORD <u>God sent him forth from the garden of Eden, to till the ground from whence he was taken</u>.**"*

Here we see the **law**, and the **judgment that resulted** due to the law being broken.

Exodus 7, beginning with verse 3 states; *"And **I will harden Pharaoh's heart, and multiply my signs and my wonders in the land of Egypt.** 4) But Pharaoh shall not hearken unto you, that I may lay my hand upon Egypt, and bring forth mine armies, and my people the children of Israel, out of the land of Egypt **by great judgments**."*

Also, look at Exodus 4:22-23, *"And thou shalt say unto Pharaoh, Thus saith the LORD, **Israel is my son, even my firstborn: 23) And I**"* say unto thee, **Let my son go,** that he may serve me: and **if thou refuse to let him go, behold, I will slay thy son, even thy firstborn."**

God is saying right here, in chapter 4, **Let my son, my firstborn, go... or I will slay yours, your firstborn! And He did just that!**

Ten different plagues God brought upon Egypt, proving to Pharaoh that **His Supremacy was above all else**! That's why God deliberately hardened Pharaoh's heart numerous times, to not only force Pharaoh to free His people once and for all, but to make a point!

Look at Exodus 14:17-18, *"And I, behold, **I will harden the hearts of the Egyptians,** and they shall follow them: **and I will get me honour upon Pharaoh, and upon all his host, upon his chariots, and upon his horsemen.** 18) And <u>the Egyptians shall know that I am the LORD, when I have gotten me honour upon Pharaoh, upon his chariots, and upon his horsemen.</u>"*

God continued to harden Pharaoh's heart each time another plague was unleashed so **Pharaoh would know that He alone was the LORD God**. He devastated everything in Egypt, not only to prove His supremacy over Pharoah, but **all the gods of Egypt**.

Look at Exodus 12:12, which states; *"For I will pass through the land of Egypt this night, and will smite all the firstborn in the land of Egypt, both man and beast; **and against all the gods of Egypt I will execute judgment:** I am the LORD."*

Each plague that God unleashed was a direct assault against specific gods or goddesses, to prove that His powers were greater than any of theirs, singularly or combined.

Look at the force of His wrath... **His judgments**.

1)   Chapter 7, verses 17-21... **turned all the waters of Egypt to blood.**

2) Chapter 8, verses 2-14... **overrun by frogs.**

3) Chapter 8, verses 16-18... **lice**.

4) Chapter 8, verses 21-31... **swarms of flies**.

5) Chapter 9, verses 3-7... **"a grievous murrain" that killed cattle, horses, asses, camels, oxen and sheep. ("murrain" is a "fatal cattle disease"**. Int'l Standard Bible Encyclopedia).

6) Chapter 9, verses 8-11... **boils breaking forth on man and beast**.

7) Chapter 9, verses 18-34... **grievous thunder, hail and fire that killed everything, man, beast, crops... that was exposed**.

8) Chapter 10, verses 4-19... **locust**.

9) Chapter 10, verses 21-23... **complete darkness for three days. "They saw not one another"**, that's how dark it was!

And the last one, number 10, was **the LORD God passing over with the plague of death, killing all of the firstborn of Egypt, man and beast**. (Chapters 11 and 12)

Can you imagine living through this? Which, **it only affected the Egyptians, not the Israelites**.

Scientists have tried to provide explanations for the water being turned to blood, and how that forced all of the frogs to leave the rivers, streams, ponds and pools. Which, in turn, caused the flies, which then led to the diseases in the livestock, and so on... But, if that were the case, why did each plague stop when Moses cried unto God to stop it? Stop believing their lies and give God the recognition and credit that He deserves.

There is a great chart available at **biblecharts.org** titled, **The 10 Plagues – Jehovah Versus the Gods of Egypt,** which provides a diagram of the different plagues, and the gods and goddesses that were targeted by each. Examples include, Osiris; the **Nile was his bloodstream**. Hapi; **Frog goddess to Egypt**. Uatchit; **The fly god of Egypt**. Sekhmet; **Egyptian goddess of Epidemics**. Serapis and Imhotep; **Egyptian gods of healing**. Re, Amon-re, Aten, Atum and Horus; **Egyptian sun gods**... and several more. Very interesting, as well as significant. Check it out.

Even though God executed these judgments against the gods of Egypt using these plagues, the horrific consequences were endured by all of Egypt, great and small. Just try to imagine the aftermath that remained each time, which putrefied everything! Talk about judgments!!

Exodus 22:22-24, *"Ye shall not afflict any widow, or fatherless child. 23) If thou afflict them in any wise, and they cry at all unto me, I will surely hear their cry; 24) And my wrath shall wax hot, and I will kill you with the sword; and your wives shall be widows, and your children fatherless."*

Leviticus chapter 18 pertains to **Marriages of Near Relations Unlawful**. Beginning with verse 2, it states; *"Speak unto the children of Israel, and say unto them, I am the LORD your God. 3) After the doings of the land of Egypt, wherein ye dwelt, shall ye not do: and after the doings of the land of Canaan, whither I bring you, shall ye not do: neither shall ye walk in their ordinances. 4) Ye shall do my judgments, and keep mine ordinances, to walk therein: I am the LORD your God. 5) Ye shall therefore keep my statutes, and my judgments: which if a man do, he shall live in them: I am the LORD. 6) None of you shall approach to any that is near of kin to him, to uncover their nakedness: I am the LORD."*

Then, the next 10 verses elaborate in detail as to who all their **near of kin** are. Not only does it specify the **near of kin** relations, but also includes **thy neighbour's wife** (verse 20), man **lying with mankind, as with womankind: "it is an abomination"** (verse 22), or **lying with any beasts** (verse 23).

Picking up with verse 24, of Leviticus 18; *"Defile not ye yourselves in any of these things: for in all these the nations are defiled which I cast out before you:... 26) Ye shall therefore keep my statutes and my judgments, and shall not commit any of these abominations; neither any of your own nation, nor any stranger that sojourneth among you:... 28) That the land spue not you out also, when ye defile it, as it spued out the nations that were before you. 29) For whosoever shall commit any of these abominations, even the souls that commit them shall be cut off from among their people. 30) Therefore shall ye keep mine ordinance, that ye commit not any one of these abominable customs, which were committed before you, and that ye defile not yourselves therein: I am the LORD your God."*

This is definitely a law that pertains to moral and ethical behaviour, with a severe judgment attached, i.e., punishment.

And, is it possible that sometimes **Judgments** just pertain to using good judgment, and doing what is right?

Look at Numbers 27, beginning with verse 8. It states; *"And thou shalt speak unto the children of Israel, saying, If a man die, and have no son, then ye shall cause his inheritance to pass unto his daughter. 9) And if he have no daughter, then ye shall give his inheritance unto his brethren. 10) And if he have no brethren, then ye shall give his inheritance unto his father's brethren. 11) And if his father have no brethren, then ye shall give his inheritance unto his kinsman that is next to him of his family, and he shall possess it: and it shall be unto the children of Israel a statute of judgment, as the LORD commanded Moses."*

And sometimes they pertain to the humane way of handling situations that involve rendering judgment.

Look at Numbers chapter 35, which speaks of **Cities of Refuge Appointed for Homicides**. The scripture elaborates in detail regarding the suburbs of the cities designated for refuge (a city in which no one can harm a slayer), and the differences between murder that is deliberate (intentional) and that which is accidental. Death is the penalty for all intentional murder. But for those that slay a person unintentionally, they are to be relocated to a refuge until they can stand before the congregation in judgment. (Numbers 35:12).

Then, verse 29 states; *"So these things shall be for a statute of judgment unto you throughout your generations in all your dwellings."*

However, in most cases, **Judgment** pertains to punishments by God for our disobedience.

1st Kings 11:6-13, *"And **Solomon did evil in the sight of the LORD**, and went not fully after the LORD, as did David his father. 7) Then* did ***Solomon build a high place for Chemosh, the abomination of Moab***, *in the hill that is before Jerusalem*, ***and for Molech, the abomination of the children of Ammon***. *8) And **likewise did he for all his strange wives**, which **burnt incense and sacrificed unto their gods**... 11) Wherefore the LORD said unto Solomon, Forasmuch as this is done of thee, and **thou hast not kept my covenant and my statutes, which I have commanded thee, <u>I will surely rend the kingdom from thee, and will give it to thy servant</u>**. 12) Notwithstanding in thy days I will not do it for David thy father's sake: but **I will rend it out of the hand of thy son**. 13) Howbeit I will not rend away all the kingdom; **but will give one tribe to thy son for David my servant's sake**, and for Jerusalem's sake which I have chosen."*

The actions and consequences of this **judgment** ended up having long term effects still today. I'm speaking of Solomon's ties to Freemasonry, and how they are making ready for their Supreme Being's arrival.

Jeremiah 25:5-11, *"... **Turn ye again now every one from his evil way, and from the evil of your doings, and dwell in the land that the LORD hath given unto you and to your fathers for ever and ever: 6) And go not after other gods to serve them, and to worship them, and provoke me not to anger with the works of your hands; and I will do you no hurt**. 7) **Yet ye have not hearkened unto me, saith the LORD**; that ye might provoke me to anger with the works of your hands to your own hurt. 8) Therefore thus saith the LORD of hosts; **Because ye have not heard my words, 9) Behold, I will send and take all the families of the north, saith the LORD, and Nebuchadrezzar the king of Babylon, my servant, and will bring them against this land, and against the inhabitants thereof, and against all these nations round about, and will utterly destroy them, and make them an astonishment, and an hissing, and perpetual desolations**... 11) And this whole land shall be a desolation, and an astonishment; **and these nations shall serve the king of Babylon seventy years**."*

And now, 2nd Chronicles 36:19-21, *"**And they burnt the house of God, and brake down the wall of Jerusalem, and burnt all the palaces thereof with fire, and destroyed all the goodly vessels**"* *thereof. 20) And them that had escaped from the sword carried he away to Babylon; where they were servants to him and his sons until the reign of the kingdom of Persia: 21) To fulfil the word of the LORD by the mouth of Jeremiah, until the land had enjoyed her sabbaths: for as long as she lay desolate she kept sabbath, to fulfil threescore and ten years."*

Disobedience has repercussions!

Isaiah 66:4, *"I also will choose their delusions, and will bring their fears upon them; because when I called, none did answer; when I spake, they did not hear: but they did evil before mine eyes, and chose that in which I delighted not."*

Psalm 119:75, *"I know, O LORD, that thy judgments are right, and that thou in faithfulness hast afflicted me."*

Psalm 119:84, *"How many are the days of thy servant? when wilt thou execute judgment on them that persecute me?"*

~

Ordinance - **Chuqqah** (Hebrew), "something prescribed, enactment, **usually with reference to matters of ritual... The word generally has a religious or ceremonial significance."** (International Standard Bible Encyclopedia Online)

* "An ordinance may signify a decree, edict or rescript. The commandments, statutes, decrees, and requirements of God are properly defined as the ordinances of God." (Kingdom Dynamics)

* "An ordinance never changes." (KD)

* "An ordinance of God is everything ordained and established by God's authority with the intent that it be applied in the lives of His children." (KD)

Scriptures pertaining to **Ordinances**;

Genesis 17:10-13, *"This is my covenant, which ye shall keep, between me and you and thy seed after thee; Every man child among you shall be circumcised. 11) And ye shall circumcise the flesh of your foreskin; and it shall be a token of the covenant* *betwixt me and you. 12) And **he that is eight days old shall be circumcised among you, every man child in your generations, he that is born in the house, or bought with money of any stranger, which is not of thy seed. 13) He that is born in thy house, and he that is bought with thy money, must needs be circumcised: and my covenant shall be in your flesh for an everlasting covenant.***"

Even though there is no mention of an **ordinance**, this is a religious ritual, or ceremony that takes place. The Jewish people call it a **Brit Milah**, also known as a **Bris.** It is the "religious ceremony in which the child is brought into the covenant community by means of the circumcision and the accompanying blessings, prayers which put the 'medical' procedure into a religious context." (reformjudaism.org) It's performed on the eighth day of life, by a **Mohel.**

In chapter 12 of Exodus, the scripture speaks of the requirements for the **Passover**, describing the lamb that was to be sacrificed, being without a blemish. The age of the lamb, how long to keep it, and on what day the lamb was to be killed and the blood of it placed upon the door posts.

Verses 8-11 describes how the lamb should be roasted, with bitter herbs, and unleavened bread. And that meal is what the Jewish people celebrate every year.

Exodus 12:14, **"And this day <u>shall be unto you for a memorial;</u> and ye shall keep it a feast to the LORD throughout your generations; <u>ye shall keep it a feast by an ordinance for ever.</u>"**

The **pass over**, where God smote all of the firstborn of Egypt, and the ritual that the Israelites had to perform to protect themselves, was so significant that God made it a **memorial!** Then, to honour it, He made it an **ordinance for ever.**

Exodus 12:17, *"And **ye shall observe the feast of unleavened bread; for in this selfsame day have I brought your armies out of the land of Egypt: therefore shall ye observe this day in your generations by an ordinance for ever.***"

Numbers 33:3, *"And **they departed from Rameses in the first month, on the fifteenth day of the first month; on the morrow after the passover the children of Israel went out with a high hand in the sight of all the Egyptians**."*

Numbers 33:3 confirms the day on which the children of Israel came out of Egypt. And, as stated in Exodus 12:17, *"**ye observe this day in your generations by an ordinance for ever**".*

The **Feast of the Passover** was to be carried out each year on the 14th day of the month of Abib, with the **Feast of Unleavened Bread** officially beginning the day after.

Which means that there are **two different ordinances** involved here. One being in honour of the Passover meal, in which the lamb was slain and its blood marking the door posts as a sign to the LORD, when He passed over, to protect them. And the second in honour of the Unleavened Bread they had to eat, which was the bread of affliction (Deuteronomy 16:3).

Chapter 15 of Numbers pertains to offerings made unto the LORD. Verse 3 states; *"<u>And will make an offering by fire unto the LORD, a burnt offering, or a sacrifice</u> **in performing a vow, or in a freewill offering, or in your solemn feasts**<u>, to make a sweet savour unto the LORD, of the herd, or of the flock</u>:"*

After which, God tells them exactly how to prepare their offering. Then, verse 12 states; *"According to the number that ye shall prepare, so shall ye do to every one according to their number. 13) **All that are born of the country shall do these things after this manner,** <u>in offering an offering made by fire, of a sweet savour unto the LORD</u>. 14) **And if a stranger sojourn with you, or whosoever be among you in your generations, <u>and will offer an offering made by fire, of a sweet savour unto the LORD</u>; as ye do, so he shall do.**"*

Numbers 15:15, *"**One ordinance shall be both for you of the congregation, and also for the stranger that sojourneth with you, an ordinance for ever in your generations**: as ye are, so shall the stranger be before the LORD."*

Here we see God accepting and honouring their vows and offerings, even including the **stranger that sojourneth with you**, as long as their offerings were prepared as stated. And, the **ordinance** was, for it to be done in this manner every time, whether it be by one of the congregation, or by a stranger.

My last example is extremely significant to this day and time. The **Ritual of the Red Heifer**, also called the **Ceremony of Purifying the Unclean**, found in the 19th chapter of Numbers.

Beginning with verse 2, it states; *"**This is the ordinance of the law which the LORD hath commanded**, saying, Speak unto the children of Israel, that they **bring thee a red heifer without spot, wherein is no blemish, and upon which never came yoke**:"*

From the start, God makes it clear that this is an **Ordinance**.

Then, verses 3-6 speaks of the heifer being presented to the priest, the slaying of the heifer outside the camp (before the face of the priest), how the priest shall sprinkle her blood directly before the Tabernacle of the Congregation seven times, and then burn the heifer in the priest's sight, including her skin, her flesh, her blood, and her dung. And the priest shall take cedar wood, hyssop and scarlet, and cast it into the midst of the burning of the heifer.

Verses 7-8 speaks of how the priest, and he that burneth her, shall wash their clothes and bathe their flesh, and be unclean until evening.

Then, verse 9 states; *"**And a man that is clean shall gather up the ashes of the heifer, and lay them up without the camp in a clean place, and it shall be kept for the congregation of the children of Israel for a water of separation: it is a purification for sin.** 10) And he that gathereth the ashes of the heifer shall wash his clothes, and be unclean until the even: **and it shall be unto the children of Israel, and unto the stranger that sojourneth among them, for a statute for ever.**"*

Beginning with verse 11 it tells us what these ashes would be used for, or the uncleanness that would require such a purification.

Verse 11 states; *"He that toucheth the dead body of any man shall be unclean seven days. 12) He shall purify himself with it on the third day, and on the seventh day he shall be clean: but if he purify not himself the third day, then the seventh day he shall not be clean. 13) Whosoever toucheth the dead body of any man that is dead, and purifieth not himself, defileth the tabernacle of the LORD; and that soul shall be cut off from Israel: because the water of separation was not sprinkled upon him, he shall be unclean; his uncleanness is yet upon him."*

Verse 14 states; *"This is the law, **when a man dieth in a tent: all that come into the tent, and all that is in the tent, shall be unclean seven days. 15) And every open vessel, which hath no covering bound upon it, is unclean. 16) And whosoever toucheth one that is slain with a sword in the open fields, or a dead body, or a bone of a man, or a grave, shall be unclean seven days."***

Bear in mind that all of the Children of Israel lived in tents at that time. Therefore, in today's language, it would be a room, or possibly even the entire house.

Verse 17 then states; *"And **for an unclean person they shall take of the ashes of the burnt heifer of purification for sin, and running water shall be put thereto in a vessel: 18) And a clean person shall take hyssop, and dip it in the water, and sprinkle it upon the tent, and upon all the vessels, and upon the persons that were there, and upon him that touched a bone, or one slain, or one dead, or a grave: 19) And the clean person shall sprinkle upon the unclean on the third day, and on the seventh day: and on the seventh day he shall purify himself, and wash his clothes, and bathe himself in water, and shall be clean at even."***

This purification ritual is extremely important to God. In fact, verse 20 states; *"**But the man that shall be unclean, and shall not purify himself, that soul shall be cut off from among the congregation, because he hath defiled the sanctuary of the LORD: the water of separation hath not been sprinkled upon him; he is unclean. 21) And it shall be a perpetual statute unto them, that he that sprinkleth the water of separation shall wash his clothes; and he*** *that toucheth the water of separation shall be unclean until even."*

I felt it necessary to quote the majority of this scripture due to the significance of the **Ashes of the Red Heifer**, and how it relates to this day and time.

A video, titled; **Prophetic Anticipation Builds as Unblemished Red Heifers for Temple** Ceremony... is a news clip from CBN NEWS LIVE. The date is approx. 8 months ago, which would be the February 2023 timeframe. The video discusses how they are preparing to build the 3rd Temple.

It was stated, "The 5 red heifers are now in a secure, undisclosed location in Israel. Plans include moving them sometime soon to a visitor's center in Shiloh, where the Tabernacle of the LORD once stood for nearly 400 years."

It then quotes the scripture from Numbers 19:1-5, saying how the ashes were used to purify priests for their service in the Temple.

It was then stated that, "These heifers are now between 1 1/2 to 2 years old, but to replicate the ceremony mentioned in the Bible, they need to be at least 3 years old. And within that time span they cannot have a blemish, or anything that would disqualify them from the ceremony, even one white or black hair".

Chris Mitchell, a news reporter from CBN News, said, "According to those working on the project, the ceremony of the red heifer needs to be performed on the Mount of Olives, and in a place that would have looked directly into where the Temple stood. The land I'm standing on, bought 12 years ago, fits both of those standards."

He continued, "Rabbi Yitshak Mamo owns the land here, on the Mount of Olives."

It was said that "Mamo says the ceremony needs priests who have not been defiled by touching anything dead."

Mamo stated, "The Temple Institute actually has 9 pure priests... born at home... Because they are priests... they don't go into any cemetery... and their parents keep them in a situation that they would not get into a cemetery... or into any problematic place... We have the priests, we have the red heifers, we have the land, and we have everything ready. We just need to wait another one and a half years." (Some of the quote was illegible due to his accent).

Byron Stinson of BONEH ISRAEL stated that they believe that the ceremony will happen "somewhere in the area of Passover of 2024 and out to the possibility of Shavuot 2024"... the cows would be old enough and it would be the proper timeline for that ceremony.

It was stated that Byron Stinson "helped find the red heifers in the US. He says these would be the first in 2000 years."

Mamo said according to the Jewish sage Maimonides, "there were nine red heifers from Moses to the 2nd Temple". He stated, "we know that the messiah will make the 10th".

The fact that they now have 5 red heifers that meets the criteria for this ceremony, leads the Temple Institute to believe that the ceremony will finally take place. Only one heifer is needed, which means they have 4 backups should anything develop that would disqualify any one of them.

Once again, the ashes are necessary to purify the priest before he can enter in to the Temple. And, as previously stated, these red heifers have been the first to be born in 2000 years.

I encourage everyone to watch the video and seek out any additional information you can regarding this event. For many it's not only history in the making, but another prophetic sign that the end is near.

But... I'm skeptical! The only discussions that I've seen in the Old Testament regarding another Temple, were those speaking of the new one, along with the new city that will come down from heaven.

Need I remind you that God told Solomon; *"But if ye turn away, and forsake my statutes and my commandments, which I have set before you, and shall go and serve other gods, and worship them; "Then will I pluck them up by the roots out of my land which I have* *given them; and **this house, which I have sanctified for my name, will I cast out of my sight, and will make it to be a proverb and a byword among all nations**."* (2 Chronicles 7:19-20)

And every time that they have rebuilt the Temple, God destroyed it! So, why do the Jews believe that God wants them to build it again? I see no evidence of that in His Word. Also, bear in mind that the Hebrew Bible is only the first five Books of any other Bible, and that being the case, they possibly don't acknowledge the prophetic statements regarding the **New City and Temple coming down from heaven** found in the books of Isaiah, Ezekiel, and Zechariah.

In Matthew 24:15 it states; ***"When ye therefore shall see the abomination of desolation, spoken of by Daniel the prophet, stand in the holy place, (whoso readeth, let him understand:)"***. Which many believe that Daniel is prophesying about this occurring in the **End Times**. But, searching the scriptures in Daniel, this statement is never made.

Daniel 9:24-27 is speaking of the "seventy weeks" (called as such in the KJV), or the "seventy sevens" (in the NIV). But nowhere does it say anything about an "abomination standing in the temple".

Daniel 12:11, *"And from the time that the daily sacrifice shall be taken away, and the abomination that maketh desolate set up, there shall be a thousand two hundred and ninety days."*

An **abomination that maketh desolate set up** is something totally different than an **abomination standing in the temple**. The abomination that maketh desolate, in my understanding, is speaking of the **mark of the beast**.

I believe that this was nothing that was prophesied in the Old Testament, but by Jesus alluding to it, he can discredit the true Messiah that may come. **Or, he is speaking of himself, because when he shows up standing in any temple, just know that he is the abomination that he, himself, spoke of!**

Regardless, there is no Biblical requirement spoken of in the Old Testament about the need for a third Temple to be built. Any need

169

for such would only be necessary for Jesus to fulfil his plan of **standing in it, showing himself to be God** as spoken of in 2nd Thessalonians 2:4... *"Who opposeth and exalteth himself above all that is called God, or that is worshipped; so that he as God sitteth in the temple of God, shewing himself that he is God."*

The video I spoke of moments ago regarding the red heifer can be found at: (https://youtu.be/euwx-g1Cx3s?si=yTDICusxh_7JOHHT), or just perform a search under YouTube using the title of the video that I cited at the beginning of this segment.

Aside from this, the examples provided throughout this chapter were to help explain the meanings of each of these terms. And, again I will stress that God's definitions of many terms are very different from what man has defined them as, especially at this day and time.

Proof of that statement is found in the 119th Palm. The title of the chapter is **An Acrostic Psalm of Meditation on the Law**, and is comprised of 176 verses which are broken up into 22 subsections, with each having its own subtitle.

Each subsection contains 8 verses, and within those verses are references to each of the terms that we have just covered, making it clear that each term means something different to God. Allow me to provide some examples of that which I speak of.

Beginning with the first subsection, which is titled **ALEPH**. Verse 1 states; *"BLESSED are the undefiled in the way, who walk in the **law** of the LORD. 2) Blessed are they that keep his **testimonies**, and that seek him with the whole heart. 3) They also do no iniquity: they walk in his ways. 4) Thou hast commanded us to keep thy **precepts** diligently. 5) O that my ways were directed to keep thy **statutes**! 6) Then shall I not be ashamed, when I have respect unto all thy **commandments**. 7) I will praise thee with uprightness of heart, when I shall have learned thy righteous **judgments**. 8) I will keep thy **statutes**: O forsake me not utterly."*

The next subsection is titled **BETH**. Verse 9 states; *"Wherewithal shall a young man cleanse his way? by taking heed thereto according to thy word. 10) With my whole heart have I sought thee:*

*O let me not wander from thy **commandments**. 11) Thy word have I hid in mine heart, that I might not sin against thee. 12) Blessed art thou, O LORD: teach me thy **statutes**. 13) With my lips have I declared all the **judgments** of thy mouth. 14) I have rejoiced in the way of thy **testimonies**, as much as in all riches. 15) I will meditate in thy **precepts**, and have respect unto thy ways. 16) I will delight myself in thy **statutes**: I will not forget thy word."*

The next subsection is titled **GIMEL**, but let's skip forward to the 4th one, **DALETH**. It contains 6 of the different terms. Verse 25 states; *"My soul cleaveth unto the dust: quicken thou me according to thy word. 26) I have declared my ways, and thou heardest me: teach me thy **statutes**. 27) Make me to understand the way of thy **precepts**: so shall I talk of thy wondrous works. 28) My soul melteth for heaviness: strengthen thou me according unto thy word. 29) Remove from me the way of lying: and grant me thy **law** graciously. 30) I have chosen the way of truth: thy **judgments** have I laid before me. 31) I have stuck unto thy **testimonies**: O LORD, put me not to shame. 32) I will run the way of thy **commandments**, when thou shalt enlarge my heart."*

I'll stop here, because, as I have already said, this continues for 176 verses. But hopefully, you now see what I was speaking of. It's evident that the writer of this Psalm was knowledgeable of the differences between these terms. And with his elaboration continuing at such length, it is no fluke.

The subtitles are, what is called, the Hebrew Alphabetic Acrostics. And, as stated by eBible.com, are Hebrew letters. I'm not going to try to explain this, because each word not only represents a Hebrew letter, but has a meaning as well. For example, the meaning of the letter Aleph "literally means 'to study' and shows this priority in the life of the Jews. Beth means understanding, Gimel means path, Dalet means door or gate." (scielo.org.za>ote)

I encourage anyone that would like to know more, to begin by reading the entire 119th Psalm, and then searching online the meanings of the various letters used as subtitles throughout the scripture.

Hopefully I have shown that these terms do have very specific meanings to God, and do differ from one another unlike the definitions provided in various sites which show terms overlapping.

Also, throughout this chapter I have tried to utilize scripture from numerous books of the Old Testament to show that God's commandments, judgments, statutes and testimonies are evident in all aspects of His Word.

My closing thoughts regarding this chapter are that everything that God wants us to do, or not to do, can be found in the first 5 Books of the Old Testament, also called the Books of Moses, and the Torah. No other Commentaries, Codices, Textbooks or Exegesis are necessary to interpret God's Word.

All of these are just other people's opinions, just as this is mine. The difference being, I have trusted only God for my understanding. That's all that's necessary. That's all the anyone should ever do. It's good to listen, and or read, other people's opinions, but we should never take it as the gospel.

As always, I encourage everyone to read and pray, and do your own research. Use the common sense that God has given you, and stop letting other people tell you what to believe! Trust only God!

Plagiarizing the Prophets

As I have already pointed out, numerous times, Jesus has taken credit for many, so called, "prophecies". Several of which were not even prophecies!

On one occasion during the Sabbath, I was reading chapter 7 in the book of Daniel when I began to notice similarities between it and the book of Revelation. I had actually noticed it before, back during the 2005-2006 time frame when I first began to read the Bible.

Like most people, I was already pretty familiar with the New Testament, and John's vision in Revelation. But never having read much of the Old Testament, it really jumped out at me upon reading Daniel chapter 7, the similarities regarding the beasts of each, that is.

But on this particular day, little did I realize when I first began to reread it, that God took me there for a reason. He knew that with my eyes, now being wide open, I would **see** many similarities that I had no clue of during my first reading.

Allow me to share my findings. I ask you to please understand that I may jump around a little bit. I will try to keep it in order as much as possible. But bear in mind that it is the similarities that I wish to focus on, and not the order of it.

Also, focus on the highlighted portions. Just as I did in **Book 2, chapter 7,** when explaining who the **Assyrian** was, based on the scripture found in Ezekiel 31:3-18. I highlighted with bold type all of the significant verses. Then, upon reassembling them, it became very obvious who the scripture was speaking of.

I guess the technique would be similar to **"Reading between the lines"**, but instead, we are reading the bold lines.

We'll begin by comparing the descriptions of Daniel's beasts to that of Revelation, and then move into other aspects of John's vision that is found elsewhere.

*Daniel 7, beginning with verse 1 states; *"In the first year of Belshazzar king of Babylon Daniel had a dream and visions of his head upon his bed: then he wrote the dream, and told the sum of the matters. 2) Daniel spake and said, I saw in my vision by night, and, behold, the four winds of the heaven strove upon the great sea. 3) And **four great beasts came up from the sea, diverse one from another**. 4) **The first was like a lion, and had eagle's wings**: I beheld till the wings thereof were plucked, and it was lifted up from the earth, and made stand upon the feet as a man, and a man's heart was given to it. 5) And behold **another beast, a second, like to a bear, and it raised up itself on one side, and it had three ribs in the mouth of it between the teeth of it**: and they said thus unto it, Arise, devour much flesh. 6) After this I beheld, and lo **another, like a leopard, which had upon the back of it four wings of a fowl; the beast had also <u>four heads</u>; and dominion was given to it."*

Stopping here for a moment, let's look now at Revelation chapter 13, beginning with verse 1. It states; *"And I stood upon the sand of the sea, and **saw a beast rise up out of the sea**, having <u>**seven heads**</u> and <u>**ten horns**</u>, and upon his horns ten crowns, and upon his heads the name of blasphemy. 2) And **the beast which I saw was like unto a leopard, and his feet were as the feet of a bear, and his mouth as the mouth of a lion...".*

In Revelation 13:2 we see all 3 beasts present, but comprised as one entity. The **leopard**, the **bear**, and the **lion**. Furthermore, if we take a head count, you will see that Daniel's three beasts have a total of **six heads**. And upon reading verse 7, the fourth beast brings that total to **seven**.

Moving forward with Daniel 7:7, *"After this I saw in the night visions, and behold a **fourth beast,** dreadful and terrible, and strong exceedingly; and it had great iron teeth: it devoured and brake in pieces, and stamped the residue with the feet of it: and it was diverse from all the beasts that were before it; and **it had <u>ten horns</u>.**"*

Here we see that both Daniel's beast (spoken of in verse 7), and Revelation's beast (spoken of in verse 1), each have **ten horns.**

Now let's add Daniel 7:8, *"I considered the horns, and, behold, there came up among them **another** little **horn, before whom there were three of the first horns plucked up by the roots**: and, behold, in this horn were eyes like the eyes of man, **and a mouth speaking great things."***

Before we continue any further, let's jump ahead to Daniel 7:15. These verses will tie together Revelation's description of its beast along with Daniel's.

Daniel chapter 7, beginning with verse 15 states; *"I Daniel was grieved in my spirit in the midst of my body, and the visions of my head troubled me. 16) I came near unto one of them that stood by, and asked him the truth of all this. So he told me, and made me know the interpretation of the things. 17) **These great beasts, which are four, are four kings, which shall arise out of the earth.** 18) But the saints of the most High shall take the kingdom, and possess the kingdom for ever, even for ever and ever. 19) **Then I would know the truth of the fourth beast, which was diverse from all the others,** exceeding dreadful, whose teeth were of iron, and his nails of brass; which devoured, brake in pieces, and stamped the residue with his feet; 20) **And of the ten horns that were in his head, and of the other which came up, and before whom three fell;** even of that horn that had eyes, **and a mouth that spake very great things,** whose look was more stout than his fellows. 21) **I beheld, and the same horn made war with the saints, and prevailed against them;"***

Now look at Revelation 13, beginning with verse 3; *"And I saw one of his heads as it were wounded to death; and his deadly wound was healed: and all the world wondered after the beast. 4) And they worshipped the **dragon which gave power unto the beast**: and they worshipped the beast, saying, Who is like unto the beast? who is able to make war with him? 5) **And there was given unto him a mouth speaking great things** and blasphemies; and power was given unto him to continue forty and two months. 6) And he opened his mouth in blasphemy against God, to blaspheme his name, and his tabernacle, and them that dwell in heaven. 7) **And it was given unto him to make war with the saints, and to overcome*** *them:* and power was given him over all kindreds, and tongues, and nations."

For those of you that have read **Book 1**, you know who this scripture is speaking of...

Revelation 13:8, *"**And all that dwell upon the earth shall worship him,** whose names are not written in the book of life of the Lamb slain from the foundation of the world."*

Who is everyone worshipping? **Jesus!** Who is the **dragon**? **Lucifer!** And the **dragon gave power unto the beast**! **Lucifer gives power unto Jesus.**

Next look at Daniel 7, beginning with verse 23; *"Thus he said, **The fourth beast shall be the fourth kingdom upon earth,** which shall be diverse from all kingdoms, and shall devour the whole earth, and shall tread it down, and break it in pieces. 24) And **the ten horns out of this kingdom are ten kings that shall arise: and another shall rise after them; and he shall be diverse from the first, and he shall subdue three kings.**"*

Now, Revelation 17, beginning with verse 12; *"**And the ten horns which thou sawest are ten kings, which have received no kingdom as yet; but receive power as kings one hour with the beast. 13) These have one mind, and shall give their power and strength unto the beast.**"*

This explains why Revelation 13:1 describes the beast as *"a beast"*, a single entity with seven heads and ten horns. Daniel sees it as **four individual beasts**, which, as he explains, is **four kingdoms**. And **three will be eliminated by the fourth**.

If we look at the world powers that exist at this day and time, we have Great Britain and the United States, which I believe is the first beast as stated in Daniel 7:4.

*"**The first was like a lion, and had eagle's wings:** I beheld till the wings thereof were plucked, and it was lifted up from the earth, and made stand upon the feet as a man, and a man's heart was given to it."*

The rampant lion is England's crest, and the eagle belongs to the US. The **wings** being **plucked** is symbolic of the US breaking free from Great Britain, and **was lifted up from the earth** being separated from the eastern hemisphere.

Daniel 7:5 states; *"And behold **another beast, a second, like to a bear, and it raised up itself on one side, and it had three ribs in the mouth of it between the teeth of it**: and they said thus unto it, Arise, devour much flesh."*

This beast makes me think of Russia. Which, if you Google **"What animal symbolizes Russia?"**, its response is; **The Russian Bear**. The **three ribs in its mouth** makes me believe that these represent three countries that are under Russian control.

I Googled **What countries are under Russian control?** The Wikipedia states; "Russian-occupied territories are lands under Russian military occupation. The term is applied to territories in **Georgia** (Abkhazia and South Ossetia), **Moldova** (Transnistria), and parts of **Ukraine**."

It's interesting that these **three countries** are the only countries that showed up. The symbology of being **ribs in the mouth of it, between the teeth**, verses being one of the **heads** (like that of the **leopard**), indicates positions of power, or lack thereof. If you're a **rib between a bear's teeth,** you are not there by your choosing!

Furthermore, look at Ezekiel 38, beginning with verse 2, it states; *"Son of man, **set thy face against Gog, the land of Magog**, the chief prince of Meshech and Tubal, and prophesy against him, 3) And say, Thus saith the Lord GOD; Behold, I am against thee, O Gog, the chief prince of Meshech and Tubal: 4) And I will turn thee back, and put hooks into thy jaws, **and I will bring thee forth, and all thine army, horses and horsemen, all of them clothed with all sorts of armour, even a great company with bucklers and shields, all of them handling swords: 5) Persia, Ethiopia, and Libya with them**; all of them with shield and helmet:... 18) **And it shall come to pass at the same time when Gog shall come against the land of Israel,** saith the Lord GOD, that my fury shall come up in my face. 19) For in my jealousy and in the fire of my wrath have I spoken, **Surely in that day there shall be a great shaking in the land of***

Israel; 20) So that the fishes of the sea, and the fowls of the heaven, and the beasts of the field, and all creeping things that creep upon the earth, and all the men that are upon the face of the earth, shall shake at my presence, and the mountains shall be thrown down, and the steep places shall fall, and every wall shall fall to the ground. 21) And I will call for a sword against him throughout all my mountains, saith the Lord GOD: every man's sword shall be against his brother. 22) And I will plead against him with pestilence and with blood; and I will rain upon him, and upon his bands, and upon the many people that are with him, an overflowing rain, and great hailstones, fire, and brimstone. 23) Thus will I magnify myself, and sanctify myself; and I will be known in the eyes of many nations, and they shall know that I am the LORD."

Here's the significance of **Magog**. As stated by the Wikipedia under **Magog** - **Ancient and Medieval Views**, Magog possibly refers to the Mongols. Scythians, "throughout the Middle Ages, they were variously identified as the Vikings, Huns, Khazars, Mongols, Turanians or other nomads, or even the Ten Lost Tribes of Israel."

The article continues; "Scythians or Scyths... were an ancient Eastern Iranian equestrian nomadic people who had migrated from Central Asia to the Pontic Steppe in **modern day Ukraine and Southern Russia** from approximately the 7th century BC until the 3rd century BC."

What the article is basically saying, is that the **land of Magog** is now what we call **modern day Ukraine and Southern Russia**. How interesting is that?

Ezekiel's prophecy regarding **Magog** is very significant in who **Magog** represents, i.e., **Ukraine** and **Southern Russia**, and the threat that **Russia** poses at this day and time.

Continuing with Daniel. Chapter 7, verse 6 states; *"After this I beheld, and lo **another, like a leopard, which had upon the back of it four wings of a fowl; the beast had also <u>four heads</u>; and dominion was given to it.**"*

178

Based on the **four heads**, this beast is four countries that join forces. Possibly like that of the middle eastern Arab countries, coupled with **portions of Africa**. Some of which may include; Israel, **Iran**, Iraq, Syria, Jordan, Saudi Arbia, Lebanon, Egypt, and **Libya**.

If you Google **"What country is symbolized by the leopard?"** The first article that pops up pertains to the **snow leopard**. However, if you scroll down under **People also ask:** and click on **What countries are associated with leopard?** It states; **"The range of the leopard is the most widespread of all the big cats. Their range covers a large stretch of the Middle East, and Asia, including China, India, and eastern Russia."**

I realize that the above quote actually pertains to areas where leopards are prevalent, but if you eliminate **eastern Russia** and add northern Africa, that puts it at four specific areas that could be represented.

Also, look again at Ezekiel 38, verse 5; *"Persia, Ethiopia, and Libya with them..."*. Here we see three of the possibilities listed. Which, just so you know, **Persia** is present day Iran, and **Ethiopia** is located in Africa.

And I knew that China had to be present amongst the super powers somewhere! Let's face it, the US, Great Britain, Russia and China definitely top the list of world powers!

An interesting quote made by Napoleon Bonaparte is found at the beginning of the 2018 movie, **Crazy Rich Asians.** It states; **"Let China sleep, for when she wakes, she will shake the world."** What a profound statement made by an Emperor who died over 200 years ago! Not only profound, but more than possibly very true!

I must stress though, these **three beasts**, or conglomerates, will be eliminated by the **fourth beast**. Which, I believe, is the New World Order that will be established. It will implement a One World Government, a One World Military, and a One World Currency. It will probably be at this point when the **Mark** will become mandatory, that we will not be able to **buy or sell** without it.

Which, again, explains Revelation 17, beginning with verse 12; *"And the ten horns which thou sawest are ten kings, which have received no kingdom as yet; but receive power as kings one hour with the beast. 13) These have one mind, and shall give their power and strength unto the beast."*

These **kings** will be in power long enough to give complete control of their countries to the **beast, the leader of the New World Order**, which I feel strongly could possibly be **Lucifer.**

*Look next at Daniel 7:25, *"And he shall speak great words against the most High, and shall wear out the saints of the most High, and think to change times and laws: and they shall be given into his hand until a time and times and the dividing of time."*

Let's compare that to Revelation 13, beginning with verse 5; *"And there was given unto him a mouth speaking great things and blasphemies; and power was given unto him to continue forty and two months. 6) And he opened his mouth in blasphemy against God, to blaspheme his name, and his tabernacle, and them that dwell in heaven. 7) And it was given unto him to make war with the saints, and to overcome them:".*

In verse 25 when Daniel states, *"a time and times and the dividing of time"*, it varies based on what *"a time"* is considered to be. It, too, is a metaphor, which can have multiple meanings. However, let's view *"a time"* as one year. Then, *"times"* would be multiples of that amount, with a *"dividing of time"* to be only half of the original amount of *"time"*.

With that said, if *"time"* was one year, and *"times"* (in this case) was twice that, or two more years, which would bring the total to three. And the *"dividing of time"* would be a half of a year, or six months. We would then be looking at a total of 3 and 1/2 years.

Comparing this to Revelation 13:5, which states *"forty and two months"*. 42 months would also equate to 3 and 1/2 years.

When Daniel 25 states, *"speak great words against the most High"*, it's not a compliment! It means just what Revelation 13:5 states, *"speaking great things and blasphemies".*

180

Again, the word **great** has a different meaning, biblically, then what we have been taught to understand.

Daniel 7:26 states; *"But the judgment shall sit, and they shall take away his dominion, to consume and to destroy it unto the end."* We'll come back to it in just a moment.

From this point on, the beginning of a new comparison will be designated with an asterisk (*). Any verses containing multiple comparisons will continue to be explained until all are discussed. After which point, another * will indicate a new comparison, or grouping.

*Take a look at Daniel 7:27, which states; ***"And the kingdom and dominion, and the greatness of the kingdom under the whole heaven, shall be given to the people of the saints of the most High,*** *whose kingdom is an everlasting kingdom, and all dominions shall serve and obey him."*

Don't confuse this with Revelation 13:7, which, again, states; *"And it was given unto him to make war with the saints, and to overcome them:* ***and power was given him over all kindreds, and tongues, and nations."*** The ***"him"*** spoken of in this verse, that **power was given to over all kindreds, and tongues, and nations**, is referring to the **beast**. The first part of that verse confirms what I'm saying.

It's interesting, but not surprising, that I found no scripture in Revelation that makes that statement, that the **kingdom shall be given to the people of the saints...** And, I believe that Jesus would never say that, because he would never want to give the kingdom away to anyone! He's worked too hard for it! But look at this...

Isaiah 60:21, ***"Thy people also shall be all righteous: they shall inherit the land for ever, the branch of my planting, the work of my hands, that I may be glorified."***

Isaiah confirms that it is part of God's plan, for His people to ***"inherit the land for ever"***.

*Let's back up to Daniel 7. **As you read the following comparisons, pay close attention to the verses that are underlined in like manner.**

Verses 9-14 of Daniel, chapter 7 states; *"I beheld till the thrones were cast down, and **the Ancient of days did sit, whose garment was white as snow, and <u>the hair of his head like the pure wool</u>**: his throne was like the fiery flame, and his wheels as burning fire. 10) A fiery stream issued and came forth from before him: **thousand thousands ministered unto him, and <u>ten thousand times ten thousand stood before him</u>: <u>the judgment was set, and the books were opened</u>.*"*

Stopping here for a moment. Look at Revelation 20, beginning with verse 11; *"And **I saw a great white throne, and him that sat on it, <u>from whose face the earth and the heaven fled away</u>**; and there was found no place for them. 12) And I saw <u>the dead, small and great, stand before God</u>; <u>and the books were opened</u>: and **another book was opened, which is the book of life: and <u>the dead were judged</u> out of those things which were written in the books, according to their works.*"*

Look at Isaiah 34:4, *"<u>**And all the host of heaven shall be dissolved...**</u>"*.

*Also, notice where I have Daniel 7:9 underlined; *"<u>**the hair of his head like the pure wool**</u>".* Look now at Revelation 1:14 where John's vision is describing the one, who's voice it was that spoke with him. It states; *"<u>**His head and his hairs were white like wool, as white as snow...**</u>"*.

What does **white** symbolize? That which is **pure!**

*It is at this point that Daniel 7:26 comes into play. It states; *"**But the judgment shall sit, and <u>they shall take away his dominion, to consume and to destroy it unto the end</u>.**"*

Daniel 7:11 states; *"I beheld then because of the voice of the great words which the horn spake: **I beheld even till the beast was slain, and his body destroyed, and given to the burning flame. 12) As*** concerning the rest of the beasts, they had their dominion taken away: yet their lives were prolonged for a season and time."

Now, look at Revelation 19:20, **"And the beast was taken, and with him the false prophet** that wrought miracles before him, with which he deceived them that had received the mark of the beast, and them that worshipped his image. These both were cast alive into a lake of fire burning with brimstone."

And, also Revelation 20:10, **"And the devil that deceived them was cast into the lake of fire and brimstone, where the beast and the false prophet are, and shall be tormented day and night for ever and ever."**

Their lives are **prolonged** due to their **torment** that they must suffer **for ever and ever.**

*Take a look at Daniel 7:13, *"I saw in the night visions, and, **behold, one like the Son of man came with the clouds of heaven,** and came to the Ancient of days, and they brought him near before him."*

Now, Revelation 14:14, *"And I looked, and **behold** a white cloud, and **upon the cloud one sat like unto the Son of man,** having on his head a golden crown..."*.

*Next, Daniel 7:14, *"And **there was given him dominion, and glory, and a kingdom, that all people, nations, and languages, should serve him: his dominion is an everlasting dominion, which shall not pass away, and his kingdom that which shall not be destroyed."***

Now, Revelation 17:14, *"These shall make war with the Lamb, and **the Lamb shall overcome them: for he is Lord of lords, and King of kings: and they that are with him are called, and chosen, and faithful."***

And, Revelation 19, beginning with verse 11; *"And I saw heaven opened, and **behold a white horse; and he that sat upon him was called Faithful and True, and in righteousness he doth judge and make war.** 12) His eyes were as a flame of fire, and **on his head were many crowns**; and he had a name written, that no man knew,* *but he himself. 13) And he was clothed with a vesture dipped in blood: and his name is called The Word of God. 14) And the armies which were in heaven followed him upon white horses, clothed in fine linen, white and clean. 15) And <u>out of his mouth goeth a sharp sword, that with it he should smite the nations</u>: and he shall rule them with a rod of iron: and he treadeth the winepress of the fierceness and wrath of Almighty God. 16)* **And he hath on his vesture and on his thigh a name written, KING OF KINGS, AND LORD OF LORDS."**

Even though Daniel uses different terminology, I think it's quite obvious that the one that was given **"dominion, and glory, and a kingdom"**, is referring to the same person that Revelation is speaking of. The fact that Revelation 19:12 tells us that **"on his head were many crowns"** confirms that he was given **"dominion"** over **"all people, nations, and languages"**.

*Another interesting observation is found in Revelation 19:15, where I have underlined **"<u>out of his mouth goeth a sharp sword, that with it he should smite the nations</u>".**

Look at Revelation 2:16, where Jesus states; **"Repent; or else I will come unto thee quickly, and will fight against them with the sword of my mouth."**

We know that Jesus is the rider of the red horse, which Revelation 6:3 tells us **"there was given unto him a great sword".** And, we know from Matthew 10:34 that Jesus, himself, states that *"I am not come to send peace on earth,* **but a sword".**

However, looking back at Revelation 1:16 it tells us, **"... and out of his mouth went a sharp two-edged sword".** Which, looking at verse 17, it confirms that this scripture is speaking of Jesus. It states; **"... Fear not; I am the first and the last: 18) <u>I am he that liveth, and was dead</u>; and, behold, <u>I am alive for evermore,</u> Amen; <u>and have the keys of hell and of death</u>."**

For those that have read **Book 1**, you are already aware of my take on who this person is... Jesus! And, as I also stated in **Book 1**, "A **'two-edged sword'** can represent a mouth that speaks words that cut both ways, or it, metaphorically, can represent a forked tongue that speaks lies".

Is it just a coincidence that Jesus has a **sword** that went out of his mouth, just as the rider of the white horse in Revelation 19:15 has, that *"he should smite the nations"* with?

I want everyone to understand that we are dealing with mirror images. Meaning, Jesus is the mirror image of the true **Lamb of God**, the **Son of man**, just as Lucifer is the mirror image of the **LORD God**.

With that said, Jesus has painted himself to be the true Lamb of God, the rider of the white horse, having a **sword** that he will smite the nations with. When, in reality, his **sword** is the *"two-edged"* one, as stated in Revelation 1:16, the forked one, like a serpent, which speaks lies!

Please... stay with me, because I have plenty more to come!

*Let's talk about Revelation 21, verses 10-23 which describes the **new Jerusalem coming down from heaven**.

Beginning with verse 10; *"And he carried me away in the spirit to a great and high mountain, and shewed me that great city, the holy Jerusalem, descending out of heaven from God, 11) Having the glory of God: and <u>her light was like unto a stone most precious, even like a jasper stone, clear as crystal;</u> 12) **And had a wall great and high, and had twelve gates**, and at the gates twelve angels, **and names written thereon, which are the names of the twelve tribes of the children of Israel: 13) On the east three gates; on the north three gates; on the south three gates; and on the west three gates.***"

Stopping here for a moment, first of all look where I have underlined verse 11. I Googled what a **jasper** stone looks like? According to the Wikipedia, it is "an aggregate of microgranular quartz and/or cryptocrystalline chalcedony... an opaque, impure variety of silica, usually red, yellow, brown or green in color; and rarely blue."

185

Then I had the thought to scroll down to see if it provided a Biblical description, and sure enough it did! It states; **"The Jasper stone in the context of (Rev 4) is the finest form of Diamond..."**. (australianopalcutters.com)

I knew when I read the description provided by the Wikipedia that something was amiss based on the exact wording of verse 11, when it states; *"even like a jasper stone, clear as crystal"*. So, based on the Biblical interpretation, a **jasper** stone is a **diamond**.

*Look now at Ezekiel, chapter 48. Beginning with verse 31, it states; *"And **the gates of the city shall be after the names of the tribes of Israel: three gates northward**; one gate of Reuben, one gate of Judah, one gate of Levi. 32) And at **the east side** four thousand and five hundred: and **three gates**; and one gate of Joseph, one gate of Benjamin, one gate of Dan. 33) And at **the south side** four thousand and five hundred measures: and **three gates**; one gate of Simeon, one gate of Issachar, one gate of Zebulun. 34) At **the west side** four thousand and five hundred, with their **three gates**; one gate of Gad, one gate of Asher, one gate of Naphtali."*

Revelation 21:14 follows; *"And the wall of the city had twelve foundations, and in them the names of the twelve apostles of the Lamb."* I have found nothing in any of the Old Testament books that speaks of *"twelve foundations"* that were named after Jesus' *"twelve apostles"*. And doubt that I will!

*Revelation 21, verse 15 then continues; *"And he that talked with me had a golden **reed to measure the city, and the gates thereof, and the wall thereof**. 16) And the city lieth **foursquare**, and the length is as large as the breadth: and he measured the city with the reed, twelve thousand furlongs. The length and the breadth and the height of it are equal."*

Allow me to say at this point that the book of Ezekiel, chapters 40 through 48, all the way through to the end of the book, discusses the new city. Complete with layout, dimensions, and descriptions of the Temple, the gates, the inner courts, chambers, porches, the altar... everything. Revelation is very limited in its description, but I will make mention of all those that I have found elsewhere.

I say elsewhere because Isaiah, also, contains limited descriptions of the **New Earth, Zion and Jerusalem** scattered throughout some of its chapters, beginning around 55, but more so in 65 through 66. I plan to touch on some of those verses as well.

Picking up where we left off, Revelation 21, verse 17 states; *"And he measured the wall thereof, a hundred and forty and four cubits, according to the measure of a man, that is, of the angel."*

According to Quora.com, "a cubit 'biblical measurement' is approximately 18" therefore (144x18) / 12 = 216ft". Which means, 144x18" = 2,592"÷12 (# of inches in a foot) = 216 feet.

It sounds like there were 12 sections, with each section (gate included) measuring 12 cubits in length.

Now, looking at Ezekiel 40, verse 5 states; *"And behold a wall on the outside of the house round about, and in the man's hand a measuring reed of six cubits long by the cubit of a hand breadth: so he measured the breadth of the building, one reed; and the heigth, one reed. 6) Then came he unto the gate which looked toward the east... and measured the threshold of the gate, which was one reed broad...".*

So, each gate was **six cubits**, and each section of wall between the gates were also **six cubits. This means, the entire wall, including the 12 gates, was 144 cubits!** Humm!

Furthermore, given the fact that each side consisted of three gates with equal size walls in between, **the entire structure, round about, would have been foursquare, as stated in Revelation 21:16.**

FYI, the number 144 just happens to be a very significant number. **As in 144,000**, the number that were **sealed** in chapter 7 of Revelation... 12,000 from each of the 12 Tribes. It's all multiples of 12!

*The next 4 verses of Revelation 21, verses 18-21, provides a description of the **great city.** Beginning with verse 18, it states; *"And the building of the wall of it was of __jasper__: and the city was **pure gold**, like unto clear glass. 19) And the foundations of the wall* *of the city were garnished with all manner of precious stones. The first foundation was **jasper**; the second, **sapphire**; the third, a **chalcedony**; the fourth, an **emerald**; 20) The fifth, **sardonyx**; the sixth, **sardius**; the seventh, **chrysolite**; the eighth, **beryl**; the ninth, a **topaz**; the tenth, a **chrysoprasus**; the eleventh, a **jacinth**; the twelfth, an **amethyst**. 21) And the twelve gates were twelve pearls; every several gate was of one pearl: and the street of the city was pure gold, as it were transparent glass."*

I have checked the books of Isaiah, Ezekiel, and Zechariah looking through their descriptions of walls that were **"garnished with all manner of precious stones"**. I even checked in both 2nd Kings and 2nd Chronicles where it provides descriptions of the original Temple built by Solomon. I have yet to find anything that pertains specifically to the walls and gates decorated as such.

However, I will say that much of Solomon's Temple was made of **pure gold**, as Revelation 21:18 describes.

Something I did find, were numerous scriptures which consistently speaks of many of these same stones, but in different contexts. Allow me to share my findings.

Let's start with Ezekiel 28:13. It states; **"Thou hast been in Eden the garden of God; every precious stone was thy covering, the *sardius*, *topaz*, and the *diamond*, the *beryl*, the *onyx* (sardonyx), and the *jasper*, the *sapphire*, the *emerald*, and the carbuncle, and *gold*: the workmanship of thy tabrets and of thy pipes was prepared in thee in the day that thou wast created."**

It's interesting how Ezekiel lists both the **diamond** and the **jasper** as though they are two different stones, which technically they are. Look at that Biblical definition again, "The Jasper stone **in the context of (Rev 4)** is the finest form of Diamond...".

Revelation 4:3 states; **"And he that sat was to look upon like a *jasper* and a sardine stone: and there was a rainbow round about the throne, in sight like unto an emerald."**

Again, this is Jesus' vision that he gave to John, so who knows what is meant by his use of a **jasper** stone??

Now look at Isaiah 54:12, *"And I will make thy windows of agates, and thy gates of carbuncles, and all thy borders of pleasant stones."*

As stated by the **International Gem Society**, **"Agate is a variety of chalcedony that exists in many colors..."**.

Also, the **Wikipedia** states, **"Chrysoprase, chrysophrase, or chrysoprasus is a gemstone variety of chalcedony"**.

Looking back at Revelation 21, verse 19 speaks of **chalcedony,** and verse 20 speaks of **chrysoprasus**, which is just a variety of **chalcedony.** So, two of the twelve stones listed are basically the same thing, which both end up being the same as the **agates** found in Isaiah 54:12.

And lastly, look at Exodus 28, beginning with verse 17. It states; *"And thou shalt set in it settings of stones, even four rows of stones: the first row shall be a **sardius**, a **topaz**, and a **carbuncle**: this shall be the first row. 18) And the second row shall be an **emerald**, a **sapphire**, and a **diamond**. 19) And the third row a **ligure**, an **agate**, and an **amethyst**. 20) And the fourth row a **beryl**, and an **onyx** (sardonyx), and a **jasper**: they shall be set in gold in their inclosings."*

This scripture is speaking of Aaron's **breastplate**. And, of the twelve stones that are listed, ten of them are found in Revelation 21's description. However, notice that Moses lists both the **diamond** and the **jasper** just as Ezekiel did. With that said, that makes 11 out of 12 stones present. Which, a **ligure** is "One of the twelve precious stones in the breastplate of the Jewish high priest, thought to be yellow **jacinth".** (Collins Dictionary)

My point with these scriptures is to show that all of these **precious stones** are found with frequency in passages that describe places and items that are significant to God. Therefore, it's not surprising that Jesus would use them in his description of the **great city, holy Jerusalem**, as well.

189

*Moving on to Revelation 21:22. It states; **"And _I saw no temple_ _therein_: for the Lord God Almighty and the Lamb are the temple of it."**

As I previously stated, Ezekiel chapters 40-48 discusses the plans for the new city and Temple, among many other details. In fact, the title of chapter 40 states, **Ezekiel's Vision of a New Temple**. The title of chapter 41 is, **Plan and Dimensions of the Future Temple**. Chapter 42 is titled, **How the Temple would be Kept from Polution**. Chapter 43, **The Glory of God to Fill the Future Temple**. Chapter 44, **Aliens to be Excluded from the Future Temple**. And it continues, all the way to the end of the book of Ezekiel.

I don't know about you, but it sure does appear to me that God has definite plans for a new Temple!

*Moving next to Revelation 21:23. It states; _"And **the city had no need of the sun, neither of the moon, to shine in it: for the glory of God did lighten it**, and the Lamb is the light thereof."_

Now look at Isaiah 60, beginning with verse 19; **"The sun shall be no more thy light by day; neither for brightness shall the moon give light unto thee: but the LORD shall be unto thee an everlasting light, and thy God thy glory. 20) Thy sun shall no more go down; neither shall thy moon withdraw itself: for the LORD shall be thine everlasting light,** and the days of thy mourning shall be ended."

The only difference in these two scriptures is that portion of Revelation 21:23 which I've underlined. The part about the **Lamb** being **the light thereof.** Which, of course, Jesus being the **Lamb** of this rendering. But nowhere else because God is the only **everlasting light!**

*My last comparison in Revelation, chapter 21, pertains to verse 25. It states; _"And **the gates of it shall not be shut at all by day**: for there shall be no night there."_

Look now at Ezekiel 44:1-2, _"Then he brought me back **the way of the gate of the outward sanctuary which looketh toward the east; and it was shut**. 2) Then said the LORD unto me; **This gate shall be**_ *shut, it shall not be opened, and no man shall enter in by it; because the LORD, the God of Israel, hath entered in by it, therefore it shall be shut."*

This is a comparison that proves to be a contradiction, which we found a couple of so far.

*Moving on to Revelation 22, beginning with verse 1. It states; **"And he shewed me a pure river of water of life, clear as crystal, proceeding out of the throne of God and of the Lamb."***

The entire 47th chapter of Ezekiel pertains to **The Healing Waters from the Temple**.

*Revelation 22:2, *"In the midst of the street of it, and on either side of the river, was there the tree of life, **which bare twelve manner of fruits, and yielded her fruit every month: and the leaves of the tree were for the healing of the nations."***

Look now at Ezekiel 47:12, *"And by the river upon the bank thereof, on this side and on that side, shall grow all trees for meat, whose leaf shall not fade, neither shall the fruit thereof be consumed: **it shall bring forth new fruit according to his months**, because their waters they issued out of the sanctuary: and the fruit thereof shall be for meat, **and the leaf thereof for medicine."***

How can all of this be a coincidence? That all of these prophecies from the books of Daniel, Ezekiel, Zechariah and Isaiah just happened to show up in a vision that Jesus gave to John? How is that? It's no coincidence... It's plagiarism!

*Hopefully, those that have read **Book 1** remember my breakdown and interpretations of John's vision from Revelation. One in particular pertained to the **four beasts** spoken of in chapter 4, beginning with verse 6.

I must say, at the time of my interpretation, linking it to Ezekiel chapter 10, I had no clue of the extent of which Jesus had usurped Ezekiel's vision.

For the sake of those that haven't read **Book 1**, let's look at it again. Revelation, chapter 4, verse 6 states; *"And before the* *throne there was a sea of glass like unto crystal: and in the midst of the throne, and round about the throne, were __four__ beasts full of eyes before and behind. 7) "And the first beast was <u>like a lion</u>, and the second beast <u>like a calf</u>, and the third beast <u>had a face as a man</u>, and the fourth beast was <u>like a flying eagle</u>. 8) "And the four beasts <u>had each of them six wings about him; and they were full of eyes within</u>: and they rest not day and night, saying, Holy, holy, holy, Lord God Almighty, which was, and is, and is to come."*

The following is a quote from **Book 1**. I state, "In Ezekiel, chapter 10 is speaking of 'The Vision of the Cherubim and the Wheels'. This flying contraption, based on the description, appears to have a throne (verse 1), and a house for the LORD (verse 4), with an outer court (verse 5). It has 4 wheels with cherubs by each wheel (verse 9), and there are several *'cherubim'*, as they are called."

That statement is immediately followed by the scripture which I spoke of. I began it at verse 12 in **Book 1**, but backing up to verse 10 we'll see the exact number of Cherubim the scripture speaks of.

Verse 10 states; *"And as for their appearances, **they <u>four</u> had one likeness**, as if a wheel had been in the midst of a wheel... 12) **And their whole body, and their backs, and their hands, and their wings, and the wheels, were full of eyes round about... 14) And every one had four faces: the first face was the <u>face of a cherub</u>, and the second face was the face of a man, and the third face of a lion, and the fourth face of an eagle**."*

Both scriptures indicate **four** Cherubim. With that said, the only real difference between the two, is that Revelation 4:7 uses the **face of a calf** in place of Ezekiel's **face of a cherub**.

*Before we move on, I'd like to comment on verses 4 and 5 of Revelation's chapter 4. I'll start by quoting the scripture and go from there. Verse 4 states; *"And round about the throne **were four and twenty seats: and upon the seats I saw four and twenty elders sitting**, clothed in white raiment; and they had on their heads crowns of gold."*

I have searched high and low trying to find any Old Testament scripture that speaks of God's throne being surrounded by **24** elders. I even Googled, specifically asking, **Where in the bible does it talk about the 24 elders**. Which, as stated by the Wikipedia, **"The Twenty-Four Elders appear in the Book of Revelation (4:4) of the Christian Bible."**

It's interesting that the Wikipedia is only aware of the one recorded occurrence. Hmm!

I did, however, find several locations in the Old Testament that speaks of the **elders**. But not in the same context that Revelation 4:4 alludes to.

Allow me to provide some examples. First of all, look at Exodus 24:1. It states; *"And he said unto Moses, Come up unto the LORD, thou, and Aaron, Nadab, and Abihu, **and seventy of the elders of Israel**; and worship ye afar off."*

Also, verse 9; *"Then went up Moses, and Aaron, Nadab, and Abihu, and **seventy of the elders of Israel**:"*

Who are these **elders**? Let's keep reading and find out. Verse 10 states; *"And they saw the God of Israel: and there was under his feet as it were a paved work of a sapphire stone, and as it were the body of heaven in his clearness. 11) **And upon the <u>nobles</u> of the children of Israel he laid not his hand**: also they saw God, and did eat and drink."*

They are the **nobles** of the tribes. Those that are wise due to their age and experience.

Look at Numbers 11:16, *"And the LORD said unto Moses, **Gather unto me <u>seventy men</u> of the elders of Israel, whom thou knowest to be the elders of the people**, and officers over them; and bring them unto the tabernacle of the congregation, that they may stand there with thee. 17) And I will come down and talk with thee there: and **I will take of the spirit which is upon thee, and will put it upon them**; and they shall bear the burden of the people with thee, that thou bear it not thyself alone."*

These **elders** were **anointed** by God, look where I have underlined verse 17. He took some of the spirit which was upon Moses, and put it upon them so they could help Moses.

Also, notice where I have verse 16 underlined, it states **seventy men**. And how many were stated in Exodus 24, verses 1 and 9? **Seventy**!

Look at 1st Samuel 8:4, *"Then all of the **elders of Israel** gathered themselves together..."*.

Ezekiel 8:1, *"And it came to pass in the sixth year, in the sixth month, in the fifth day of the month, as I sat in mine house, and the **elders of Judah** sat before me, that the hand of the Lord GOD fell there upon me."*

Every passage I've read that speaks of the **elders**, is referring to the older, wiser, more experienced men of the tribes/cities.

But... during the Sabbath, as I was reading my Bible, God led me to something interesting. He always answers my prayers! Trust me when I say that I don't just sit here, constantly pouring over the scriptures, looking for ammunition to use against Jesus. God guides me to these things, pointing it out as though He were standing right next to me saying, **Look at that**!

I'm constantly praying, asking for confirmation of the things that I have been guided to understand, or for validation of the things that I am uncertain of. And, He always responds! He wants this information to be known, and because so, He wants it to be accurate.

So, on the Sabbath I found myself in the book of 1st Chronicles, looking for information pertaining to David. When suddenly I discovered what appeared to be the **24 elders.**

Look at 1st Chronicles, chapter 24. Beginning with verse 1, it states; *"Now these are the divisions of the sons of Aaron. The sons of Aaron; Nadab, and Abihu, Eleazar, and Ithamar. 2) But Nadab and Abihu died before their father, and had no children: therefore **Eleazar and Ithamar executed the priest's office**. 3) **And David distributed them, both Zadok of the sons of Eleazar, and Ahimelech of the sons of Ithamar, according to their offices in their service**. 4) And there were more chief men found of the sons of Eleazar than of the sons of Ithamar; and thus were they divided.*

*Among the sons of Eleazar there were <u>sixteen chief men</u> of the house of their fathers, <u>**and eight**</u> among the sons of Ithamar according to the house of their fathers. 5) Thus were they divided by lot, one sort with another; for **the governors of the sanctuary, and governors of the house of God, were of the sons of Eleazar, and of the sons of Ithamar.** 6) And Shemaiah the son of Nethaneel the scribe, one of the Levites, wrote them before the king, and the princes, and Zadok the priest, and Ahimelech the son of Abiathar, and before the chief of the fathers of the priests and Levites: one principal household being taken for Eleazar, and one taken for Ithamar."*

Sixteen chief men of Eleazar, and eight of Ithamar equals 24! I believe that this is the precedent that was established, which Jesus is imitating.

*Look now at Revelation 4:5, "And out of the throne proceeded lightnings and thunderings and voices: **and there were seven lamps of fire burning before the throne, which are the seven Spirits of God.**"*

First of all, let's start with Exodus 25, beginning with verse 31. It states; *"**And thou shalt make a candlestick of pure gold: of beaten work shall the candlestick be made:** his **shaft**, and his branches, his bowls, his knops, and his flowers, shall be of the same. 32) **And six branches** shall come out of the sides of it; three branches of the candlestick out of the one side, and three branches of the candlestick out of the other side:"*

According to the scripture just quoted, this **candlestick** includes the **shaft** and **six branches**, three on each side. Then, the next 3 verses continue to elaborate on the design and details.

Picking back up with verse 36, it states; *"Their knops and their branches shall be of the same: **all it shall be one beaten work of pure gold.** 37) And thou shalt make the **seven lamps thereof**: and they shall light the lamps thereof, that they may give light over against it."*

I made sure to include that last verse so you could see that this is speaking of **one candlestick with seven lamps.**

Exodus chapter 25 pertains to God providing instructions to Moses about the Tabernacle, and the items that must be displayed therein. One on which, of course, was the **candlestick with seven lamps**.

This scripture doesn't tell us the significance of the **candlestick with seven lamps**, but Zechariah chapter 4 does.

Verse 2 states; *"And said unto me, What seest thou? And I said, I have looked, and behold **a candlestick all of gold**, with a bowl upon the top of it, **and his seven lamps thereon**, and seven pipes to the seven lamps, which are upon the top thereof:"*

Now, skipping down to verse 10 of chapter 4, Zechariah tells us; *"For who hath despised the day of small things? for they shall rejoice, and shall see the plummet in the hand of Zerubbabel **with those seven; they <u>are the eyes of the LORD</u>, <u>which run to and fro through the whole earth</u>."***

So, these verses tell us that the **candlestick all of gold** with the **seven lamps thereon** are the **eyes of the LORD which run to and fro through the whole earth**.

Look at Revelation 5:6, *"And I beheld, and, lo, **in the midst of the throne** and of the four beasts, and in the midst of the elders, stood a Lamb as it had been slain, having **seven horns** and **seven eyes, <u>which are the seven Spirits of God</u> sent forth into all the earth**."*

If I'm understanding correctly, the **seven eyes** are different from the **seven Spirits of God.**

Look at Zechariah 3:9. It states; *"**For behold the stone that I have laid before Joshua; <u>upon one stone shall be seven eyes</u>**: behold, I will engrave the graving thereof, saith the LORD of hosts, and I will remove the iniquity of that land in one day."*

The number **7** is very significant to God. And, even though Jesus is attempting to represent himself as the *"**Lamb as it had been slain**"* standing before God, look at the **seven horns**, the **seven eyes**, and the **seven Spirits of God!**

If Jesus was using other people's material, it would be very easy for him to mimic all of this. Especially, making references to the number **seven** when speaking of God, or those items which are significant to Him.

Going all the way back to Genesis, chapter 1, it is evident that the number **seven** has significance based on the day in which God ended His work, and rested. So don't be amazed by Jesus' supposed prophetic statements involving the number **seven**, or any of those numbers that are of significance to God, ie., **1, 2, 3, 4, 7, 12, 24, 40, 70, 144,** and **144,000.**

*And, just to validate who the real **Lamb** is, that is standing before God, look at Daniel 7:13, *"I saw in the night visions, and, behold, **one like the Son of man** came with the clouds of heaven, and **came to the Ancient of days, and they brought him near before him**. 14)* *"And there was given him dominion, and glory, and a kingdom..."*.

A quick sidenote... in case you haven't read **Book 1,** the **Lamb** is **Abel!** When Revelation 13:8 states; *"... whose names are not written in the book of life of the Lamb <u>slain from the foundation of the world</u>"*, it means **from the very beginning**... the **first to be slain.**

The definition of **foundation**, means; "... the act of founding or establishing, or the state of being founded or established." (Dictionary.com)

The **foundation of the world** means **from the beginning!** And, the first to be **slain** was **Abel.**

*Let's talk about the **seven Spirits of God** referenced in Revelation 5:6. The Wikipedia states, "Including the **Spirit of the Lord**, and the Spirits of **wisdom**, of **understanding**, of **counsel**, of **might**, of **knowledge** and of **fear of the LORD**, <u>here are represented the seven Spirits, which are before the throne of God</u>."

For confirmation, look at Isaiah 11, verse 2. It states; *"And **the spirit of the LORD** shall rest upon him, **the spirit of wisdom** and **understanding, the spirit of counsel** and **might, the spirit of knowledge** and of **the fear of the LORD**;"*

So, we have the **LORD God** and **His seven Spirits**, which includes; 1) the **Spirit of the LORD**, 2) the **Spirit of wisdom**, 3) the **Spirit of understanding**, 4) the **Spirit of counsel**, 5) the **Spirit of might**, 6) the **Spirit of knowledge**, and 7) the **Spirit of fear of the LORD**.

Nothing is said anywhere about them being the **eyes of the LORD God.**

I previously stated in **Book 1,** that the **Spirit of the LORD**, also called the **Spirit of God** (Genesis 1:2) was His female counterpart. While researching the information just provided about the **seven spirits**, I stumbled across the following...

According to the Wikipedia, **"The grammatical gender of the word for 'spirit' is feminine in Hebrew** (רוּחַ, *rūaḥ*).

Continuing, the same article referenced above also states, "The Holy Spirit was furthermore equated with the (grammatically feminine) **Wisdom of God** by two early Church fathers, **Theophilus of Antioch** (d. 180) and by **Irenaeus** (d. 202/3)."

Regarding **Ruah,** the same source states; **"Ruah or ruach, a Hebrew word meaning 'breath, spirit'."**

It's always nice to see additional validation of the interpretations that God has guided me to understand.

*Now, backing up to verse 5 of chapter 5, still discussing Revelation, let's touch on that for a moment. It states; *"And one of the elders saith unto me, Weep not: **behold, the Lion of the tribe of Juda, the Root of David, hath prevailed to open the book,** and to loose the seven seals thereof."*

This, I believe, is another one of those inclusions that Jesus has added to the vision, in an effort to tie himself into it. After all, he does claim to be the **lion and the lamb**! I even thought if this could possibly be someone that I hadn't considered. A descendant of David based on the wording. But, it is **based on the exact wording** that took that thought from my mind as quickly as it came. What does Jesus call himself in Revelation 22:16? *"... I am the root and the offspring of David..."*. And there's the key!

*Let me remind those that have read **Book 1**, of my interpretation provided of the **Two Olive Trees** (Revelation 11:4-12) when discussing the Book of Revelation in the **End Times** chapter. An understanding that was, in part, based on scripture from Zechariah 4:3, and 4:11-14.

Quoting first from Revelation 11:4, *"These are the two olive trees, and the two candlesticks **standing before the God of the earth.**"*

Now, Zechariah 4:14, *"... These are the two anointed ones, that stand by the Lord of the whole earth."*

Verse 14 was the response given by the angel when Zechariah asked two times, first in verse 11, and again in verse 12, *"What are these two olive trees...?"*

Is it just a coincidence that the **Two Olive Trees** are spoken of in both books, with an almost identical response given in each?

*Revelation 3:7, "... he that hath **the key of David, he that openeth, and no man shutteth; and shutteth, and no man openeth;"**.*

And now, Isaiah 22:22, *"And **the key** of the house **of David** will I lay upon his shoulder; so **he shall open, and none shall shut; and he shall shut, and none shall open."***

Even the little things add up!

*Look at Revelation 17:5, "And upon her forehead was a name written, **MYSTERY, BABYLON THE GREAT, THE MOTHER OF HARLOTS AND ABOMINATIONS OF THE EARTH."***

Now, Zechariah 5, beginning with verse 5, states; *"Then the angel that talked with me went forth, and said unto me, Lift up now thine eyes, and see what is this that goeth forth. 6) And I said, What is it? And he said, **This is an ephah that goeth forth.** He said **moreover, This is their resemblance through all the earth.** 7) And, behold, there was lifted up a talent of lead: **and this is a woman that sitteth in the midst of the ephah.** 8) And he said, **This is wickedness.** And he cast it into the midst of the ephah; and he cast the weight of lead upon the mouth thereof."*

199

An **ephah**, in most definitions, is "an ancient Hebrew unit of dry measure equal to 1/10 homer or a little over a bushel." (Merriam-Webster). But, clearly this is not what Zechariah is referring to.

According to **"brill.com>article-p289_6"**, **"The ephah is a stand-in for its contents, the woman who is wickedness."**

Continuing with Zechariah 5, verse 9, *"Then lifted I up mine eyes, and looked, and, and, behold, there came out two women, and the wind was in their wings; for they had wings like the wings of a stork: and* ***they lifted up the ephah between the earth and the heaven.*** *10) Then said I to the angel that talked with me,* ***Whither do these bear the ephah?*** *11) And he said unto me,* ***To build it a house in the land of Shinar: and it shall be established, and set there upon her own base.*** *"*

According to the Wikipedia, **"The name Sin'ar occurs eight times in the Hebrew Bible in which it refers to Babylonia. That location of Shinar is evident from its description as encompassing both Babel/Babylon (in northern Babylonia)** and Erech/Uruk (in southern Babylonia)."

So, this **ephah** is a **stand-in**, or semblance of the **woman who is wickedness** that was **lifted up** and **established in the land of Shinar,** aka, **Babylon.** Sure does sound like the description provided in verse 5 of Revelation 17 to me!

*Now, skipping down to Revelation 18, verse 21. It states; *"**And a mighty angel *took up a stone like a great millstone, and cast it into the sea, saying, Thus with violence shall that great city Babylon be thrown down, and shall be found no more at all.*"**

Notice how that verse is very similar to Zechariah 5:8, *"**This is wickedness.** And he cast it into the midst of the ephah; **and he cast the weight of lead upon the mouth thereof.**"*

*In **Book 1**, the **End Times** chapter, I explain that Revelation is speaking of the **Church**. The **Church** is the metaphorical equivalent of the **great whore** that chapter 17 speaks of. Pay close attention to the description provided by verses 3 and 4. Verse 3 states; *"So he carried me away in the spirit into the wilderness: and I saw **a** *woman sit upon a scarlet coloured beast, full of names of blasphemy, having seven heads and ten horns."*

The **seven heads** represents the **seven core religions**, with the **horns being branches** thereof.

What is Lucifer's plan, as stated by Isaiah 14:12-14? *"I will exalt my throne above the stars (angels) of God: I will sit also upon the mount of the congregation... I will be like the most High".*

Also, 2nd Thessalonians 2;4, *"Who opposeth and exalteth himself above all that is called God, or that is worshipped; so that he as God sitteth in the temple of God, shewing himself that he is God."*

The **Church** is the **woman** that sits upon the **scarlet coloured beast, full of names of blasphemy** because he is calling himself God, and being worshipped as God.

Revelation 17, verse 4 states, *"And **the woman was arrayed in purple and scarlet colour, and decked with gold and precious stones and pearls**, having a golden cup in her hand full of abominations and filthiness of her fornication:"*

For those that have read **Book 2**, hopefully you recall my discussion about the **robes, also called cassocks**, worn by the Catholic bishops and cardinals. One quote states; **"During liturgical ceremonies a bishop or cardinal will wear the 'choir' cassock, which is entirely purple or red; otherwise, the cassock worn is the 'house' cassock, which is black with purple or red buttons and fascia, or sash."**

And, think about "all of the **red inside the sanctuaries, the bench cushions, the cushions on the altar chairs, and the curtains hung at the baptismal fonts** (pools)."

Why? Knowing that these are the very colours that the **great whore** is described in, why would the Church choose these colours for their furnishings?

Because, as I clarified in **Book 2**, Exodus chapters 26, 27, and 28 provides God's explicit instructions to Moses about the construction of the Tabernacle, and how every curtain, hanging, and vail, as well as all robes, ephods, and other priestly attire, were all to be linens of *"blue, **and purple, and scarlet"**.*

Chapter's 35, 36, 38 and 39 also reiterates the use of these colours, once again, when elaborating about the assembly of the Tabernacle.

Therefore, **when His Church became a harlot, purple and scarlet became colours that represented whoredom.** This due to the fact that all churches have been taken over by the Devil, stealing not only God's identity, but everything that was meaningful to Him. Which, explains their use of the colours **purple and scarlet**.

So, as you can see, this description is the same of that which is spoken of in Zechariah 5:6. Because the **Church** is the **woman** which is the **ephah**, or the **stand-in**, that is the **image** of **wickedness**.

As we are comparing these scriptures, keep the following in mind... *"... <u>for by thy sorceries were all nations deceived</u>. **24) And in her was found the blood of prophets, and of saints, and of all that were slain upon the earth."*** (Revelation 18:23-24)

If these scriptures in Revelation were not speaking of the **Church**, then what else explains their reference to the above statement, ***"And in her was found the blood of prophets, and of saints"**?* I'm not looking for an answer, just making you think!

*Is it also just a coincidence that the colours of horses spoken of in Revelation chapter 6, verses 1-8, just happens to be the same colours as horses drawing chariots in Zechariah, also chapter 6, and also spoken of in verses 1-8?? The only difference being that Zechariah uses the term **grizzled and bay** instead of **pale.**

Zechariah, chapter 6, beginning with verse 1 states; *"And I turned, and lifted up mine eyes, and looked, and, behold, there came four chariots out from between two mountains; and the mountains were mountains of brass. 2) In **the first chariot were red horses;** and in **the second chariot black horses;** 3) And in **the third chariot white horses;** and in **the fourth chariot grisled and bay horses.** 4) Then I answered and said unto the angel that talked with me, What* *are these, my lord? 5) And the angel answered and said unto me,* **These are the four spirits of the heavens, which go forth from standing before the Lord of all the earth...".**

Researching the term **grizzled coloured horses in the bible**, I was surprised to see that others have written about this very comparison!

One quote from an article titled **Grizzled Horses in Zechariah**, by Floyd Nolen Jones (Th.D., Ph.D.), states; "The third colour of horse present is said to be speckled here, in other places they are referred to as dappled or grizzled (hail spotted). Grizzled is from grizzly which means pale but spotted."

He states that **Black represents Famine. White is for victory or triumph. Red is the colour for war and bloodshed.** And, **dappled or grizzled horses (spotted, speckled, splotched...) symbolically represents wholesale death from sources OTHER than just war and famine, such as plagues, pestilence, epidemics... (sword, famine, beasts and pestilence. Ezekiel 14:21).**

Merrill F. Unger (1909-1980), "suggests that **white indicates victory** (Revelation 6:2; also, Revelation 19:11, and 14), **red stands for bloodshed** (Revelation 6:4), **black represents judgment** (Revelation 6:5-6), **and the dappled colour signifies death** (Revelation 6:8)."

In **Book 1**, I state that "the **'white horse'**, which white has always been a symbol of **'purity'**, or that which is **'righteous'**. As far as the rider of the horse, and speaking in a literal sense, I believe it is referring to the **Spirit of God, which is literally stirring in people throughout the world at this time.**"

Regarding the **red horse**, Revelation 6:4 tells us; *"another horse that was red: and power was given to him that sat thereon to take peace from the earth, and that they should kill one another: and there was given unto him a great sword."*

I tie Jesus into this verse, given the fact that he tells us in Matthew 10:34, *"Think not that I am come to send peace on earth, but a sword."*

The verse, itself, states that people **should kill one another**, so clearly **bloodshed** is represented here.

Regarding the **black horse** I state; "This *'pair of balances in his hand'* takes me back to the Book of Daniel, chapter 5 where King Belshazzar of Babylon sees a hand write upon the wall 'MENE, MENE, TEKEL...'. Then the king asks Daniel to interpret it for him, and Daniel states in verse 26, '... **MENE;** *God hath numbered thy kingdom, and finished it.* 27) **TEKEL;** *Thou art weighed in the balances, and art found wanting*'."

The fact that they are *"weighed in the balances, and art found wanting"*, symbolizes **judgment!**

And, as anyone that has read either one of my previous books already knows, I have made it very clear that the **pale horse is death**, which is **Lucifer.**

Zechariah chapter 1, beginning with verse 8, also speaks of the horses. It states; *"I saw by night, and behold a man riding upon a **red horse**, and he stood among the myrtle trees that were in the bottom; and behind him were there **red horses, speckled,** and **white**. 9) Then said I, O my lord, what are these? And the angel that talked with me said unto me, I will shew thee what these be. 10) And the man that stood among the myrtle trees answered and said,* <u>*These are they whom the LORD hath sent to walk to and fro through the earth.*</u>"

*** Notice how verse 10 states that they **walk to and fro.** Whereas, previously when we were discussing chapter 4, verse 10 of Zechariah, the **candlestick all of gold** with the **seven lamps thereon**, and that they were the **eyes of the LORD which run to and fro through the whole earth.**

Look at the specific wording... it is no mistake. When you stop and think about it, our **eyes** move much faster than our legs, or even the legs of **horses.**

I referenced this scripture in **Book 2**, tying it to Satan as him being one of the horsemen. Which is based on that portion of 4:10 that I have underlined.

204

The following is a quote from **Book 2**, regarding these passages just quoted. I state; "What I'm understanding here, is that there are **4 horsemen, that** ride/**walk to and fro through the earth. They are God's eyes who watch and report back to Him. And based on the responses that Satan gives in Job 1:7, and again in Job 2:2, he is one of the four horsemen.**"

In Job 1:7 and 2:2, Satan is asked by God *"from whence comest thou?"* And both times Satan replies, *"From going to and fro in the earth, and walking up and down in it."*

His response coupled with Zechariah 4:10's last statement is what ties the verses together, and validates my theory regarding Satan/Lucifer being one of the **four horsemen.**

Furthermore, God has **eyes** everywhere! We just discussed the **candlestick with seven lamps thereon**, which are the **eyes of the LORD** (Zech. 10:4&10). And, the **stone**, which "**upon one stone there shall be seven eyes**" (Zech. 3:9).

He sees everything!

It's all about connecting the dots!

*Revelation 6:12, "And I beheld when he had opened the sixth seal, and, lo, there was a great earthquake; and **the sun became black as sackcloth of hair, and the moon became as blood;**"

Look at Joel 2, beginning with verse 30; *"And I will shew wonders in the heavens and in the earth, blood, and fire, and pillars of smoke. 31) **The sun shall be turned into darkness, and the moon into blood,** before the great and the terrible day of the LORD come."*

*Also, Revelation 6:13-14, "And **the stars of heaven fell unto the earth, even as a fig tree casteth her untimely figs,** when she is shaken of a mighty wind. 14) And **the heaven departed as a scroll when it is rolled together**; and every mountain and island were moved out of their places."*

Now, Isaiah 34:4, *"And all the host of heaven shall be dissolved, and the heavens shall be rolled together as a scroll: and all their host shall fall down*, as the leaf falleth off from the vine, and **as a falling fig from the fig tree.**"

*Revelation 7:16-17, "**They shall hunger no more, neither thirst any more; neither shall the sun light on them, nor any heat.** 17) **For the Lamb which is in the midst of the throne shall feed them, and shall lead them unto living fountains of waters**: and God shall wipe away all tears from their eyes."*

Now, Isaiah 49:10, "**They shall not hunger nor thirst; neither shall the heat nor sun smite them: for he that hath mercy on them shall lead them, even by the springs of water shall he guide them.**"

The only difference between these two scriptures is the word **Lamb** in Revelation 7:17, compared to Isaiah's use of **he**. Again, with Jesus being the one to impart the vision to John, he is, more than likely, trying to make it about himself, being the **Lamb**.

*Revelation 8:5, "And the **angel took the censer, and filled it with fire of the altar,** and cast it into the earth: and there were voices, and thunderings, and lightnings, and an earthquake."*

Now, Isaiah 6:6, "*Then flew **one of the seraphims** unto me, **having a live coal in his hand, which he had taken** with the tongs **from off the altar:**"*

*And let's not forget Revelation 9:14-19, and 16:12, where it speaks of the **four angels which are bound in the great river Euphrates, and upon it drying up they are loosed. And the army of horsemen that were two hundred thousand thousand. That's 200,000,000!**

In **Book 1**, I tie this event in to Joel 2:1-11. Beginning with verse 4 it states; "**The appearance of them is as the appearance of horses; and as horsemen, so shall they run. 5)** Like the noise of chariots on the tops of mountains shall they leap, like the noise of a flame of fire that devoureth the stubble, as a strong people set in battle array. 6) **Before their face the people shall be much pained: all faces shall gather blackness. 7) They shall run like mighty men; they shall climb the wall like men of war; and they shall march every one on his ways, and they shall not break their ranks: 8)**

Neither shall one thrust another; they shall walk every one in his path: and when they fall upon the sword, they shall not be wounded. 9) They shall run to and fro in the city; they shall run upon the wall, they shall climb up upon the houses; they shall enter in at the windows like a thief. 10) The earth shall quake before them; the heavens shall tremble: the sun and the moon shall be dark, and the stars shall withdraw their shining: 11) And the LORD shall utter his voice before his army: for his camp is very great: for he is strong that executeth his word: for the day of the LORD is great and very terrible; and who can abide it?"

*Look at Revelation 10:4, *"And when the seven thunders had uttered their voices, I was about to write: and I heard a voice from heaven saying unto me, **Seal up those things** which the seven thunders uttered, and write them not... 7) **But in the days of** the voice of the seventh angel, when he shall begin to sound, the mystery of God should be finished, as he hath declared to his servants the prophets."*

And now, Daniel 12:9, *"And he said, Go thy way, Daniel: **for the words are closed up** and **sealed till the time of the end**."*

Also, Habakkuk 2:2-3, *"And the LORD answered me, and said, Write the vision, and make it plain upon tables, that he may run that readeth it. 3) For **the vision is yet for an appointed time, but at the end it shall speak**, and not lie: though it tarry, wait for it; because it will surely come, it will not tarry."*

*Revelation 10:9-10, *"And I went unto the angel, and said unto him, Give me the little book. And **he said unto me, Take it, and eat it up**; and it shall make thy belly bitter, but it shall be in thy mouth sweet as honey. 10) And I took the little book out of the angel's hand, **and ate it up**; and **it was in my mouth sweet as honey**: and as soon as I had eaten it, my belly was bitter."*

Ezekiel 3:1-3, *"Moreover **he said unto me**, Son of man, eat that thou findest; **eat this roll**, and go speak unto the house of Israel. 2) So I opened my mouth, and he caused me to eat that roll. 3) And he said unto me, Son of man, cause thy belly to eat, and fill thy bowels with this roll that I give thee. Then **did I eat it**; and **it was in my mouth as honey for sweetness**."*

*Revelation 11:11, *"And after three days and a half the Spirit of life from God entered into them, and they stood upon their feet; and great fear fell upon them which saw them."*

Now, Hosea 6, verses 1 and 2; *"Come, and let us return unto the LORD: for he hath torn, and he will heal us; he hath smitten, and he will bind us up. 2) After two days will he revive us: in the third day he will raise us up, and we shall live in his sight."*

Moving on to Revelation, chapter 12. Which again, was already interpreted in **Book 1.**

*Revelation 12:1, *"And there appeared a great wonder in heaven; a woman clothed with the sun, and the moon under her feet, and upon her head a crown of twelve stars: 2) And **she being with child cried, travailing in birth, and pained to be delivered.**"*

Now, Isaiah 66, beginning with verse 7. The LORD states; *"**Before she travailed, she brought forth; before her pain came, she was delivered of a man child.** 8) Who hath heard such a thing? Who hath seen such things? **Shall the earth be made to bring forth in one day? (The "woman" is Jerusalem) Or shall a nation be born at once? for as soon as Zion travailed, she brought forth her children.** 9) Shall I bring to the birth, and not cause to bring forth? saith the LORD: **shall I cause to bring forth, and shut the womb?** saith thy God. 10) **Rejoice ye with Jerusalem, and be glad with her, all ye that love her...** 11) That ye may suck, and be satisfied with the breasts of her consolations; that ye may milk out, and be delighted with the abundance of her glory. 12) For thus saith the LORD, Behold, I will extend peace to her like a river, and the glory of the gentiles like a flowing stream: **then shall ye suck, ye shall be borne upon her sides, and be dangled upon her knees. 13) As one whom his mother comforteth, so will I comfort you...**"*.

The following is a statement I made in **Book 1**, following the scripture that was just quoted.

"The long quote was necessary for you to see that God is talking about the *'woman'* of Revelation, chapter 12, which is Jerusalem. The *'child'* that was brought forth represents His people".

*Continuing with Revelation 12, verse 3 states; *"And there appeared another wonder in heaven; and **behold a great red dragon, having seven heads and ten horns, and seven crowns upon his heads**. 4) And his tail drew the third part of the stars of heaven, and did cast them to the earth: and the dragon stood before the woman which was ready to be delivered, for to devour her child as soon as it was born. 5) And she brought forth a man child, who was to rule all nations with a rod of iron: and her child was caught up unto God, and to his throne."*

This is the same **beast** that we previously discussed, at the beginning of this chapter. Only this time, this chapter makes it very clear that it is speaking of Lucifer.

Look at the following verses. Verse 7 states; *"And **there was war in heaven**: Michael and his angels fought against the dragon; and the dragon fought and his angels, 8) And prevailed not; **neither was their place found any more in heaven. 9) And the great dragon was cast out, that old serpent, called the Devil, and Satan, which deceiveth the whole world: he was cast out into the earth, and his angels were cast out with him.** "*

The **war in heaven** resulted in Lucifer being **cast out into the earth**. Isaiah 14:12 tells us, *"**How art thou fallen from heaven, O Lucifer, son of the morning! how art thou cut down to the ground, which didst weaken the nations!**"*

Look also at Isaiah 27:1, *"**In that day the LORD with his sore and great and strong sword shall punish leviathan the piercing serpent, even leviathan that crooked serpent; and he shall slay the dragon** that is in the sea."*

Now, back to Revelation 12, verse 12, *"Therefore rejoice, ye heavens, and ye that dwell in them. **Woe to the inhabiters of the earth and of the sea! for the devil is come down unto you, having great wrath, because he knoweth that he hath but a short time. 13) And when the dragon saw that he was cast unto the earth, he persecuted the woman which brought forth the man child.**"*

And, as I stated just moments ago, the woman is Jerusalem (Zion), and her child that she gave birth to was God's people.

Then, after the **dragon** was **cast unto the earth,** he had a score to settle, **so he went after God's people.**

*Look at Revelation 14:2, **"And I heard a voice from heaven, as the voice of many waters...".**

Also, Revelation 19:6, *"And I heard as it were the voice of a great multitude, **and as the voice of many waters...".***

Ezekiel 43:2, *"... the glory of **the God of Israel** came from the way of the east: and **his voice was like a noise of many waters."***

*Look at Revelation 14:15, *"And another angel came out of the temple, crying with a loud voice to him that sat on the cloud, **Thrust in thy sickle, and reap: for the time is come for thee to reap; for the harvest of the earth is ripe."***

Compare it to Joel 3:13, *"**Put ye in the sickle, for the harvest is ripe**: come, get you down; for the press is full, the fats overflow; for their wickedness is great."*

*Now, Revelation 14:19-20, *"And the angel thrust in his sickle into the earth, and gathered the vine of the earth, **and cast it into the great winepress of the wrath of God. 20) And the winepress was trodden without the city, and blood came out of the winepress,** even unto the horse bridles, by the space of a thousand and six hundred furlongs."*

Also, Revelation 19:15, *"**... and he treadeth the winepress of the fierceness and wrath of Almighty God."***

Now, Isaiah 63:3, *"**I have trodden the winepress** alone; and of the people there was none with me: **for I will tread them in mine anger, and trample them in my fury; and their blood shall be sprinkled upon my garments, and I will stain all my raiment."***

*More comparisons: Revelation 15:3, *"And **they sing the song of Moses** the servant of God, and the song of the Lamb, saying, Great and marvellous are thy works, Lord God Almighty; **just and true are thy ways**, thou King of saints."*

In Deuteronomy 31:16 God tells Moses that after his demise, the children of Israel will *"go a whoring after the gods of the strangers of the land."*

Then, verse 17 states; *"**Then my anger shall be kindled against them in that day, and I will forsake them, and I will hide my face from them,** and they shall be devoured, **and many evils and troubles shall befall them; so that they will say in that day, Are not these evils come upon us, because our God is not among us? ...19) Now therefore <u>write ye this song for you, and teach it the children of Israel</u>: put it in their mouths, that this song may be a witness for me against the children of Israel."***

The actual **song** is the entire 32nd chapter of Deuteronomy. It's the scripture where God refers to Himself as their **Rock**, saying how they are **unmindful** of Him. Talking about how they **have moved Him to jealousy with that which is not God**, (Verse 21). Which ends with Him saying that **their Rock has sold them**! (Verse 30).

It is my understanding that this is the **song** referenced in Revelation 15:3, because it's being sung by the **saints**, the **144,000**, after they have ascended to heaven, and God's wrath is getting ready to pour down!

*Next, look at Revelation 16, verses 14 and 16, which states; *"For they are the spirits of devils, working miracles, which go forth unto **the kings of the earth and of the whole world, to gather them to the battle of that great day of God Almighty...** 16) And he gathered them together into a place called in the Hebrew tongue Armageddon."*

Now, Zephaniah 3:8, *"Therefore wait ye upon me, saith the LORD, until the day that I rise up to the prey: for my determination is **to gather the nations, that I may assemble the kingdoms, to pour upon them mine indignation, even all my fierce anger: for all the earth shall be devoured** with the fire of my jealousy."*

*Revelation chapter 18 elaborates on the destruction of Babylon. Verse 2 states; *"**And he cried mightily with a strong voice, saying, Babylon the great is fallen, is fallen, and is become the habitation** *of devils, and the hold of every foul spirit, and a cage of every unclean and hateful bird."*

Now, Isaiah 21:9, *"...Babylon is fallen, is fallen...".*

*Revelation 18:3, *"For **all nations have drunk of the wine** of the wrath of her fornication, and the kings of the earth have committed fornication with her, and the merchants of the earth are waxed rich through the abundance of her delicacies."*

Now, Jeremiah 51:7, *"Babylon hath been a golden cup in the LORD'S hand, that made all the earth drunken: **the nations have drunken of her wine**; therefore the nations are mad."*

*Revelation 18:4, *"And I heard another voice from heaven, saying, **Come out of her, my people, that ye be not partakers of her sins, and that ye receive not of her plagues."***

Jeremiah 51:6, *"**Flee out of the midst of Babylon, and deliver every man his soul: be not cut off in her iniquity;** for this is the time of the LORD'S vengeance; he will render unto her a recompence."*

*Revelation 18:5, *"**For her sins have reached unto heaven,** and God hath remembered her iniquities."*

Jeremiah 51:9, *"We would have healed Babylon, but she is not healed: forsake her, and let us go every one into his own country: **for her judgment reacheth unto heaven,** and is lifted up even to the skies."*

*Also, Revelation 18:7, *"**How much she hath glorified herself,** and lived deliciously, so much torment and sorrow give her: **for she saith in her heart, I sit a queen, and am no widow,** and shall see no sorrow. 8) **Therefore shall her plagues come in one day, death, and mourning, and famine; and she shall be utterly burned with fire**: for strong is the Lord God who judgeth her."*

Compared to Isaiah 47:7, *"And thou saidst, **I shall be a lady for ever**: so that thou didst not lay these things to thy heart, neither didst remember the latter end of it. 8) Therefore hear now this, thou that art given to pleasures, that dwellest carelessly, **that sayest in thine heart**, I am, and none else beside me; **I shall not sit*** *as a widow*, neither shall I know the loss of children... 10) For thou hast trusted in thy wickedness: thou hast said, None seeth me. Thy wisdom and thy knowledge, it hath perverted thee; and thou hast said in thine heart, I am, and none else beside me. 11) **Therefore shall evil come upon thee**; thou shalt not know from whence it riseth: **and mischief shall fall upon thee**; thou shalt not be able to put it off: **and desolation shall come upon thee suddenly**, which thou shalt not know."

I believe that everything underlined in Revelation 18:8 falls within the parameters of **evil, mischief, and desolation** as stated in Isaiah 47:11.

*Look next at Revelation 18:11-19. Verse 11 states; "**And the merchants of the earth shall weep and mourn over her**; for no man buyeth their merchandise any more: 12) The merchandise of **gold**, and **silver**, and **precious stones**, and of pearls, and **fine linen, and purple**, and silk, and scarlet, and all thyine wood, and all manner vessels of **ivory**, and all manner vessels of most precious wood, and of **brass**, and **iron**, and marble, 13) And **cinnamon**, and odours, and ointments, and frankincense, **and wine, and oil, and fine flour, and wheat**, and beasts, and sheep, and **horses, and chariots**, and **slaves, and souls of men**. 14) And the fruits that thy soul lusted after are departed from thee, and all things which were dainty and goodly are departed from thee, and thou shalt find them no more at all. 15) **The merchants of these things, which were made rich by her, shall stand afar off for the fear of her torment, weeping and wailing**, 16) And saying, Alas, alas, that great city, that was **clothed in fine linen**, and **purple**, and scarlet, and decked with gold, and **precious stones**, and pearls! 17) For in one hour so **great riches** is come to nought. **And every shipmaster, and all the company in ships, and sailors, and as many as trade by sea, stood afar off. 18) And cried when they saw the smoke of her burning, saying, What city is like unto this great city! 19) And they cast dust on their heads, and cried, weeping and wailing**, saying, Alas, alas, **that great city, wherein were made rich all that had ships in the sea by reason of her costliness**! for in one hour is she made desolate."

Now, that compared to Ezekiel 27:12-33. Again, continue to focus only on those parts that I've highlighted with bold type, and have underlined in like manner.

Beginning with verse 12, it states; " *... thy merchant by reason of the **multitude of all kind of riches; with silver, iron, tin, and lead, they traded in thy fairs.** 13) ... they were thy merchants: **they traded the persons of men** and **vessels of brass** in thy market. 14) ... traded in thy fairs with **horses and horsemen and mules.** 15) ... they brought thee for a present horns of **ivory** and ebony. 16) ... they occupied in thy fairs with **emeralds, purple, and broidered work, and fine linen, and coral, and agate.** 17) ... they traded in thy market **wheat** of Minnith, and Pannag, and honey, **and oil, and balm.** 18) ... for the multitude of all riches; in the **wine** of Helbon, and white wool... 22) ... they occupied in thy fairs with **chief of all spices,** and with **all precious stones, and gold**... 24) These were thy merchants in all sorts of things, in blue clothes, and broidered work, and in chests of rich apparel, bound with cords, and made of cedar, among thy merchandise... 27) Thy riches, and thy fairs, thy merchandise, thy mariners, and thy pilots, thy calkers, and the occupiers of thy merchandise, and all thy men of war, that are in thee, and in all thy company which is in the midst of thee, shall fall into the midst of the seas in the day of thy ruin... 29) **And all that handle the oar, the mariners, and all the pilots of the sea, shall come down from their ships, they shall stand upon the land; 30) And shall cause their voice to be heard against thee, and shall cry bitterly, and shall cast up dust upon their heads, they shall wallow themselves in the ashes:** 31) And they shall make themselves utterly bald for thee, and gird them with sackcloth, and **they shall weep for thee** with bitterness of heart **and** bitter **wailing.** 32) And in their wailing they shall take up a lamentation for thee, and lament over thee ... 33) When thy wares went forth out of the seas, thou filledst many people; **thou didst enrich the kings of the earth with the multitude of thy riches and of thy merchandise."*

Ezekiel is speaking of the destruction of Tyre. It appears to me that two different people are telling the same story, but each in their own words.

*How about Revelation 18:22, *"**And the voice of <u>harpers</u>, and musicians, and of pipers, and trumpeters, <u>shall be heard no more</u> at all in thee;** and no craftsman, of whatsoever craft he be, shall be found any more in thee; and the sound of a millstone shall be heard no more at all in thee;"*

Now, Ezekiel 26:13, *"**And I will cause the noise of thy songs to cease; and the sound of thy <u>harps</u> <u>shall be no more heard</u>.**"*

Look at the big picture! How is it that there are so many similarities? Big and small! Especially with the books of Ezekiel and Zechariah.

*Look now at Revelation 19:17 & 18. It states; *"And I saw an angel standing in the sun; and he cried with a loud voice, **saying to all the fowls that fly in the midst of heaven, Come and gather yourselves together unto the supper of the great God; 18) That ye may eat the flesh of kings, and the flesh of captains, and the flesh of mighty men,** and **the flesh of horses, and of them that sit on them,** and **the flesh of all men,** both free and bond, both **small and great.**"*

Let's compare that to Ezekiel 39:17 & 18. It's interesting that the verse numbers are even the same! It states; *"And, thou son of man, thus saith the Lord GOD; **Speak unto every feathered fowl, and to every beast of the field, Assemble yourselves, and come; gather yourselves on every side to my sacrifice that I do sacrifice for you,** even a great sacrifice upon the mountains of Israel, that ye may eat flesh, and drink blood. 18) **Ye shall eat the flesh of the mighty, and drink the blood of the princes of the earth,** of rams, of lambs, and of goats, of bullocks, all of them fatlings of Bashan. 19) And ye shall eat fat till ye be full, and drink blood till ye be drunken, of my sacrifice which I have sacrificed for you. 20) **Thus ye shall be filled at my table with horses** and chariots, **with mighty men, and with all men of war, saith the Lord GOD.**"*

*Revelation 21:1-4, *"And **I saw a new heaven and a new earth:** for the first heaven and the first earth were passed away; and there was no more sea... 3) And I heard a great voice out of heaven saying, **Behold, the tabernacle of God is with men, and <u>he will dwell with them</u>, and <u>they shall be his people, and God himself</u>**

215

shall be with them, and be their God. 4) *And God shall wipe away all tears from their eyes; and there shall be no more death, neither sorrow, nor crying,* neither shall there be any more pain: *for the former things are passed away.*"

And, Revelation 21:7, "*He that overcometh shall inherit all things; and I will be his God, and he shall be my son.*"

Look first at Exodus 29:45, "*And I will dwell among the children of Israel, and will be their God.*"

What's really amazing about this verse is that it was stated right after God had given Moses very detailed instructions about the construction of the **Tabernacle**.

Now, Isaiah 65:17, "*For, behold, I create new heavens and a new earth: and the former shall not be remembered, nor come into mind. 19) And I will rejoice in Jerusalem, and joy in my people: and the voice of weeping shall be no more heard in her, nor the voice of crying.*"

Ezekiel 36:28, "*And ye shall dwell in the land that I gave to your fathers; and ye shall be my people, and I will be your God.*"

Jeremiah 32:38, "*And they shall be my people, and I will be their God:*"

Again, I have underlined all like verses in a similar manner.

*Look at Revelation 21:2, "... saw the holy city, new Jerusalem, coming down from God out of heaven, **prepared as a bride adorned for her husband.**" And, 21:9, "**... Come hither, I will shew the bride, the Lamb's wife.**"

Isaiah 54:5, "**For thy Maker is thine husband;** the LORD of hosts is his name; and thy Redeemer the Holy One of Israel; The God of the whole earth shall he be called.*"

Again, Jesus is trying to pass himself off as the **Lamb**, and the new **Jerusalem as his bride!** **God**, Himself, **is** thy **Maker** and **thine husband!**

Everything belongs to God!

*Here's a big one... Revelation 22:13, **"I am Alpha and Omega, the beginning and the end, the first and the last."**

This is Jesus speaking of himself. Remember, he has said **I and my Father are one** (John 10:30), and here he even states that he is the **beginning and the end.** This same statement is also found in Revelation 1, verse 8.

But, Isaiah 48:12 makes it very clear, *"Hearken unto me, O Jacob and Israel, my called; I am he; **I am the first, I also am the last**."*

The LORD God is the only first and last!

Also, Jesus' statement is just 3 verses away from the truth of his true identity. Revelation 22:16, *"I Jesus have sent mine angel to testify unto you these things in the churches. I am the root and the offspring of David, and **the bright and morning star**."*

Isaiah 14:12, **"How you have fallen from heaven, O morning star, son of the dawn".** (NIV)

Furthermore, look now at Revelation 2:26-28, *"And he that overcometh, and keepeth my works unto the end, to him will I give power over the nations: 27) And he shall rule them with a rod of iron; as the vessels of a potter shall they be broken to shivers: even as I received of my Father. 28)* **And I will give him the morning star."**

Who's the **morning star**? **Lucifer.**

These are Jesus' words. If you doubt me, and you have a Bible that's a Red Letter Edition, take a look and you will see that the above scripture is in **red** type. If you don't have a Red Letter Edition, just Google **kingjamesbibleonline.org**.

Based on these comparisons, it is my opinion that much of the vision given to John by Jesus is nothing more than Jesus, once again, using someone else's material!!

Daniel was among the captives that were taken by Nebuchadnezzar when Babylon besieged Israel and Judah beginning sometime between 442-441 BCE. That date comes from the Creation Chart that I made using all of the lineage and other events as outlined in the Old Testament, which can be found on page 179 of **Book 1**.

Daniel was taken captive during the first siege based on chapter 1, of the Book of Daniel, verses 1-6. Verse 1 states; *"In the third year of the reign of Jehoiakim king of Judah came Nebuchadnezzar king of Babylon unto Jerusalem, and besieged it."*

Now, skipping down to verse 6, it states; *"Now among these were of the children of Judah, Daniel,* Hananiah, Mishael, and Azariah".

Verse 1 of chapter 7 states, *"In the first year of Belshazzar king of Babylon Daniel had a dream and visions...".*

Again, based on the Creation Chart on page 179 of **Book 1**, and the detailed history I provide on pages 181-187, Belshazzar began his reign in approximately 375 BCE. **That's 375 years before the birth of Jesus**.

Ezekiel, too, was taken captive by Nebuchadnezzar. The Book of Ezekiel, chapter 1, beginning with verse 1 states; *"Now it came to pass in the thirtieth year, in the fourth month, in the fifth day of the month, as I was among the captives by the river of Chebar, that the heavens were opened, and I saw visions of God. 2) In the fifth day of the month, which was the fifth year of king Jehoiachin's captivity,"*

Jehoiachin was taken captive during Nebuchadnezzar's 2nd invasion in approximately 434-433 BCE, and this vision took place during the 30th year of their captivity. That would put it at approximately 404-403 BCE.

The vison that was given to John by Jesus occurred at least 400 years after Daniel's vision took place, and yet... how can anyone say that they are not speaking of the same events? And that's just the events of Daniel's vision. That doesn't even factor in the events taken from Isaiah, Ezekiel and Zechariah.

I believe that Jesus knew about these visions of the **End Times,** and after splicing them together, gave it to John. Need I remind you of the numerous examples I've previously provided of him doing this

218

very thing in the past. Most of which involved king David, even calling him a prophet!

And, given the fact that all of these visions are well documented, would make it easy for him to do so. Not only that, I feel certain that Jesus' father, Lucifer, helped to fill in any gaps that were necessary.

I would estimate that 90% of the entire vision of Revelation is plagiarized? I believe that there are portions of the Devil's plan, which have been included, that are truthful to him, the Devil. And, who better to provide those details than the Devil's son... Which again, as Jesus has told us, *"I and my Father are one"!!* (John 10:30).

Anyone being of average intelligence and impartial, who were to compare these visions would have to agree that the number of similarities, and their precision of detail are too numerous to deny!

Please don't misunderstand, the events of Revelation are not in question. They are going to happen! What is questionable, is the origins of the vision.

I'd like to close this chapter with a quote from Leonardo da Vinci...

"There are three classes of people: those who see, those who see when they are shown, those who do not see."

Which one are you?

Calling the 144,000

Revelation, chapter 7, beginning with verse 9; *"After this I beheld, and, lo, **a great multitude**, which no man could number, of all nations, and kindreds, and people, and tongues, **stood before the throne,** and before the Lamb, **clothed with white robes**, ain their hands; 10) And cried with a loud voice, **saying, Salvation to our God which sitteth upon the throne**, and unto the Lamb. 11) And all the angels stood round about the throne, and about the elders and the four beasts, and fell before the throne on their faces, and worshipped God, 12) Saying, Amen: Blessing, and glory, and wisdom, and thanksgiving, and honour, and power, and might, be unto our God for ever and ever. Amen. 13) And one of the elders answered, saying unto me, **What are these which are arrayed in white robes? and whence came they?** 14) And I said unto him, Sir, thou knowest. And he said to me, **These are they which came out of great tribulation,** and have washed their robes, and made them white in the blood of the Lamb. 15) Therefore are they before the throne of God, and serve him day and night in his temple: and he that sitteth on the throne shall dwell among them. 16) They shall hunger no more, neither thirst any more; neither shall the sun light on them, nor any heat. 17) For the Lamb which is in the midst of the throne shall feed them, and shall lead them unto living fountains of waters: and God shall wipe away all tears from their eyes."*

These are those **which came out of great tribulation**.

Tribulation is defined as **"a cause of great trouble or suffering."** (Oxford Languages)

Chapter 7 of Revelation pertains to the **sealing of the 144,000**. The heading beneath the chapter number states; **Pause while Israel and the Gentiles are Sealed**. And, given the fact that the scripture quoted above, verses 9-17, are found within chapter 7, that pertains to the 144,000, I understand these verses to be speaking of them as well.

The 144,000 are those **which came out of great tribulation**, and they are standing before the throne of God because they were

220

slain by the beast, as stated in **Revelation 13:7**, and have now ascended into heaven.

That scripture states; *"And __it was given unto him to make war with the saints, and to overcome them...__"*.

For those that have read **Book 1**, I make it very clear that **no one is raptured out of here before all of the bad stuff happens**... the **tribulation**.

I explain in the last chapter, **End Times**, that the **two witnesses** spoken of in Revelation chapter 11, beginning with verse 3, is also referring to the 144,000.

My understanding was based on verses 7, 9 and 11, of Revelation 11. Beginning with verse 7, it states; *"And **when they shall have finished their testimony, the __beast that ascendeth out of the bottomless pit shall make war against them, and shall overcome them, and kill them__**...".*

Stopping here for a moment. Comparing Revelation 13:7 to that just stated, we see in both that the beast **shall make war with God's chosen, and kill them**.

Continuing, verse 8 states; *"**And their dead bodies shall lie in the street** of the great city, which spiritually is called Sodom and Egypt, where also our Lord was crucified. 9) And they of **the people and kindreds and tongues and nations shall see their dead bodies three days and a half, and shall not suffer their dead bodies to be put in graves.**"*

Stopping again... Think about what verse 9 is saying. That's a whole lot of people that *"shall see their dead bodies"*... **the bodies of just two people!** I realize that television would provide *"people and kindreds and tongues and nations"* the opportunity to witness this event. But, all of this attention given to the deaths of just two people... Worldwide coverage?

However, if the **two witnesses** were symbolic of 144,000 people being killed, and their bodies lying dead in the streets **for 3 1/2 days**... that would be a **spectacle!!** And talk about worldwide coverage... **Breaking News! Top of the Headlines! All of the** *"people and kindreds and tongues and nations"* **would be watching!**

Finishing up the scripture, verse 11 states; *"And **after three days and a half the Spirit of life from God entered into them, and they stood upon their feet; and great fear fell upon them which saw them**. 12) **And they heard a great voice from heaven saying unto them, Come up hither. And they ascended up to heaven in a cloud; and their enemies beheld them.**"*

After 3 1/2 days they stand up, and are called to Heaven by God. Again, something like this involving only 2 people could be easily missed by the world, or even covered up. But not when it involves 144,000 people! There's no hiding that!

My reason for understanding that **two could become 144,000** is twofold. Let's look at the specific wording of Revelation 11, verses 3 and 4.

Beginning with verse 3, it states; *"And I will give power unto my **two witnesses**, and they shall prophesy a thousand two hundred and threescore days, clothed in sackcloth. 4) **These are the two olive trees, and the two candlesticks** standing before the God of the earth."*

First of all, Revelation 1:20 tells us what a **candlestick** is. It states; *"The mystery of the seven stars which thou sawest in my right hand, and the seven golden candlesticks. The seven stars are the angels of the seven churches: and **the seven candlesticks which thou sawest are the seven churches.**"*

A **candlestick** represents a church. And, given the fact that there are **seven candlesticks**, means there are **seven churches**. Which, as I explain in **Book 1**, even though Revelation, chapters 2 and 3, identifies those churches, once again they are metaphors.

And, those metaphors are speaking of the **7 original core religions of the world.** I realize that more than 7 exist today, but most are factions that have branched off of the original 7. I even share my thoughts on who those **7 core religions possibly are** in **Book 1.**

Based on there being only **two candlesticks** referenced in Revelation 11:4, tells me that there are **portions of only two core religions represented**.

Secondly, as for the **two olive trees**, it too is another metaphor. Going back to Genesis 8:11, when Noah sent a dove out to see if the waters had abated, it returned with **an olive leaf plucked off**.

So, **an olive leaf is a sign from God**. And, given the fact that there are **two olive trees**, tells me that **there are many leaves that symbolizes messengers of God**!

Additional validation is found in Zechariah 4, beginning with verse 2. It states; *"And said unto me, What seest thou? And I said, I have looked, and behold a candlestick all of gold, with a bowl upon the top of it, and his seven lamps thereon, and seven pipes to the seven lamps, which are upon the top thereof: 3)* **And two olive trees by it, one upon the right side of the bowl, and the other upon the left side thereof.***"*

Then, after this exchange back and forth between Zechariah and the angel, verse 11 continues; *"Then answered I, and said unto him,* **What are these two olive trees upon the right side of the candlestick and upon the left side thereof***? 12) And I answered again, and said unto him,* **What be these two olive branches which through the two golden pipes empty the golden oil out of themselves***? 13) And he answered me and said, Knowest thou not what these be? And I said, No, my lord. 14) Then said he,* <u>These are the two anointed ones, that stand by the Lord of the whole earth</u>.*"*

Verse 14 is speaking literally of the **two olive trees being the two anointed ones...** My point with this scripture is to show that metaphorically, **olive trees** are **anointed ones**.

Therefore, between the **candlesticks** that are **portions of the two core religions,** and the **leaves of the olive trees, all are messengers of God, or anointed ones... the 144,000.**

Furthermore, **two bodies lying dead in the streets for 3 1/2 days would not create the spectacle that Lucifer would endeavour to make. He wants to get everyone's attention... make a statement!**

Not only that, beginning with verse 10 of chapter 11, the scripture tells us; *"And they that dwell upon the earth shall rejoice over them, and make merry, and shall send gifts one to another; because these two prophets tormented them that dwelt on the earth."*

Verse 10 is saying that all of the people will **rejoice over their deaths**! To the point of **sending gifts to one another**! That's pretty sad. But, trust me when I say that the Christian population hate my books! I finally stopped advertising them on Amazon under search results pertaining to **Christian books, apparel and gifts**.

It's not my plan to hold the books back from them indefinitely, I just needed to shut down, or limit the negative reviews that **Book 1** was initially receiving, that would have discouraged others from reading it. God guides me every step of the way!

However, as Revelation 11:11 tells us, *"after three days and an half the Spirit of life from God entered into them, and they stood upon their feet; and great fear fell upon them which saw them. 12) And they heard a great voice from heaven saying unto them, Come up hither. And they ascended up to heaven in a cloud; and their enemies beheld them."*

Now we see God's response to that! Again, **two people standing up and ascending to heaven**, easy to be overlooked, or covered up! But, **144,000 standing up and ascending to heaven... What a spectacular sight to see! One that would definitely cause great fear to fall upon all of them** watching!

Let's backup for a moment to Revelation 11, verses 5 & 6. The scripture states; *"And if any man will hurt them, fire proceedeth out of their mouth, and devoureth their enemies: and if any man will hurt them, he must in this manner be killed. 6) These have power to shut heaven, that it rain not in the days of their prophecy: and have power over waters to turn them to blood, and to smite the earth with all plagues, as often as they will."*

Again, the scripture is speaking in metaphors. The **"fire proceedeth out of their mouth"** could be symbolic of their words convicting people of their sinful ways, damning all who refuse to believe.

The **"power to shut heaven, that it rain not"** could mean that the bowls of wrath will not rain down from heaven until they have finished their prophesying.

The **"power over waters to turn them to blood"** could be referring to people's fates being doomed because they believed not their message. Revelation 17:15 tells us that **'waters'** are people.

Bear in mind, metaphors enable multiple interpretations. So, the possibility exists that the literal interpretations could happen as well, which also applies to the **two witnesses**. It's very likely that there will be two people that witness something significant. That may be required to testify to that, which they saw.

Back to the metaphors of 11:5 & 6. Remember our previous discussion about the plagues that God unleashed upon Egypt. He used Moses to accomplish that. Meaning that Moses was the go-between that God used to, not only communicate through, but to bring about the onset of each plague.

Look at Exodus 7, beginning with verse 1. It states, *"And **the LORD said unto Moses, See, I have made thee a god to Pharaoh: and Aaron thy brother shall be thy prophet. 2) Thou shalt speak all that I command thee: and Aaron thy brother shall speak unto Pharaoh,** that he send the children of Israel out of his land. 3) **And I will harden Pharaoh's heart, and multiply my signs and my wonders in the land of Egypt**."*

Now, same chapter, verse 19 states, *"And **the LORD spake unto Moses, Say unto Aaron, Take thy rod, and stretch out thine hand upon the waters of Egypt,** upon their streams, upon their rivers, and upon their ponds, and upon all their pools of water, **that they may become blood; and that there may be blood throughout all the land of Egypt,** both in vessels of wood, and in vessels of stone."*

Also, chapter 8, verse 5, ***"And the LORD spake unto Moses, Say unto Aaron, Stretch forth thine hand with thy rod over the*** *streams, over the rivers, and over the ponds, and cause frogs to come up upon the land of Egypt."*

And this happened with each plague. God accomplished His Will through Moses. With that said, who knows what abilities these **"anointed ones"** will have at that time.

Who are the 144,000?

Revelation 14, beginning with verse 1; *"And I looked, and, lo, a Lamb stood on the mount Zion, and with him **a hundred forty and four thousand**, having his Father's name written in their foreheads. 2) And **I heard a voice from heaven, as the voice of many waters, and as the voice of a great thunder:** and I heard the voice of harpers harping with their harps:"*

Stopping here for a moment. The **voice** that verse 2 is speaking of is the **voice of God.** Look at those portions which I've underlined. They are describing a single voice.

Look at Ezekiel 43:2, **"**... *the glory of **the God of Israel** came from the way of the east: and **his voice was like a noise of many waters.**"*

Continuing with Revelation 14, verse 3; *"And **they sung as it were a new song** before the throne, and before the four beasts, and the elders: **and no man could learn that song but the hundred and forty and four thousand, which were redeemed from the earth.**"*

Verse 3 makes it clear that they **were redeemed from the earth.** The definition of **redeemed** means, "a sum of money or **other payment demanded or paid for the release** of a prisoner. "

Just as it was with the Israelites, God had to pay a ransom for them. The cost being all of the firstborn of Egypt, man and beast.

With that said, there will be a price to pay. The deaths of many, probably scattered throughout the world. And, the Book of Revelation alludes to that very thing in many passages.

Their song is a **new song.** It's not the **song of Moses** that is spoken of in Revelation 15:3. Let's take a look...

Revelation 15, beginning with verse 2; *"And I saw as it were a sea of glass mingled with fire: and them that had gotten the victory over the beast, and over his image, and over his mark, and over the number of his name, stand on the sea of glass, having the harps of God. 3)* **And they sing the song of Moses the servant of God,** *and the song of the Lamb, saying, Great and marvellous are thy works, Lord God Almighty; just and true are thy ways, thou King of saints. 4) Who shall not fear thee, O Lord, and glorify thy name? for thou only art holy: for all nations shall come and worship before thee;* **for thy judgments are made manifest.** *"*

The **song of Moses** spoken of, is found in Deuteronomy, and covers almost the entire 32nd chapter, verses 1-47.

For context, let's begin with Deuteronomy, chapter 31, so you will understand what brought this about. Beginning with verse 16, it states; *"And the LORD said unto Moses, Behold, thou shalt sleep with thy fathers; and* **this people will rise up, and go a whoring after the gods of the strangers of the land,** *whither they go to be among them,* **and will forsake me, and break my covenant which I have made with them. 17) Then my anger shall be kindled against them in that day, and I will forsake them, and I will hide my face from them, and they shall be devoured, and many evils and troubles shall befall them; so that they will say in that day, Are not these evils come upon us, because our God is not among us?** *18) And I will surely hide my face in that day for all the evils which they shall have wrought, in that they are turned unto other gods. 19)* **Now therefore <u>write ye this song for you, and teach it the children of Israel: put it in their mouths, that this song may be a witness for me against the children of Israel.</u>** *"*

I have already quoted large portions of Deuteronomy 32 in my last two books, so I'll just recap some of the highlights.

It's the scripture where God refers to Himself as their **Rock**, and states beginning with verse 18, *"**Of the Rock that begat thee thou art unmindful, and hast forgotten God that formed thee...** 20) And he said,* **I will hide my face from them, I will see what their end shall be:** *for they are a very froward generation, children in whom is no faith. 21)* **They have moved me to jealousy with that which is**

not God; *they have provoked me to anger with their vanities: and **I will move them to jealousy with those which are not a people**; I will provoke them to anger with a foolish nation."*

In fact, it is in verse 30 that it becomes known that **their Rock has sold them**! The **song** ends at verse 43. And, verse 44 then states; *"**And Moses came and spake all the words of this song in the ears of the people**, he, and Hoshea the son of Nun."*

This **song** is definitely speaking about the **judgments** of God, and unlike the songs that we have come to know, this one is not joyful at all!

So, what is the **song** that Revelation 14, verse 3 speaks of?

These words that I have written, within these three books, this is the "song that no man could understand". And, if you understand these words, the truth about God and how Lucifer and Jesus have deceived everyone, and all of the lies that I have uncovered regarding the Church and its ties to the Devil, if all of this makes sense to you, then you are one of God's chosen, one of the 144,000.

And, that being known, it's time for all of those that have been awakened, pulled out from under the **Strong Delusion**, to pray to the LORD God for forgiveness, and Repent of your sins. Get your life right with God, and start keeping His Sabbaths.

Revelation 14, verse 4, *"**These are they which were not defiled with women;** for they are virgins. These are they which follow the Lamb whithersoever he goeth. These were redeemed from among men, being the firstfruits unto God and to the Lamb. 5) **And in their mouth was found no guile: for they are without fault before the throne of God.**"*

When verse 4 states that they *"**were not defiled with women**"*, **women** means **churches.** They probably were at one time, but came out of the Church after learning the truth.

Look at Isaiah 43:25, *"**I, even I, am he that blotteth out thy transgressions for mine own sake, and will not remember thy sins.**"*

228

So, whatever sins they may have had in the past, they have been forgiven by God, and will be **defiled no more!** Their past **transgressions are non-existent.** That's why they are now **virgins, pure. Their robes have been washed, and are now white as snow.**

When verse 5 states, *"in their mouth was found no guile"*, it means **lie,** or **deception.**

The definition of **guile** means; "insidious cunning in attaining a goal; crafty or artful deception; duplicity." (dictionary.com)

However, when I Googled the question, **What does guileless mean in the Bible?** One of the responses provided stated, **"free of deceit".** (thefreedictionary.com)

They **are without fault before God,** because He has **blotted out their sins.**

Look at Isaiah 44:22, *"I have blotted out, as a thick cloud, thy transgressions, and, as a cloud, thy sins: return unto me; for I have redeemed thee."*

I know the day is coming that Revelation 11:7 will be fulfilled, that the **beast that ascendeth out of the bottomless pit,** the **Dragon, Lucifer, will slay the 144,000.** But the thought of it doesn't really scare me. Because I know that God will be with His saints to the end.

This is something that must happen, just as its stated in Revelation 6, verses 9-11. The scripture tells us, *"And when he had opened the fifth seal, I saw under the altar **the souls of them that were slain for the word of God, and for the testimony which they held: 10) And they cried with a loud voice, saying, How long, O Lord, holy and true, dost thou not judge and avenge our blood on them that dwell on the earth?** 11) And white robes were given unto every one of them; and it was said unto them, that they should rest yet for a little season, **until their fellowservants also and their brethren, that should be killed as they were, should be fulfilled."***

The **number of souls that were slain for the word of God must be fulfilled!**

And, Yes! I was a sinner... My rags were filthy! And God took those filthy rags from me. And now I can only hope that my efforts in changing my life have earned me a white robe. Who knows, maybe writing these books to help others has been part of my penance.

Furthermore, unlike God not being there for Jesus when he was crucified, because he supposedly had all of the sins of the world upon him, and God can't look upon sin?? I have no doubt that God will be right there with me until my end. With all of His saints!

And, knowing that God is with me, goes a long way. Especially, taking into consideration the content matter of these books I write. I feel certain that Jesus and Lucifer are not happy with me one bit, for bringing all of their lies to light. But the **LORD God is the only Light! The true Light!** And, He's com'in to snuff 'em out!!

Jesus states in Revelation 2:11, *"... He that overcometh shall not be hurt of the second death."* Hopefully this is one of the true things that he said. If so, my first death took place back in 2006, when the full impact of the truth came crashing down upon me.

Suddenly the realization of everything that you have ever been taught to believe your whole life, was all a complete lie, and it hit me and my daughter like a ton of bricks! Just like I stated about my sister, when I shared the story of her waking up in **Book 1.** I was talking with her on the phone, and prior to that day, had been working on her, off and on, for quite some time.

Then, out of the blue, something just clicked inside her! And I could hear the reality of it crashing in on her, and recognized it immediately! She was fumbling for the words to speak, because her mind was unable to comprehend the enormous reset that had just taken place. I remember all too well.

Then, a couple of days later I went to check on her. And, she had now reached the stage of empowerment, and was filled with this sense of urgency to clean out her house, getting rid of every semblance of Jesus... **I mean smashing and trashing!!** And taking great pleasure in it! It was truly exciting to watch! Hopefully others have experienced the same thing.

But, here's the bottom line... Look at Revelation 17:17, *"**For God hath put in their hearts to fulfil his will, and to agree, and give their kingdom unto the beast, until the words of God shall be fulfilled.**"*

All of this is part of God's plan. He *"**hath put in their hearts to fulfil his will**"*. He has allowed this earthly kingdom to be taken over by evil *"**until the words of God shall be fulfilled.**"*

What are the words of God? Look at Isaiah 24:5-6, *"**The earth also is defiled under the inhabitants thereof; because they have transgressed the laws, changed the ordinance, broken the everlasting covenant.** 6) **Therefore hath the curse devoured the earth, and they that dwell therein are desolate:** therefore the inhabitants of the earth are burned, and few men left.*"

God knew that all of this would happen. Just like He told Moses in Deuteronomy 31:16, *"And the LORD said unto Moses, Behold, **thou shalt sleep with thy fathers; and this people will rise up, and go a whoring after the gods of the strangers of the land, whither they go to be among them, and will forsake me, and break my covenant which I have made with them**... 21) ... **for I know their imagination which they go about, even now, before I have brought them into the land which I sware.**"*

He knew then, the hearts of men. And, He still knows.

Deuteronomy 28:58-59, *"**If thou wilt not observe to do all the words of this law that are written in this book, that thou mayest fear this glorious and fearful name, THE LORD THY GOD; 59) Then the LORD will make thy plagues wonderful, and the plagues of thy seed, even great plagues, and of long continuance, and sore sicknesses, and of long continuance.**"*

Deuteronomy 29:20, *"**The LORD will not spare him, but then the anger of the LORD and his jealousy shall smoke against that man, and all the curses that are written in this book shall lie upon him, and the LORD shall blot out his name from under heaven.**"* (Curses are found in chapters 27 and 28.)

Deuteronomy 31:17-18, *"**Then my anger shall be kindled against them in that day, and I will forsake them, and I will hide my face from them, and they shall be devoured, and many evils and troubles shall befall them**; so that they will say in that day, **Are not these evils come upon us, because our God is not among us?** 18) And I will surely hide my face in that day for all the **evils which they shall have wrought, in that they are turned unto other gods**."*

I realize that many who read this will think that these verses have come to pass long ago. And, they have! But, bear in mind that verses such as these speak to all generations. They continue to replay until all the words of this book are fulfilled. Which, the grand finale is soon to come.

Isaiah 59:2-4, *"**But your iniquities have separated between you and your God, and your sins have hid his face from you, that he will not hear. 3) For your hands are defiled with blood, and your fingers with iniquity; your lips have spoken lies, your tongue hath muttered perverseness. 4) None calleth for justice, nor any pleadeth for truth: they trust in vanity, and speak lies; they conceive mischief, and bring forth iniquity**."*

Isaiah 40:28, *"... **there is no searching of his understanding**."*

Isaiah 13:11, *"**And I will punish the world for their evil, and the wicked for their iniquity**; and I will cause the arrogancy of the proud to cease, and will lay low the haughtiness of the terrible."*

Isaiah 5:20-21, *"**Woe unto them that call evil good, and good evil; that put darkness for light, and light for darkness; that put bitter for sweet, and sweet for bitter! 21) Woe unto them that are wise in their own eyes, and prudent in their own sight!**"*

Isaiah 26:8-11, *"Yea, **in the way of thy judgments, O LORD, have we waited for thee; the desire of our soul is to thy name, and to the remembrance of thee**. 9) With my soul have I desired thee in the night; yea, with my spirit within me will I seek thee early: **for when thy judgments are in the earth, the inhabitants of the world will learn righteousness**. 10) Let favour be shewed to the wicked, yet will he not learn righteousness: in the land of uprightness will he deal unjustly, and will not behold the majesty of the LORD. 11)*

LORD, when thy hand is lifted up, they will not see: but they shall see, and be ashamed for their envy at the people; yea, the fire of thine enemies shall devour them."

Think back to our discussion about Pharaoh of Egypt, and how the LORD God hardened his heart 11 times. And each time He did, another plague was unleashed! Pharaoh couldn't have conceded even if he wanted to, because God wanted to make certain that he not only learned his lesson, but that he also recognized the supremacy of the LORD as God, the only God!

Look at Exodus 10:3, *"And Moses and Aaron came in unto Pharaoh, and said unto him, **Thus saith the LORD God of the Hebrews, <u>How long wilt thou refuse to humble thyself before me?</u>** "*

And, Deuteronomy 10:17, *"... **the LORD your God is God of gods, and Lord of lords, a great God, a mighty, and a terrible...**".*

For God, it's no longer a question of disobedience. It has gone way beyond that. Look at all of the devotion and worship taking place today, involving **false gods, images, likenesses, and** let's not forget about **self worship**!

An article from pepperdine-graphic.com, titled **Idolatry of Self: Hurting or Helping Identity**, dated April 18, 2023 by Abby Wilt. She states; "Individuals can make idols out of several different things - money, fame, love, work, school or friends. Or, individuals can simply view themselves as their own idol - using all their time and effort to better themselves until the desire to succeed is all-consuming, rather than using that time to strengthen their faith in something larger than themselves."

"While self-idolatry may be a common concept that affects every individual in different ways, ... inward focus is not God's plan or will; God made humans in His image and for His purpose... It [idolatry] goes against the very intention of God for humanity". (Cari Meyers, Religion Professor)

Self worship has become more prevalent, at this day and time, than most all else. Even those that make a deal with the Devil, do it for self serving reasons. And, probably never realize, thinking it to be a joke, that the day will come when he collects!

Which is the very point of all of this! People do not take seriously, those commitments they make. The better word is **covenant**! Up to this point they have had no accountability. And, that mindset has been fostered by Churches leading everyone to believe that **by the blood of Jesus, they have been forgiven!** I'm here to tell you, they are in for one Hell of a rude awakening!

God continued to hammer Pharaoh, and many other kings, with plagues (judgments) until He had successfully, either bent their will to His, or destroyed them completely. And, that is exactly, what's about to happen here.

Let's take a look at what's in store...

Beginning with Revelation chapter 14, verse 1, *"And I looked, and, lo, **a Lamb stood on the mount Zion, and with him a hundred forty and four thousand, having his Father's name written in their foreheads**. 2) And I heard a voice from heaven, as the voice of many waters, and as the voice of a great thunder: and I heard the voice of harpers harping with their harps: 3) **And they sung as it were a new song before the throne, and before the four beasts, and the elders: and no man could learn that song but the hundred and forty and four thousand, which were redeemed from the earth.**"*

At this point, the 144,000 have already been slain by the beast that ascendeth from the pit, and they are singing the **new song that no man could learn.** As I stated moments ago, their song is all of this that I have been ranting about in my three books now. All of the lies that this world has been deceived by due to the **Strong Delusion** that was allowed by God.

And people just cannot believe it! It matters not how many different ways I try to explain it, it's as though I'm speaking in a foreign language that only myself and 143,999 other people can understand. And those that understand it, get it completely! Maybe not all of it initially, but once they've been awakened, their eyes begin to see the truth everywhere.

Look at verse 6, same chapter; *"And I saw another angel fly in the midst of heaven,* **having the everlasting gospel to preach unto them that dwell on the earth, and to every nation, and kindred, and tongue, and people,** *7) Saying with a loud voice,* **Fear God, and give glory to him; for the hour of his judgment is come***: and* **worship him that made heaven, and earth, and the sea, and the fountains of waters.**"

The **true gospel**... **God's truth,** is the **song that the 144,000 were singing that no one could understand.** Once they all stand up after 3 1/2 days, and ascend into heaven, many will start to wake up.

Not just for that reason, but Revelation 11:13 tells us that after they ascend into heaven, *"...* **the same hour was there a great earthquake, and the tenth part of the city fell, and in the earthquake were slain of men seven thousand: and the remnant were affrighted, and gave glory to the God of heaven.**"

Now we see that people were not only frightened by the 144,000 standing up after lying dead for 3 1/2 days, and ascending into the heavens, but within the same hour a powerful earthquake hit. So strong that 7,000 people were killed from it. And that's when those who survived became terrified, finally believing that God's wrath had begun.

Verse 18 confirms that. It states; *"And* **the nations were angry, and thy wrath is come,***"*.

However, each chapter is like the same story that's being told by different people, and each version varies due to the perspectives of those telling it. At this moment there are two versions taking place, one being chapter 11, and the other being chapter 14.

**Look at chapter 11, verse 15; *"And the seventh angel sounded; and there were great voices in heaven"*.

Now, chapter 14, verse 6; *"I saw another angel fly in the midst of heaven"*.

Chapter 11:13; *"...* **the same hour was there a great earthquake, and the tenth part of the city fell, and in the earthquake were slain of men seven thousand..."*.

Chapter 14:8; *"And there followed another angel, saying, **Babylon is fallen, is fallen, that great city** ..."*.

Look now at 11:18; *"And **the nations were angry, and thy wrath is come and **the time of the dead, that they should be judged**".*

And, chapter 14:7-8; *"Fear God, and give glory to him; for **the hour of his judgment is come**..."*.

We've all just learned that God's **judgments are punishments**, it also means **passing sentence** as well. But, at this point, I believe the **judgment** spoken of is God's **wrath**. Another clue which confirms that is found in chapter 11, verse 14. It states; *"**The second woe is past; and, behold, the third woe cometh quickly**."*

Given the fact that there are only three woes, and the **third woe cometh quickly**, that makes it clear to me, that all hell is on the verge of breaking loose!

Chapter 15 discusses the **seven vials of wrath, or **bowls** as they are called in some interpretations. One of the tricks to putting events in the proper order, is to watch for the clues. If you look at Revelation 21:9, you'll see what I mean.

It states; *"And **there came unto me one of the seven angels which had the seven vials full of the seven last plagues**, and talked with me, saying, Come hither, I will shew thee the bride, the Lamb's wife."*

Chapter 21 speaks of the vision of new **Jerusalem descending out of heaven from God.** And even though this vision is not spoken of until chapter 21, we know that, based on the specific wording highlighted in bold type, that John actually sees this before the **vials of wrath** are poured.

This proves that not all of these events are written in their proper sequence. Not just the events, but the chapters as well.

When Revelation 14:1-5 speaks of the 144,000 that now stand before God, along with the Lamb, then verse 7, just two verses away, tells us that **the hour of God's judgment has come. But, it is the deaths and ascension of God's saints that actually triggers **His judgment** (wrath) that quickly follows.

At that point, we tie chapter 11 back in. Which is where verse 13 states that a great earthquake occurs within the same hour that the 144,000 ascend into heaven. An **earthquake so great that the city of Babylon falls.** Even though these chapters are not in order, if we pay attention to the keys (key words), it will enable us to follow it.

Furthermore, please understand that the name **Babylon** is also a metaphor, symbolizing that this city is extremely corrupt and evil. I speculate in **Book 1** that this could be referring to the **Vatican.**

Much of my reasoning is based on Revelation 18, which pertains to the **fall of Babylon.** The key is found in verse 24, which states; *"**And in her was found the blood of prophets, and of saints, and of all that were slain upon the earth.**"*

It too, is highly possible that this metaphor is referring to the **Church**... **all churches,** as the **whore of Babylon.** If so, it could be representing the **Vatican, and all churches.**

However, another possibility could be, whichever city that the New World Order is set up in. This is the World government that Lucifer will establish, along with the **ten kings** spoken of in Revelation 17:12-13. Again, this is the purpose of using metaphors, it enables multiple meanings.

In verse 9, of chapter 14, it states; *"And the third angel followed them, saying with a loud voice, **If any man** worship the beast and his image, and receive his mark in his forehead, or in his hand, 10) **The same shall drink of the wine of the wrath of God**, which is poured out without mixture into the cup of his indignation; and he shall be tormented with fire and brimstone in the presence of the holy angels, and in the presence of the Lamb:"*

The key to understanding is found in verse 9, **if any man**... This means that **everyone else is here for all of the bad stuff.** There will not be a **rapture** that lifts all of the Jesus worshipping Christians out of here before the **tribulation**, or the **time of great distress** occurs. The only ones that are raptured out, are the 144,000, and they had to endure persecution and death before so.

At this point the vials of wrath begin to pour out, one by one, the details of which are found in chapter 16. I speculate in **Book 1**, that based on events that take place in chapters 6 and 8, which coincide with the opening of the seals, it sounds as though the vials begin to pour out in conjunction with some of the seals being opened.

The plagues include; verse 2 (chapter 16), *"And the **first** went, and **poured out his vial upon the earth; and there fell a noisome and grievous sore <u>upon the men which had the mark of the beast, and upon them which worshipped his image</u>."***

Verse 3, *"And the **second** angel **poured out his vial upon the sea; and it became as the blood of a dead man: and every living soul died in the sea.***"

Verse 4, *"And the **third** angel **poured out his vial upon the rivers and fountains of waters; and they became blood.***"* All our fresh water supply will disappear, no drinking water!

Verses 8-9, *"And the **fourth** angel **poured out his vial upon the sun; and power was given unto him to scorch men with fire.** 9) And men were scorched with great heat, and blasphemed the name of God, which hath power over these plagues: and they repented not to give him glory."*

Bear in mind that all the inhabitants of the world will be enduring these plagues. The only plague that is specific to those with the **mark**, is the 1st plague, the **noisome** and **grievous sores.**

Verse 10, *"And the **fifth** angel **poured out his vial upon the seat of the beast; and his kingdom was full of darkness; and they gnawed their tongues for pain,***"

Verse 12, *"And the **sixth** angel **poured out his vial upon the great river Euphrates; and the water thereof was dried up, that the way of the kings of the east might be prepared.***"

This verse tells us that the Battle of Armageddon is preparing to get underway. In fact, as I have written in **Book 1**, the **Euphrates**

River began drying up in 2014! If you had any doubts, whatsoever, that this is the time of the end, that fact should, hopefully, provide you with the proof you need.

At this point, other chapters kick in, namely, chapter 14. Verse 13 states; *"And I heard a voice from heaven saying unto me, Write,* ***Blessed are the dead which die in the Lord from henceforth: Yea, saith the Spirit, that they may rest from their labours; and their works do follow them.*** *"*

Then, verses 15-20 tells us that the inhabitants of the world, with the exception of those that had gotten the **mark,** are reaped. Verse 15 states; *"And another angel came out of the temple, crying with a loud voice to him that sat on the cloud,* ***Thrust in thy sickle, and reap: for the time is come for thee to reap; for the harvest of the earth is ripe.*** *"*

Now, I have no understanding of how this comes about, but I do know what comes next. Look at chapter 15, beginning with verse 2. It states; *"And* ***I saw as it were a sea of glass mingled with fire: and them that had gotten the victory over the beast, and over his image, and over his mark, and over the number of his name, stand on the sea of glass,*** *having the harps of God."*

This is the final rapture. All of those which had refused the **mark,** and in doing so, **gotten victory over the beast,** are now in heaven.

Look also at Revelation 19:5-7, *"And a voice came out of the throne, saying, Praise our God, all ye his servants, and ye that fear him, both small and great. 6)* ***And I heard as it were the voice of a great multitude, and as the voice of many waters,*** *and as the voice of mighty thunderings, saying, Alleluia: for the Lord God omnipotent reigneth. 7) Let us be glad and rejoice, and give honour to him: for the marriage of the Lamb is come, and his wife hath made herself ready."*

Again, **waters are people** (Revelation 17:15). And, all of God's people are now in heaven, and preparing for the **marriage of the true Lamb**. The marriage between the Lamb and the true church body of God, all of His people! They are all finally united as one!

This takes place before the battle of Armageddon, which verse 11 of chapter 19 alerts us to its onset when it states; *"And I saw heaven opened, and behold a white horse; and he that sat upon him was called Faithful and True, and in righteousness he doth judge and make war. 12) His eyes were as a flame of fire, and on his head were many crowns; and he had a name written, that no man knew, but he himself. 13) And he was clothed with a vesture dipped in blood: and his name is called The Word of God. 14) And the armies which were in heaven followed him upon white horses, clothed in fine linen, white and clean."*

All of God's armies, His people and angels, will be participants in the battle. And even though I have yet to discuss the dead rising, which is also another interpretation of 14:7, God's **judgment**, they, too, are part of His army.

As for their rising, look at 11:18, *"**And the nations were angry, and thy wrath is come, and the time of the dead, that they should be judged**, and that thou shouldest give reward unto thy servants the prophets, and to the saints, and them that fear thy name, small and great; and shouldest destroy them which destroy the earth."*

Also, John 5:28-29, *"Marvel not at this: **for the hour is coming, in the which all that are in the graves shall hear his voice**, 29) **And shall come forth; they that have done good, unto the resurrection of life; and they that have done evil, unto the resurrection of damnation."***

And, 1st Corinthians 15:52, *"**In a moment, in the twinkling of an eye, at the last trump: for the trumpet shall sound, and the dead shall be raised incorruptible**, and we shall be changed."*

They that have done good will become part of God's army, and **they that have done evil**, part of Lucifer's army.

I see no need to provide all of the details about the seals being opened, the alien invasion, the reign of the beast, the dead rising, and the battle itself, since all of this information is discussed at length in **Book 1.**

The recap that I've provided was mainly dealing with the events pertaining to the 144,000, as well as the uniting of all God's children for the final battle... the battle of Armageddon.

Everything that has happened leading up to that battle, served a purpose to God. The strong delusion was brought about by Him because of man's continued defiance and disobedience. Despite the numerous judgments that were unleashed upon His people, they just could not remain compliant. He knew their hearts...

Jeremiah 17:9-10, **"The heart is deceitful above all things, and desperately wicked: who can know it? 10) I the LORD search the heart, I try the reins, even to give every man according to his ways, and according to the fruit of his doings."**

And even though He put His laws into their hearts, drastic measures became necessary. He had to prove the hearts of mankind once and for all.

And, it's not just about His chosen people. Look at Isaiah 65:1, *"I am sought of them that asked not for me; I am found of them that sought me not: I said, Behold me, behold me, unto a nation that was not called by my name. 2) I have spread out my hands all the day unto a rebellious people, which walketh in a way that was not good, after their own thoughts; 3) A people that provoketh me to anger continually to my face; that sacrificeth in gardens, and burneth incense upon altars of brick; 4) Which remain among the graves, and lodge in the monuments, which eat swine's flesh, and broth of abominable things is in their vessels; 5) Which say, Stand by thyself, come not near to me; for I am holier than thou. These are a smoke in my nose, a fire that burneth all the day."*

Also, Isaiah 56:6, *"**Also the sons of the stranger, that join themselves to the LORD, to serve him, and to love the name of the LORD, to be his servants, every one that keepeth the sabbath from polluting it, and taketh hold of my covenant; 7) Even them will I bring to my holy mountain, and make them joyful in my house of prayer**: their burnt offerings and their sacrifices shall be accepted upon mine altar; **for mine house shall be called an house of prayer for all people**."*

God welcomes all people who are willing to **serve Him, and keep His Sabbath, and take hold of His covenant.**

Ezekiel 36, beginning with verse 26 tells us, *"A new heart also will I give you, and a new spirit will I put within you: and I will take away the stony heart out of your flesh, and I will give you a heart of flesh. 27) <u>And I will put my spirit within you, and cause you to walk in my statutes, and ye shall keep my judgments, and do them</u>."*

Notice how verse 27 states that He will **<u>cause</u> us to walk in His statutes, and keep His judgments and do them!** I don't know about you, but I'm looking forward to that. This **free will** stuff isn't all it's cracked up to be!

"Yea, truth faileth; and he that departeth from evil maketh himself a prey: and the LORD saw it, and it displeased him that there was no judgment. 16) And saw that there was no man, and wondered that there was no intercessor: therefore... **His arm brought salvation unto Him: and His righteousness, it sustained Him. For He put on righteousness as a breastplate, and a helmet of salvation upon His head; and He put on the garments of vengeance for clothing, and was clad with zeal as a cloak**.*"*
(Isaiah 59:15-17)

This is the true LORD God's Armor, and His Armor is the only Armor that we need. **His Truth, Salvation and Righteousness**!

This is God's Message, and His Message is clear...

REPENT!!

"Fear thou not; for I am with thee: be not dismayed; for I am thy God: I will strengthen thee; yea, I will help thee; yea, I will uphold thee with the right hand of my righteousness."

Isaiah 41:10

Printed in Great Britain
by Amazon

46493000R00136